WITHDRAWN

The Countryside of
Medieval England

The Countryside of Medieval England

Edited by
Grenville Astill and Annie Grant

Illustrations drawn by Brian Williams

Basil Blackwell

British Library Cataloguing in Publication Data

The countryside of medieval England.
    1. England—Rural conditions 2. England—
    Social conditions—Medieval period,
    1066–1486 3. England—Social conditions—
    16th century 4. England—Social conditions
    —17th century
    I. Astill, Grenville G. II. Grant, Annie
    942'009'734   HN398.E5
    ISBN 0-631-15091-9

Library of Congress Cataloging in Publication Data

The Countryside of medieval England.
  Bibliography: p.
  Includes index.
  1. England—Historical geography. 2. England—
  Rural conditions—History. 3. England—Social life
  and customs—Medieval period, 1066–1485. 4. Land-
  scape—England—History. 5. Land use, Rural—
  England—History. 6. Country life—England—History.
  7. Agriculture—England—History. I. Astill,
  Grenville. II. Grant, Annie.
  DA600.C664 1988   942'.009734   87–35521
  ISBN 0-631-15091-9

Typeset in 10 on 12pt Caslon
by Hope Services, Abingdon, Oxon
Printed in Great Britain
by T. J. Press Ltd,
Padstow, Cornwall

Contents

Acknowledgements

This book from conception to completion has been a collaborative effort. The editors would like to thank all the other contributors to the book, first for agreeing to write their chapters, and then for coming to the two meetings to discuss the outline of the book and the first draughts of each of the chapters. Christopher Dyer in particular has provided much useful comment. We would also like to thank Virginia Murphy of Basil Blackwell for hosting our meetings and for all her help.

While writing and editing this book, we have also received support and advice from many colleagues and friends. We would particularly like to thank Keith Bate, Barrie Bullen, John Davey, Michael Fulford, Marcus Grant, Andrew Jones and Susan Wright.

James Greig gratefully thanks his colleagues for their help, and especially Bruce Campbell and Christopher Dyer for advice on the historical sources for plants.

Paul Stamper thanks his colleagues throughout the country on the Victoria History of the Counties of England who supplied references, and in several cases texts in advance of publication. He would also like to thank Nigel Tringham for transcripts of the Bishop of Lichfield's account rolls.

We are grateful for permission to cite from the unpublished theses of P. L. Armitage, I. S. W. Blanchard, C. C. Fenwick, I. H. Goodall, F. J. Green, C. A. Morris, L. R. Poos, J. West and J. P. Williams.

D. Austin, P. Drury, D. Gadd, A. R. Hall, R. Harcourt, F. J. Green, D. Keene, G. Lambrick, L. C. Moffet, P. Murphy, M. Stephenson, P. R. Tomlinson and S. West kindly allowed us to quote unpublished information.

Figures 1.2, 2.4, 5.5, 5.6, 6.2, 6.3, 6.4, 8.3, 8.5, 8.6, 8.7, 10.2, 10.3 and 10.4 are reproduced by courtesy of the Bodleian Library, Oxford; figures 5.1, 5.4, 5.7, and 7.2 by courtesy of the British Library, London; figure 7.6 by courtesy of the Fitzwilliam Museum, Cambridge; figure 1.1 by courtesy of Warwickshire County Museum; figure 3.5 by courtesy of the Ministry of Defence (Crown Copyright reserved); figure 4.3 by courtesy of Cambridge Committee for Aerial Photography; figure 6.1 by courtesy of A. Hall, York Environmental Unit; figure 8.4 by courtesy of D. Baker and figure 10.1 by courtesy of G. Beresford.

Permission for redrawing was given by Cambridge University Press for figures 2.1, 2.3, 4.1, 4.2, 9.2 and 9.3; B. Campbell for figure 2.2; M. Aston for figures 3.2 and 4.5; Derbyshire Archaeological Society for figure 3.2; C. Hayfield for figure 3.2; P. Wade-Martins and the Norfolk Archaeological Unit of the Norfolk Museums Service for figures 3.3 and 3.4; L. Watts, P. Rahtz and the Bristol and Gloucestershire Archaeological Society for figure 3.3; Society for Medieval Archaeology for figures 3.3, 3.4 and 4.5; J. Musty and D. Algar for figure 3.4; Oxford University Press for figure 4.1; Royal Commission on Historic Monuments of England for figure 4.3; L. Poos for figure 9.1 and J. Sheail for figure 9.5. F. W. B. Charles allowed examples of tree sizes to be used in figure 7.1.

G. A. and A. G.
Reading University.

Illustrations

1

The Medieval Countryside: Approaches and Perceptions

Grenville Astill and Annie Grant

As scholarly effort has steadily enlarged our knowledge and understanding of the countryside of medieval England, the emphasis of much of this research has shifted from manors and estates to peasants, villages and rural society. The historical stress on social relationships remains, but cooperation and conflict among the peasantry are now of as much concern as the interaction between lords and peasants.

More recently a related, but clearly different kind of research has developed in order to discover more of the physical reality of the countryside, particularly in relation to the fundamental need, for both lords and peasants, to produce food. This has involved not just historians, but also archaeologists, geographers, soil scientists, botanists and zoologists.

In *The Countryside of Medieval England*, which deals specifically with rural resource exploitation and management, we reflect this recent, multidisciplinary trend, but we are also dependent on work done in the older tradition. We bring together the disparate strands of evidence for the ways in which the countryside was used, concentrating on the primary natural resources, the plants and the animals. We discuss how fields, woods and parks were used to manage these resources, and how tools were employed to help in the practice of agriculture. In addition we consider the human population of the countryside and how this organized itself in villages and settlements. The period we cover is that from approximately the late eleventh century to the late fifteenth century, within which we attempt to isolate both regional variations and chronological developments.

Our view of the countryside is inevitably conditioned by the kind of evidence that has survived. The most sustained, long-standing, and therefore sophisticated enquiry into the nature of medieval rural society has been conducted by documentary historians. By using the abundant records of central government and estate management, it has been possible to reconstruct many aspects of rural society. For example, numerous studies show how the estates of the nobility, mostly ecclesiastics, were organized. The ways lords chose to manage their lands

at different times during the medieval period give us valuable insights into how
the economy of regions, and perhaps of the country, was changing. The records
of the lords' estates also afford the most abundant information about the majority
of the population of medieval England – the peasants. We can appreciate the
wide range of social and economic status that existed within village communities,
the sizes of individual families, their interrelationships and standards of living,
and how these all changed through time. Such aspects of rural life cannot,
unfortunately, be documented for all parts of the country, nor for the entire span
of the medieval period, since the documentary record is socially, geographically
and temporally selective (pp. 12–14).

Documentary evidence emphasizes the agricultural basis of medieval society,
but it is suprising how little detailed work has been done on the ways and the
conditions under which agriculture was practised and the relationships between
population and environment. These issues have been tackled by historical
geographers, and by archaeologists. Initially the concern of medieval archaeology
was mainly with the excavation of the most obvious physical remains of the past,
but more recent work has provided a broader view of the landscape of the past.
However, the archaeological evidence is no easier to use than the documentary
and no less selective. The most plentiful information for the rural scene is that for
the buildings within settlements, because structures usually survive well
underground. It is most fragmentary about the standards of living of the
occupants, depending as it does on what was thrown out as rubbish. In most rural
settlements rubbish deposits have not survived well, simply because much of the
refuse was recycled and spread on the gardens or fields as manure. The absence of
middens in rural settlements also means that the stratification is often very
shallow (figure 1.1). The record of three hundred years of occupation may be
compressed into a series of layers that is less than one-third of a metre deep,
severely limiting the detail of reconstruction and interpretation. Although it may
be possible to identify several periods of house building, or of use, it may be
impossible to provide an absolute chronology or to characterize the nature of each
period because the finds cannot be related to particular phases of occupation. The
archaeologist is thus often in the position of being able to recognize significant
changes, and offer a relative sequence for the events, but only able to set them
within a very broad time scale, perhaps one of several hundred years.

In contrast, the excavation of urban sites which have well-preserved, deep
stratification, has provided much more accurate dating for many artefacts. This is
particularly true of waterfront sites where rubbish deposits have been dated by
dendrochronology. Urban excavations have been particularly important in
providing the environmental evidence for the countryside that is often very
scarce in the rural settlements themselves. In their role as markets, towns
collected, redistributed, processed and consumed surplus products of the
countryside so that the remains of plants and animals grown and raised in the

1.1 *Burton Dassett, Warwickshire. A modern excavation of a deserted medieval settlement showing the remains of a terrace of buildings of the fifteenth century. The position of the main walls is indicated by the stone free strips in the rubble. Note the shallow stratification. The scales have half metre divisions*
(photo: N. Palmer).

countryside are found in the rubbish pits of the towns. However, while most of the food eaten in towns was produced in the country, some could have been from the urban area itself. Animals were penned and vegetables grown in the least congested parts of the built-up area or in the town fields.

An additional complication is that the rubbish deposits archaeologists find may not be representative of the waste generated in a town. The rubbish could vary according to a district's social and economic character, while in the larger towns, from the fourteenth century onwards, the disposal of waste was increasingly regulated so that refuse no longer accumulated on the tenements where it was produced. Instead it piled up on communal waste tips on the towns' outskirts or was used to reclaim land.

All contributors to this volume have had to come to terms with the methodological problems of their own particular disciplines. Historians have great difficulties in trying to extract numerical information from their sources. Dyer's discussion of the documentary evidence for the countryside exploits quantitative data, but the ease with which these are used belies the great efforts made to obtain them. There was no standardization of terminology for units of land, nor for quantities of agricultural products or other goods. Peasant holdings, for example, were measured in units of virgates (yardlands), or bovates (oxgangs), or in wists, yokes, townlands and many other local terms. Usually these refer to a unit of agricultural resources, primarily an acreage of arable, together with a share in the meadow, pasture and woodland of the village territory. They varied with the density of population, the quality of the soil, the power of the local lord and a host of other factors that determined local customs. Historians often give 12 ha of arable as the size of a yardland, but this is an average of areas that ranged from 5 to 24 ha, and often we do not know which reckoning documents are using.

Sheaves of corn or bundles of hay were measured by the length of a man's arm or the amount he could carry on his fork, and references to 'wainloads' and 'cartloads' of hay make it impossible or at least very difficult to judge productivity. Some goods were measured with more precision – corn in bushels and quarters, cheese in stones and wool in todds – although we still cannot be sure that these measures were standardized over the whole country.

Precision and comparability are often no more straightforward for the archaeological record. For example, archaeozoologists differ in the ways that they count bone fragments to determine the relative proportions of species represented in bone assemblages; this inevitably makes intersite comparisons very difficult. And there is much debate about the methods used for, and the validity of, attempting to reconstruct live herds from the bones of dead animals.

Historians and archaeologists both encounter problems resulting from the differential survival of evidence. For some estates, most notably those of the church, detailed records have been preserved, while for others they have been lost. Animal bones and plant remains survive in some soils, but are entirely destroyed in others. Not all bones of all animals have an equal chance of survival and recovery by the archaeologist. Small bones and in particular those of fish, birds and tiny mammals are much less likely to be found than the bones of larger animals. Plant remains survive best where they are in waterlogged deposits, have been mineralized as may happen in cess pits, have been dried or occur where the soil is sufficiently acidic to favour the preservation of pollen grains. Plant remains may also be preserved by charring, but this is only likely to occur where plants have been used for fuel, or are prepared or consumed near fires. The surviving botanical material, then, cannot be assumed to be a representative sample of all the plants or plant parts that were used in the past. In many instances, valuable environmental material that was preserved has been lost during the process of excavation, because the soil was not sieved.

The treatment of individual aspects of our broad theme varies not only according to the kinds of evidence available but also to the extent to which a particular topic has already received attention. For example, Stamper's essay on woodland and parks depends a great deal on documents because these are the most prolific type of evidence, but he is also able to draw on the work of botanists to help understand the way woodland was managed. This chapter is also to a certain extent socially specific because, although wood and parkland were ubiquitous in medieval England, the right to exploit them often rested with the nobility. In contrast, Astill's essay on rural settlement, which is essentially a summary of archaeological work, tends to concentrate on peasant settlements – most villages after all did not have a resident lord. Likewise, because the peasantry were largely responsible for working the land, they naturally form the centrepiece of Smith's discussion of the human population.

Greig's and Grant's essays on plants and animals use as their main source the environmental evidence, and in providing the first major syntheses for this period must do so with a critical awareness of the quality and limitations of their material. Medieval faunal remains have, to date, received rather more attention than the botanical remains, whose systematic study has a relatively short history. This is reflected in the nature of these contributions, and both will have to be judged against the new evidence which is constantly being produced by excavations and which may confirm or contradict the conclusions that have been drawn.

For Langdon the major problem in discussing agricultural equipment is reconciling different types of information. Documentary references to tools and machinery are numerous but often cryptic. The difficulty lies in interpreting the words in terms of solid objects or of the fragments that have been excavated. The same problem recurs in Astill's chapter on fields, where much hangs on the validity of relating post-medieval maps of field systems to the earthwork evidence.

By approaching our theme from the different viewpoints of historians, archaeologists and environmentalists, we hope to be able to compensate for some of the deficiencies that each separately encounters. Sometimes the different sources are mutually supportive, at other times they appear to be discrepant. On these latter occasions it does not necessarily mean that one source is wrong, nor is it simply a question of the old and sterile debate of archaeology ranged against history; rather it means that the particular character of each of the different types of evidence needs to be taken more fully into account.

As an illustration we can consider the question of the importance of deer in the rural economy in our period. In order to answer this it is necessary to investigate many aspects of the social and economic structure of medieval England. Three contributors discuss deer from a variety of standpoints. Both Dyer and Grant discuss the importance of the animal in the medieval diet and Stamper examines hunting and poaching – the ways of obtaining venison – as aspects of life in woodland areas. All three have something to say about the way deer and the other resources of woods and waste were exploited and how these changed during the medieval period. Dyer and Stamper both show how competition over rights to the use of woods led to conflict not only among the nobility but also between lords and peasants. The view that deer hunting and the consumption of venison was primarily a prerogative of the nobility is clearly and consistently stated. The abundant and unambiguous documentary material demonstrating this is supported by significantly larger proportions of deer bones on most high status sites compared to those of lower status. And the records of the many court appearances for poaching discussed by Stamper (p. 143) are nicely brought to life by the half-butchered remains of a presumably poached deer hidden in a well at the village of Lyveden (p. 165).

Interpretations diverge however when some aspects are dealt with in greater detail, for example when assessing the relative importance of venison in the meat diet of the nobility. The documentary evidence, Dyer argues (p. 25), would encourage us to minimize the importance of game; perhaps only 7 per cent of the meat consumed in noble households came from hunted animals. The faunal remains from some castles and other high status sites would suggest otherwise. In some cases deer bones were as common as those of cattle, sheep and pig put together, which Grant interprets (p. 165) as indicating that venison formed a high proportion of the meat eaten.

The discrepancies between these views highlight the inadequacies of the information, the difficulties we have in interpreting it and the understandable tendency of both archaeologists and historians to generalize from the particular. Neither documentary nor archaeological evidence exists for the whole country and few regions have good information from both sources. The documents are particularly abundant for the south and east (p. 14), while the sites with the highest proportions of deer bones are mainly in the north and west. We may therefore merely be seeing regional differences in the exploitation of deer. However, further complications arise out of a problem already mentioned – the quality of the information. The best documentary sources are household accounts, the majority of which make no reference to goods which were not purchased or valued, thus omitting park deer from the record. Generalizations about venison consumption therefore depend on a relatively small number of cases that may not be typical.

Archaeological evidence, as we have already mentioned, suffers particularly from the accidental biases of survival and recovery. Furthermore, while the day and the year were often recorded on documents, archaeological deposits can rarely be dated to within a score of years and often only to within a century and we cannot always be clear about the length of time that the archaeological deposit has taken to accumulate. Are we dealing with the remains of a single, possibly untypical feast, or a larger number of more mundane meals? And, since castles in particular were frequently occupied by their lords for only a small part of the year, may we be seeing evidence of the exploitation of resources in a limited season that may not have been typical of the rest of the year?

Archaeologists have a tendency to concentrate perhaps too much on the inadequacies of their data and should not forget that their evidence gives them the great advantage of a long time perspective. It is likely that we may never know whether the aristocracy really consumed 7 per cent or 70 per cent of their meat as game – no doubt there was enormous individual, regional and temporal variation. However, it is very clear that, compared to many earlier periods of history, the middle ages saw a substantially increased consumption of deer, although unlike the deer that were eaten earlier, few of the medieval animals were truly wild, but were carefully managed in the parks of the period (p. 140).

Any discussion of agriculture must acknowledge the opportunities offered and the constraints and limitations set by the geology and climate of the land. While the geographical coverage of this book is limited to England, a comparatively tiny area of the world, there is within this single country a wide range of terrain, soils, natural vegetation and climate – all of which affected the nature of agricultural practices, and were themselves affected by those practices. We return to a consideration of some aspects of this inter-relationship in the final chapter.

The focus of the majority of the discussion in this book is on the practical aspects of rural life, but we must also be aware that the medieval population had feelings and sensibilities towards the natural landscape. Castles are often located in positions commanding magnificent views, but it is difficult to ascertain the extent to which this was any more than a coincidental result of their strategic defensive positions. Nevertheless, Stamper (p. 143) reminds us of the construction of the balcony at Woodstock Palace that allowed Princess Isabella a view of the park.

Literary and iconographic sources frequently suggest that medieval writers and artists responded to the natural world in a highly stylized and idealized way. The fabulous beasts included together with the ordinary animals such as dogs and chickens in medieval bestiaries and encyclopaedias (for example, Cantimpratensis 1973) show that this conception was often quite inaccurate or at least that the dividing line between the real and the imaginary was not very firmly drawn.

The idealized landscape and the enclosed garden are common visual themes and find their equivalent in descriptions in Latin and vernacular poetry and prose of human love in paradisical settings. They also had a physical reality – in 1250, Henry III ordered the queen's garden at Woodstock to be surrounded by 'two good high walls' (Pearsall and Salter 1973, 77).

Nature was a force to be contained and controlled, perhaps even embellished. Around the houses of the nobility, the sophisticated pleasure gardens were often planted with imported exotic trees (p. 136). The walled garden, in both art and life, may be in part an expression of the nobility's desire to reinforce their superior status by distancing themselves from the toil and labour of their social inferiors in the countryside.

The nobility were able to take pleasure in the natural world, or at least in the tamed wildernesses of the parks. Hunting, whether for deer or for smaller game, was not just a means of acquiring meat. The enjoyment and the ritual and even mystical aspects of hunting can be seen in the anonymous author of *Gawain*'s description of the lord 'beside himself with delight' (Barron 1974, 89) and in Tristan's instruction to the hunters on the art of 'excoriation' (von Strassburg 1960, 78f.). The importance attached to hunting is indicated by the maintenance of parks even when they were not profitable (p. 146).

Literary and pictorial evidence both suggest the beginnings of changes in attitudes to and perceptions of nature in the later part of our period. The more naturalistic and personal images of the fourteenth-century *Gawain* stand in marked contrast to those of the earlier poems of the courtly love traditions (Pearsall and Salter 1973, 152). Bernart de Ventadorn saw 'the lark moving its wings against the sun's rays, until it forgets itself and lets itself drop because of the sweetness that comes into its heart . . .' (O'Donoghue 1982, 117). By contrast, Gawain saw 'the hazel and the hawthorn . . . all tangled together, hung all over with rough, shaggy moss, with many mournful birds upon their bare branches, piping pathetically there, in pain from the cold.' (Barron 1974, 67).

Hutchinson (1974) points to evidence of an increasingly naturalistic style in manuscript illustrations from the late thirteenth century (figure 1.2). She suggests that while for practical reasons many botanical illustrations became more accurate and more carefully observed – they had to be used for the identification

1.2 *Birds from an early fourteenth-century manuscript, showing a naturalistic style of illustration (Bod. Lib. MS New College 65, fol. 73).*

of medicinal plants – new attitudes to the representation of animal forms may have been primarily aesthetic. The more accurate portrayal of nature may suggest an increasing delight in nature. However, Herbert (quoted in Hutchinson 1974, 27), writing about the early fifteenth-century Sherbourne Missal, saw the birds in that document as more than merely an attempt to decorate. He felt that 'the artist's purpose had been to make a serious contribution to ornithological science'.

We may be sure that perceptions of and attitudes to the countryside were not the same for those of different social orders. The nobility may have been permitted the luxury of idealizing it, but the relationship of the peasants to the natural world was much more pragmatic and direct. Langland's William sees on his 'smooth plain . . . some that laboured at ploughing and sowing, with no time for pleasures, sweating to produce food for the gluttons to waste' (Goodridge 1959, 63).

Some inkling of medieval attitudes to the animals that were so essential to the well-being of medieval lords and peasants alike can be gleaned from the contemporary manuals of farming practice. The author of the *Senechaucy* advised against overworking farm animals and using unskilled labour for working with animals, thereby risking injury to them (Oschinsky 1971, 271, 279, 281). None the less, examples of the callous treatment of animals may be seen in bones showing evidence of traumatic injury (for example, Grant 1977, 229; Sadler in press). After reading the *Senechaucy* and Walter of Henley's *Husbandry* (Oschinsky 1971) one is left with the impression that they advised good treatment of animals only to ensure that they could be exploited to the maximum and not from any finer feelings. Animals were clearly primarily intended to serve human needs.

However, in what was a primarily agricultural society, the high level of dependence on animals certainly encouraged intimate knowledge and understanding of them. By the early modern period, the English rural vocabulary was particularly rich in descriptive terms for animals, allowing fine distinctions to be made between animals of different ages and colorations, and even between different consistencies of cow dung (Thomas 1983, 70). Some animals were clearly valued for more than their utilitarian function. Pet keeping has a long history; in Roman Britain we find the remains of dogs whose small size strongly suggests that they can only have been kept as pets (Harcourt 1975, 408). Medieval wills, accounts and court rolls show that names were given not only to the horses of the aristocracy but also to the working horses of the peasantry (C. Dyer pers. comm.). The nature of the contact between humans and pets may foster a kind of sensibility towards the animal kingdom that is different from that engendered by animal husbandry. The attribution to animals of human impulses and motivations is common among pet owners today and in the past – indeed Thomas (1983, 121) claims that 'it was the observation of household pets which buttressed the claims for animal intelligence and character'. The movement away from a man-centred perception of nature, was traced back by Thomas to changes in the thinking of scientists, moralists and theologians in the sixteenth to eighteenth centuries, but he suggests that even in the medieval period views were being expressed that ran counter to the more generally accepted view of animals as creatures entirely subordinate to the desires and aspirations of man, particularly in regard to unnecessary cruelty (1983, 152).

Animals also figured commonly in contemporary folklore. The cat is well known as the beast of witches and sorcerers, but beliefs in supernatural attributes of animals extend to the full complement of domestic species and a wide range of wild animals, birds, reptiles, fish and even insects (Sebillot 1984).

With this range of literary, folkloric, iconographic, documentary, archaeological and environmental evidence, in comparison to that available to scholars looking at earlier periods, medievalists studying the English countryside are remarkably fortunate. They have the advantage of being able to investigate the nature of rural society in ways which are impossible for earlier periods. The superior data base should help to resolve questions which many would regard as fundamental to an assessment of a past society. Foremost might well be that of the nature of subsistence. How was it achieved? Were the same methods used in all parts of the country and did they change through time? What possibilities were there for generating surplus and what were the consequences for the environment?

We do not have answers to all these questions, because they require much multidisciplinary effort. In the past this has been rare in medieval studies, although the last decade has seen a change, most notably in the study of the landscape in which documentary historians, historical geographers and archaeologists have been involved. It is now necessary to develop this collaborative approach further so that we can tackle both wider and more basic issues. This book is intended to be a step in that direction. It is an initial collaboration, bringing together historians and archaeologists with environmentalists. Its themes are determined, and limited, by the currently available information. It is our hope that it will stimulate further work of a more integrated nature so that in the near future it will be possible to widen the discussion to all aspects of the medieval countryside.

2

Documentary Evidence:
Problems and Enquiries

Christopher Dyer

To appreciate the strengths and weaknesses of the written evidence used by historians of the countryside we must remember the limited role of writing in the middle ages. Even for the royal government, memory, oral evidence, and command by word-of-mouth did not give way decisively to the use of documents until the thirteenth century (Clanchy 1979, 41–59). Throughout the period documents were specialized artefacts, which cost a good deal to produce, because of the relatively expensive materials on which they were written, and because of the scarce skills of the clerks who knew the approved languages and the customary formulae. They did not labour for our benefit. A few medieval chroniclers purported to be aiming their works at posterity, but such narratives contain little of interest for those studying the countryside. Instead we must rely on the administrative records that were compiled for current use, containing a mass of information relevant to such tasks as managing an estate, enforcing the law, or collecting taxes. The documents appear to contain complete and impartial information, but by the nature of the bureaucratic process that produced them they are far from being comprehensive or objective.

Firstly, the evidence is socially selective. The documents served the interests of either the state or the powerful elite of landlords. They tell us a great deal about the activities of lords and governments, and we see the rest of society through their eyes, as their tenants, employees or taxpayers. Let us take two of the basic questions that we need to ask – what crops were grown and what animals kept? Thousands of manorial accounts of the thirteenth and fourteenth centuries provide us with a mass of detail, almost embarrassing in its volume, on agricultural production on the demesnes, that is, the lands reserved for the exclusive use of the lords of manors. On the back of the roll the local official, a reeve or bailiff, had to account for the goods in his charge in the same way that he accounted for money on the front of the document. He stated how much wheat, rye, barley, peas and oats had been received from the harvest, and how much he had sown, used or sold. The purpose of making the account was to check on the reeve's efficiency and honesty. If the yields were poor, he could be held responsible and be charged with the value of the grain that should, in the opinion of the auditors, have been produced. The account also included a section in which all the animals, from cart horses to doves, were listed, with the additions to the livestock from breeding or purchase, and losses from death, disease, slaughter or sale. Some accounts also included sections for goods (fleeces and tar for example) and the works owed by the tenants. The detail impressed a seventeenth-century estate administrator, John Smyth of Nibley (1883, I, 303), when he looked at the medieval account rolls in the muniment room of Berkeley Castle (Glos.):

> When the Reeve or Bayly at the end of his yeare, left his office to a successor, the inventory is so exact, what cattle of each kind, grain of each sort . . . what poultry of each sort . . . which was by writing on parchment . . . delivered over to the next, that it cannot but give us cause almost of wonder . . .

The peasant holdings, in total, produced much more grain, meat and wool than did the lords' demesnes, yet to learn about their crops and stock we have to gather crumbs of information. In a few accounts which record tithes, the grain collected indicates the crops grown by the peasants of the parish. Individual households' possessions are recorded in the detailed tax assessments of 1225–1332, which like all fiscal records are subject to omissions both of taxpayers who were exempt or who evaded payment, and of grain and animals left out of the assessment both legally and illegally. Occasionally a peasant committed a crime or fled the manor, and the lord's officials accounted for the crops and stock that he left behind. Manorial court rolls, our main source for the lives of the peasantry, record such exceptional cases, and also the more routine references to stolen crops or those damaged by animals, and animals found wandering as strays, or taken as heriots (death duties). It is possible to use these references to reconstruct the crops and animals of the village (Dyer 1980, 316–24).

Even as a source for the demesnes of landlords, the account rolls are imperfect. Church estates are better documented than those of laymen, and great lords, such as bishops and earls, have left more evidence than minor lords, the gentry. Yet the latter held (cumulatively) more manors than the magnates.

The second disadvantage of the written sources is that they vary in both quantity and quality over time. Although the eleventh-century countryside is illuminated by the great survey of 1086, and in the twelfth century there are charters and royal Pipe Rolls, the really large volume of written material begins in the thirteenth century. The manorial records, which give the most vivid insights into agriculture, are most informative in the thirteenth and fourteenth centuries. Surveys and extents survive sparsely from the twelfth century and proliferate in the thirteenth. Accounts begin for the Winchester estate in 1208 and are widespread from about 1270, as are series of court rolls. The treatises on estate management, like 'Walter of Henley', were mostly written in the thirteenth century (Oschinsky 1971). So the period around 1300 is illuminated by a concentration of good quality written evidence. Surveys become rare after 1350, and were replaced by relatively brief rentals, and accounts become less informative after the fourteenth century (Harvey, P. D. A., 1984, 35–7). Following a period of relatively poor evidence in the fifteenth century, many new sources, especially probate inventories and a great deal of contemporary comment and description, appear after 1500.

Thirdly, there is a geographical inequality in the records, with a bias towards the east and south. Estate records are especially thin in the north-west. The unevenness of distribution partly reflects the variations in literate culture, and in the location of large bureaucratically run estates, as well as the degree of destructive disorder, endemic in the case of the Scottish border. Some counties, like Cheshire and Durham, are omitted from the state records because they were governed separately.

Finally, the documents are slanted towards production rather than consumption, so we can calculate from the manorial accounts the rate of sowing of seed, or the number of bushels of grain harvested from each demesne acre, or the number of piglets produced by a sow. Our information on the eventual use of the produce is much less complete. The survival of dozens of household accounts tells us about the eating habits of the higher aristocracy, but again we must use such indirect evidence as the toll-corn from mills, or the agreements for the maintenance of retired peasants, to gain a little information about the food eaten by the lower classes. For example, peasants grew substantial amounts of peas. Did they eat them themselves? Or feed them to animals? Or sell them to the poor? No certain answer can be given.

The documents are, then, very imperfect sources, and they must be used with care. They can yield evidence that is unobtainable elsewhere. Above all, they are capable of providing an overview of the whole country, enabling us both to gain a general picture, and to define regional differences. Domesday Book of 1086 gives the first 'description' of the kingdom, at a remarkably early date by European standards because of the advanced and centralized character of the English royal government. It provides statistics for each manor of the numbers of tenants, slaves and ploughs. A critical approach to Domesday forces us to treat the figures, especially of tenants, as minima, and it is now believed that the 'ploughlands', once regarded as a guide to the cultivated area, were a fiscal assessment (Harvey, S. P. J., 1985, 86–103). The ploughs recorded for the demesne and tenants do appear to have had a basis in reality, so that their distribution, mapped by Darby (1977, 127) allows us to gain some notion of regional variations in land use (figure 2.1). A belt of country with a high commitment to arable farming ran across the centre of England from the south-

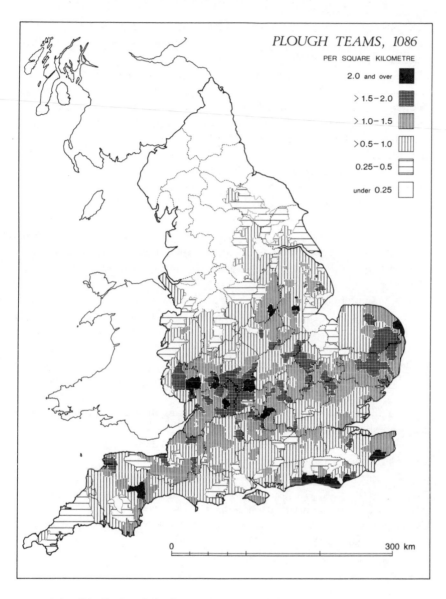

PLOUGH TEAMS, 1086

PER SQUARE KILOMETRE

2.0 and over

> 1.5 – 2.0

> 1.0 – 1.5

> 0.5 – 1.0

0.25 – 0.5

under 0.25

0   300 km

2.1   *Distribution of plough teams in 1086, calculated from Domesday Book*
(source: Darby 1977).

west, through the midlands to Norfolk and Suffolk, with significant concentrations also in the Trent Valley, Thames Valley, east Kent, and the coast of
Sussex.

Attempts have been made to estimate the arable of the whole country in 1086,
with totals varying from 2 million to 3.4 million ha. Lennard's figure of 2.9
million ha is plausibly argued from an assumption of 40 ha (100 acres) per
plough (1959, 393). In the localities with the highest densities, such as east
Norfolk or north Gloucestershire, arable land exceeded 70 per cent of the total,
and in much of the midlands and East Anglia it is reasonable to estimate that
more than half of the land was ploughed.

Domesday's record of ploughs seems consistent and systematic, which is
certainly not true of the patchy figures for meadow and pasture. The woodland
statistics, though imperfect, have allowed an informed estimate of a nationwide
coverage of 15 per cent, totalling 1.6 million ha (Rackham, O., 1980, 126).
The distribution of woodland is to some extent complementary to that of the
ploughs, with high densities in the north and in the south-east (Darby 1977,
171–94).

Such an ambitious survey as Domesday was not repeated, though one of its
functions, to inform the central government about the resources of the king's
tenants-in-chief, was performed from the thirteenth century by the extents
attached to Inquisitions *Post Mortem*. Every death of a tenant-in-chief (mostly the
higher secular aristocracy) was followed by an official enquiry into the lands of
the deceased by a local jury. Though the surveys are formalized, and
underestimate the value of the lands, they can be used to draw comparisons
between different regions. They are currently being studied by Campbell, whose
map of arable demesnes is a foretaste of future research (figure 2.2). This does
not measure directly the proportion of land used as arable. It shows the
percentage of large and small arable demesnes, which is partly determined by the
size of lay manors, and partly by the extent of lords' interest in arable cultivation.
The largest demesnes are shown to be concentrated in the midlands, south and
East Anglia. Extensive arable demesnes also existed on the large church estates of
the south-west midlands, and Norfolk was very much an arable farming area, but
its demesnes tended to be small.

Inquisitions record grazing land inexactly because lords often held rights in
common pastures rather than specific acreages of 'several' (separate or enclosed)
pasture. The difference between Devon Inquisitions of the late thirteenth and
early fourteenth century, where about one-fifth of the land was said to be pasture
or waste, and those for Gloucestershire of similar date, in which only about 5 per
cent was described as pasture and moor, simply reflects the prevalence of enclosed
pastures in one county and open commons in the other (Fox, H. S. A., 1975,
185; Madge and Fry 1903–10). Some sense of the variations in the ratio between
arable and pastoral resources can be derived from the areas of arable and meadow

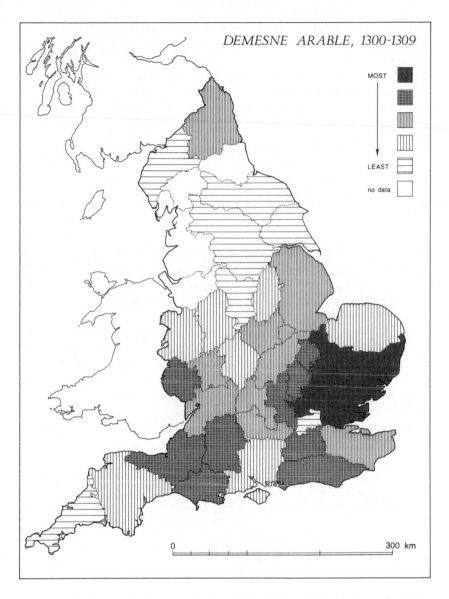

DEMESNE ARABLE, 1300-1309

MOST

LEAST

no data

0   300 km

2.2 *Distribution of demesne arable in 1300–1309, calculated from Inquisitions*
Post Mortem
(source: B.M.S. Campbell).

given for demesnes. Those for Lincolnshire and Nottinghamshire cover many types of agrarian landscape.

Table 2.1 *Percentages of arable and meadow in Inquisitions Post Mortem of the thirteenth century, for Lincolnshire and Nottinghamshire*

	Arable, %	Meadow, %
Marshland (Lincs.)	52	48
Fenland (Lincs.)	73	27
Clayland (Lincs.)	75	25
River valley (Notts.)	87	13
Limestone (Lincs.)	89	11
Woodland (Notts.)	97	3

source: Platts 1985, 106–7; Standish 1914, 20–104

The extensive meadows of the marshes provided unusually abundant grazing and hay for animals. The much lower percentage for the woodland was perhaps more typical of the limited availability of meadow over much of the country.

Another record of land use is provided by the feet of fines, which were conveyances of freehold land (usually between substantial landholders, including manorial lords) registered in the royal courts. Like the Inquisitions they give formalized round numbers, and omit common pastures and woods, but can still be used to compare different agricultural patterns. A national study of these sources has not yet been made. The potential is indicated by comparing the Feldon district of south and east Warwickshire with the wooded Arden to the north and west, as in table 2.2.

Table 2.2 *Land use from Warwickshire feet of fines, 1300–13*

	Hectares (%)				
	Arable	Meadow	Pasture	Wood	Total
Feldon	1,076 (94)	19 (1.5)	6 (0.5)	47 (4)	1,148
Arden	1,007 (85)	55 (5)	24 (2)	101 (8)	1,187

source: Stokes and Drucker 1939

The preponderance of arable in the Feldon is characteristic of a champion district, that is one in which nucleated villages cultivated large tracts of open fields. The Arden is typical of many woodland districts where trees and grass were relatively plentiful, together with a good deal of arable.

The figures obtained from the Inquisitions and feet of fines allow comparisons to be made between different regions, but they do not provide absolute figures for the use of land. Close analysis of surveys, with the help of modern maps and a good deal of guesswork, suggests that in the north of England as little as 5 to 20 per cent of the land was arable in the thirteenth century (Miller 1975, 1–16); in individual parishes in the champion midlands 80 per cent of the land was used as arable.

Finally, figure 2.3 shows the division of England into farming regions made by Thirsk, based on such sources as probate inventories (1967a, 1–112). A complex patchwork of agrarian economies is shown, with a large 'mixed farming' area in midland, southern and eastern England, open pasture regions in the north and west, and localised wood pasture districts breaking up the mixed farming areas.

Three general conclusions can be drawn from the these studies of regional differences. Firstly, England can be divided into areas which were primarily oriented towards arable farming (though with animals playing a vital role as suppliers of pulling power and manure), and those regions in the north and west which had a more pastoral emphasis. Secondly, beneath these broad patterns lie many small districts which were infinitely varied in their use of land and methods of farming. The probate inventories of the sixteenth century, and such medieval documents as the Inquisitions point to the fine texture of a countryside with many types of *pays* (such as wood pasture, fenland, champion). Closer analysis usually reveals that no one *pays* is ever quite like another. The various woodland districts, and the many 'wolds' stretching from the Gloucestershire Cotswolds to those of east Yorkshire, all had distinctive characters.

Thirdly, there was a broad continuity of regional types over time. The areas with the highest plough team densities in 1086 tend to show a bias towards arable farming in the subsequent periods. Of course there were changes. A campaign of woodland clearance in 1086–1300 may have increased the cultivated area by 400,000 ha (Rackham, O., 1980, 134). The amount of land under cultivation also expanded at the expense of heaths, moors and pastures, and areas of wetlands were drained for conversion to arable. But these changes did not transform woodlands and pastoral districts into champion country. In the woodlands, for example, the proportion of arable rose, but enough trees and grassland survived to maintain a distinctive economy. After the demographic and economic crises of the fourteenth century the trends favoured grassland at the expense of arable. In the champion districts of Warwickshire the feet of fines show a drop in the percentage of arable from 94 per cent in 1300–13 to 57 per cent in *c.*1500. However, the contrast with the Arden remained, because there the amount of recorded arable declined from 85 per cent to 34 per cent in the same period (Dyer 1981, 10).

Series of manorial documents can reflect changes in agricultural production

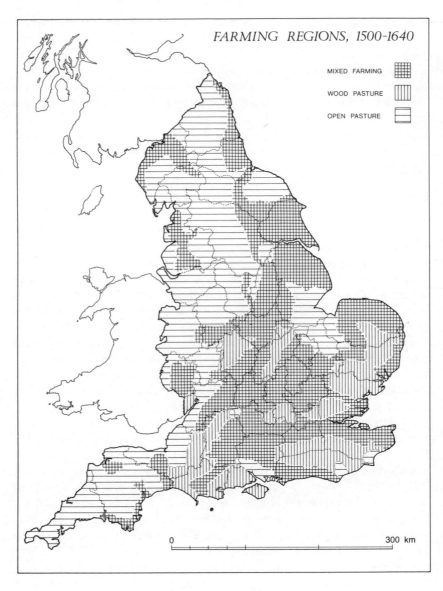

FARMING REGIONS, 1500-1640

MIXED FARMING

WOOD PASTURE

OPEN PASTURE

0   300 km

2.3   *Farming regions 1500–1640*
      (source: Thirsk 1967a).

among the peasants. Tithe receipts ought to provide a good indication of trends, though they seldom exist in very long series. In the hills of north Derbyshire the sum at which tithe corn was leased out slumped drastically after the Black Death of 1348–9, as fields which had been created in bleak upland locations in times of food scarcity were abandoned by their peasant cultivators (Blanchard 1967, 64–6). The changes in the priorities of midland peasants are suggested by the by-laws enacted in sessions of manorial courts: in the early fourteenth century a major preoccupation was the regulation of the grain harvest, forbidding activities like night carting that could have been a cloak for theft, laying down rules for gleaning and protecting crops from the depredations of animals set to graze the stubble too early. Two centuries later, and the principal concerns of those framing by-laws were problems of pastoral farming: the tethering of horses, the ringing of pigs (to prevent them rooting), and the overstocking of the commons (Ault 1972, 86, 137–8). The change in production resulted from developments in consumption, especially in diet. For example, the food given to farm servants during the harvest at Sedgeford (Norfolk) consisted mainly of barley bread in the late thirteenth century, with no more than 2 per cent of calories being provided by meat. In the century after 1340, especially after the mid-fourteenth-century plagues, the meat content rose steadily, until by the 1420s meat accounted for 23 per cent of the calories consumed (Dyer in press).

The documents therefore have the virtue of providing us with both a general spatial overview, and a picture of long-term development over time. They are also valuable for the quality of their evidence, which enables us to examine the relationship between society and its natural environment. Three aspects of this interaction will now be examined, concentrating on the well-documented thirteenth and fourteenth centuries: the social hierarchy, the efficiency with which resources were exploited, and exchange in the countryside.

Social Hierarchy and the Use of Resources

The units of agricultural production of the different social groups varied greatly in size and structure and included the peasant farm, the village, the manor and the estate.

At the peak of medieval growth, in *c.*1300 there were about a million peasant farms from which the majority of the population gained at least part of their living. They ranged from a cottage to tenements in excess of 12 ha of arable land. Holdings tended to be larger in the midlands, west and north, with many that were standard units of yardlands or half-yardlands (12 or 6 ha), or oxgangs (6 ha). In East Anglia the majority of peasants held 2 ha or less. In addition to the arable holding, each farm normally had a share of meadow, rarely more than a tenth of the total, and often also rights of common grazing: in its most fully developed form this extended over the permanent pasture, the stubble of the arable after the harvest, the fallows and the meadow after the hay had been carried. Peasants also often had common rights in woods or in places where turf could be cut (turbaries). The physical lay-out of the farm depended on the local settlement pattern and field-system. In a champion village in the midlands or north-east the peasant's house and garden formed part of a compact settlement, while his land lay scattered in strips over the open fields. In areas of dispersed settlement, either uplands and woodlands, or in the diffuse settlements of East Anglia, the house was more likely to stand in isolation or in a hamlet, and the lands would not necessarily be fragmented; they might even be arranged in a discrete block near the dwelling.

The village was not itself a unit of agricultural production, even in its developed champion form. However, it did act as a management organization, at the very least exercising control over the common pastures, and often making important decisions about crop rotations, harvesting, and the limitation of the numbers of animals (stinting). For many peasants the village territory contained all of their resources, but access to grazing and woodland might sometimes have been subject to more complex arrangements, like the intercommoning systems by which many villages shared in extensive pastures, such as in the Chiltern Hills in Oxfordshire (p. 133; figure 7.3; Roden 1973, 327).

The manor can best be described as an administrative unit, through which lords were able to levy rents, services and dues from the subordinate peasantry, with a manorial court exercising jurisdiction over the tenants. Manors often contained only a fraction of a village, so that their lords enjoyed much influence, but not control, over the village's management. The lord's demesne formed an integral part of most manors, and this indeed was a large and important unit of agricultural production. About one-third of all of the arable land in eastern England in the late thirteenth century lay in demesnes, most of it in units of between 40 and 120 ha (Kosminsky 1956, 68–151). Like peasant holdings, demesnes could either be dispersed over a field system or, very commonly, gathered into more compact blocks (Hall, D. 1985, 64–5). One specialised type of demesne, the Cistercian grange, could resemble a modern farm, consisting as it did of an isolated group of buildings sometimes surrounded by its own fields (Platt 1969, 58–65). The management of the demesne was most commonly in the hands of the lord's agent (reeve or bailiff) in the thirteenth and fourteenth centuries, and both before 1200 and after 1400 the land was leased out to a tenant who paid a fixed rent, a farm, and who was therefore known as a farmer.

A manor might be the only asset of a minor lord, but often formed a single element in a larger estate. When the lord's ability to travel was limited, as with a fixed institution like a monastery, the estate tended to lie within a radius of 30 km. Lay magnates held manors scattered over many counties. In large estates demesne production was co-ordinated; a manor well-suited to the production of oats, for example, might supply others with that grain. Seed corn would be exchanged between manors. Animals would be driven from manor to manor in a pattern of transhumance, the sheep to upland pastures in the summer, and pigs to feed on woodland acorns in the autumn. One manor with the appropriate resources might serve as a central horse stud.

To describe the agricultural units in this way gives the impression that the countryside was simply divided into farms of different sizes, peasant holdings and large demesnes, each type integrated into larger organisations, villages and estates. This would ignore the vital links of lordship that bound peasant holdings and lords' demesnes together. The peasant holding and the village could have existed without the manor and the estate: the peasant economy was autonomous. By contrast, the demesne was dependent on the tenant holdings. In the earlier centuries the peasants' labour services supplied much of the work done on the lords' arable, and both before and after the commutation of services demesne agriculture was funded from the tenants' cash rents (Hilton 1975, 174–214). The small and large productive units co-existed as part of a system for transferring wealth in the form of goods, labour and cash upwards, from the peasant producers to the aristocracy.

Competition for the control of rural resources naturally arose from this inequality of wealth and power. The disputes which can be found throughout the period seem to have reached a climax in the thirteenth century, when land was scarce in relation to increasing population, and lords were anxious to raise incomes threatened by inflation. The battlegrounds tended to be the fens, woods and wastes, the underdeveloped areas which had been shared or intercommoned in less difficult times. As lords and peasants sought to increase the intensity of the use of these lands, they found it necessary to define their rights more precisely. Such an area was Malvern Chase, more than 50 square km of wood, marsh and pasture in south-western Worcestershire. By the mid-thirteenth century, although much of the land had been colonized for agriculture and industry (it was a centre of pottery manufacture), three magnates enjoyed hunting rights there, the bishops of Hereford and of Worcester, and the earl of Gloucester. After a quarrel between Earl Gilbert and the Bishop of Hereford a compromise over hunting rights was reached in 1278, and in 1287 a boundary was drawn along the crest of the hills by means of the still visible 'Red Earl's Ditch' (Smith, B.S. 1964, 29–31).

Problems were not always settled so decisively. Nowhere were conflicts more bitter and protracted than in the fenlands of eastern England, where pressures were heavier and the rewards of agriculture greater than west of the Severn. Here drainage schemes were turning wastes (previously used profitably as common pastures and as sources of turf, reeds, rushes, sedge, fish and fowl), into improved pastures and arable for the use of the peasant communities and lords who drained the land. Crowland Abbey, as a principal promoter of such schemes, found itself locked in long-term combat with rival landowners, notably the Prior of Spalding, the Abbot of Peterborough and the Wake family (Darby 1940, 86–92).

'Waste', in the modern sense of wild land, seems to have ceased to exist by the thirteenth century. An assart, that is, a clearing made by removing trees and undergrowth, and enclosed with a hedge and ditch, encroached on many interests: if the land lay in royal forest, the crown required a fine. The landlord might also expect an entry fine and certainly an annual rent. The local churches would have tithe claims. And neighbours' grazing rights would be infringed. Village communities sometimes clashed over the improvement of wastes that had previously been subject to intercommoning, and trouble might boil up into the forcible removal of the offending fences or the mass impounding of animals (Hilton 1983, 151–2).

Villagers also became involved in unequal conflicts with landlords over pastures and woods. The balance was tipped in favour of the lords by the Statute of Merton in 1236, which gave them more control over 'lands, wastes, woods and pastures' judged to be surplus to the direct needs of the tenants (*Statutes of the Realm*, I, 2–3). An extreme example of the lords' ability to take over land for their exclusive use can be seen in the wave of imparking in the thirteenth and fourteenth centuries (Cantor and Hatherly 1979). Often the parks occupied remaining areas of wood and pasture, and the pale presented a permanent barrier against further assarting. Potentially good agricultural land, even arable, might be taken into parks and removed from cultivation. The park served as an assertion of seigneurial power, showing that a lord could declare a halt to the clearance of land, and reserve it for his private pleasure and profit. Parks became a symbol of lordly privilege which invited assault, with the result that the royal judicial documents record dozens of incidents in which bands of men broke the pales, killed deer, and drained ponds (p. 147).

On a smaller scale, struggles for resources pitted individual peasants against village communities. In their concern to protect the interests of the majority the villagers sought to prevent individuals from departing from the agreed routines of cultivation, and above all from appropriating to themselves too large a share of the common grazing. In a Wiltshire village, Monkton Deverill, a typical complaint was directed against a servile tenant called William Husee in 1308. He pastured his sheep on the stubble field immediately after the harvest, instead of waiting, as was the custom, until the first of November, so as to leave the cattle and horses to graze before the close-cropping sheep came on to the temporary pasture. He also released the sheep after they had been impounded, and took broom from common land with his cart and prevented other tenants from taking broom (presumably they used it as litter for animals) (Longleat MS. 9654). In this case, as in many others, the villagers brought the action to the lord's court, hence our knowledge of it. The lord, who had a direct interest in the grazing problem, and a less direct concern to maintain order among his tenants, supported the villagers against Husee.

In addition to direct competition for resources in terms of property divisions and common rights, the day-to-day circumstances of lordship influenced the peasants' use of land. Lords were concerned with the efficiency of the peasants' ploughs and carts, because these were periodically put to work on the demesne. Consequently peasants were supposed to obtain permission for the sale of oxen or horses, though this eventually became no more than an occasion for the levying of a toll. The growth of money rents from the twelfth century must have encouraged peasants to grow cash crops, such as wheat, instead of cheaper grain for their own consumption. Was seigneurial pressure therefore a stimulus to peasant production? This is sometimes alleged, though the contrary arguments are very strong – the diversion of labour from the holdings, especially in the critical harvest season, the appropriation of manure for the lord's fold, and above all the constant drain of cash all weakened the peasants' productive capacity.

In spite of the disadvantages of the peasants' social position, they should be given some credit as innovators. It is true that lords did adopt new techniques, such as the windmill in the decades around 1200, and the Cistercians introduced a new rationality into the organisation of agriculture in their granges. However, the great majority of assarts resulted from peasant initiative. And peasants made the various adaptations of the field systems, such as the *inhoks* which allowed more intense cultivation by planting crops in the fallow field. Also the peasants found horses more convenient means of traction at a time when the lords clung to traditional ox-power (Langdon 1986a, 172–229).

Were Resources Used Efficiently?

The medieval landscape was largely a tamed and civilized one, in which the forces of nature had come under human control. The hunting and gathering element in the economy was of relatively small consequence. Even the higher nobility, who regarded hunting as such a prestigious activity, can sometimes be estimated from household accounts to have consumed only about 7 per cent of their meat supplies in the form of game (Dyer, forthcoming). And in any case park deer, the main source of venison, were semi-domesticated animals, as were the rabbits which were kept in the sheltered environment of warrens (p. 164).

So we must turn to agriculture in order to assess the efficiency of the medieval exploitation of the countryside. Every manorial survey lists the lord's assets in terms of arable, meadow, pasture and wood. They give the impression of resources that were carefully balanced and complementary in function. The aim was to produce a combination of grain and animal products, with the two sectors interlocking because the animals provided traction and manure, and were fed from straw, grain, hay and the grazing of the stubble, as well as the permanent pasture. Closer examination often shows that the balance of resources within manors was imperfect, and in the champion midlands grazing and woodland resources were often obtained at a distance.

Priority was given to corn growing on most demesnes, the choice of crops being partly conditioned by those best suited to the local soils, and partly by the needs of the producer. So oats predominated in the north and south-west because they grew in adverse circumstances, and barley was preferred as the main crop in East Anglia. Most demesnes outside these areas of specialization grew wheat because of its high price and its almost universal use as a bread corn by the aristocracy, together with some barley or drage (barley and oats sown as a mixture), oats and peas or beans, in many varied permutations.

The treatises and accounts show that the managers of the demesnes knew of many methods for maintaining the fertility of the soil. Fallowing rested the land, and the ploughing of the fallow killed the weeds. Long fallows, in which the uncultivated ground reverted to pasture, was practised in the less fertile areas, and became more general with the reduction in the intensity of cultivation after 1349. Under the regular rotation of crops, in theory practised over much of midland England, land was fallowed every second or third year. In fact *inhoking* allowed the fallow to be partly cropped, so the fallow might occur on some land every fourth year or even less frequently. Nutrients were put into the soil by a number of different techniques: marling involved spreading on the land subsoil dug from deep pits; in the south-west sea sand was spread on the arable; in the same region, in a process called beat-burning, turf was pared off land, and then burnt and spread out before ploughing; peas and other legumes put nitrogen into the soil to benefit the next year's crop. These measures achieved some success, as can be demonstrated from comparing the yields obtained from marled land and unmarled land on the estates of Canterbury Cathedral Priory, or by noting the remarkably high productivity on Tavistock Abbey's demesnes after they had been treated with manure, sea sand, and beat-burning (Mate 1985, 23; Finberg 1969, 86–115). Manure was much the most important source of crop nutrition, whether carted from byres and yards, or trodden into the ground by flocks of sheep folded at night on the arable. The importance attached to manure by contemporaries can be judged from the space devoted to its application by the treatises, and the adoption of elaborate practices such as the East Anglian foldcourse, by which sheep flocks were moved over the fields, dunging the land in rotation (Oschinsky 1971, 362–9; Postgate 1973, 313–22).

Once the ground had been prepared, the success of the crop could be helped by effective sowing. Seed corn on well-run estates was obtained from other manors, and in some regions was sown thickly to smother the weeds (Brandon 1971, 113–34). Special skills in sowing are mentioned in Fitzherbert's *Husbandry*

(Skeat 1882, 18–24) but the only one that leaves much trace in manorial records is the dibbling of beans, that is, sowing seeds individually. Weeds presented a threat to the growing crops, and despite the weeding carried out in June, a difficult process given the broadcast method of sowing, the growth of thistles must have reduced the yield (figure 2.4; Harwood Long 1979, 459–69).

Although the arable husbandry practised by peasants is less well-documented than that of the demesnes, we can assume some similarities because the peasant holdings and the demesnes shared the same fields. Frequent references in court records to peasant marl pits and manure heaps reflect their attempts to maintain soil fertility. Peasants are often alleged to have used inefficient methods, like the scattering of strips in the field system; this was not the result of wasteful egalitarianism, but a method of ensuring fair shares of good and bad land, as a basis for cooperation among villagers. Peasants were not trapped in a mindless traditionalism. The fields, even in the most orthodox midland system, were managed flexibly, by using the internal subdivisions, the furlongs, as the cropping units, rather than the whole field. In this way peasants could choose their crops, and did not have to plant equal quantities of winter corn (wheat and rye) and spring corn (barley, peas, oats); nor did they have to leave the land fallow every two or three years (VCH 1954, 159–61). A contrast is rightly drawn between the regular fields of the midland system, and the irregular types found elsewhere. Yet in practical management the differences were not very great, because we can find land being cropped on a three-course rotation in the irregular fields, and all kinds of eccentric variations within the supposed constraints of a two- or three-field system (p. 64).

In eastern Norfolk, in an area of very fertile soils, high population density, weak lordship and peasant individualism, lords and peasants alike achieved high levels of grain production in the thirteenth and fourteenth centuries by eliminating fallows, applying much manure, sowing thickly, and using labour-intensive methods (Campbell 1983a, 26–46). Yields on demesnes as high as 3 hectolitres per ha (20 bushels per acre) were obtained for wheat, compared with about 1.5 hectolitres per ha (10 bushels per acre) on the contemporary estates of the bishopric of Winchester (Titow 1972, 82–91). Other regions did not follow this example because, presumably, they were not impelled by the same pressure of population, and they were rightly cautious of ultimately reducing yields by fallowing too infrequently and thereby losing both the benefit of the rested land and the meagre but useful grazing on the fallows.

Medieval arable farming must be judged to have performed patchily, with only some areas of success. Pastoral farming has received less attention from historians, and less criticism. Animals were sometimes specially managed, as in the vaccaries for cattle in the north, or by the provision of a sheep-reeve or master shepherd, who moved flocks from one pasture to another, and arranged for the centralized shearing and sale of wool. Sheep were worth care because their wool

2.4 *A man cutting a thistle with a weeding hook and forked stick, from a late fourteenth-century manuscript*
(Bod. Lib. MS Rawl. D. 939, Section 2).

gave an important return in cash, and their meat and manure were valuable by-products. Large sums were spent in some regions on housing sheep in sheep-cotes, often 30 m long. Some districts had their own distinctive type of sheep, one important variable being the length of the fleece. Flocks were sometimes improved by bringing rams from a distance (Trow-Smith 1957, 155). New lambs received supplementary feed of cows' milk, and even ale, while adult sheep in the winter were fed on hay, grain and peas. Walter of Henley advised that sheep should be treated gently, because a bad-tempered shephered would upset the flock, and cause some to die; he expected shepherds to attend to every detail for the sake of the lambs, like the removal of wool around the ewe's teats (Oschinsky 1971, 336–9). Attempts were made to control disease by culling sickly animals (the main criterion for choosing which young sheep to kill for meat), and by applications of tar, grease and butter, but there was no defence against the great scab epidemic of the 1270s. Outside these disastrous years, mortality rates were on average between 10 and 20 per cent, which though very much higher than the modern 2 to 5 per cent, were no worse than in any age before the advent of scientific veterinary medicine. Individual fleeces weighed usually between half and one kg, which is one-third of the modern figure (Stephenson 1983). This therefore represents a better medieval performance than in cereal cultivation, for which demesnes in the thirteenth and fourteenth centuries could attain only one-sixth or one-eighth of late twentieth-century yields. Dairy farming did not achieve such good results as sheep farming, partly because of the lack of the same cash incentive. Medieval cows, for example, produced about 40 kg of milk products a year, compared with a modern animal's 450 kg (Kershaw 1973a, 102). Perhaps the most effective example of profitable cattle farming lay in the development of long-distance droving, first recorded in the thirteenth century, whereby young beef cattle bred in the hills of Wales and the north were driven to midland pastures for fattening, and then taken on to London for slaughter (Finberg 1954, 12–14; Dyer 1981, 20).

Water control and exploitation must be judged to be an area of success in medieval management of resources. Such spectacular technical feats as Edward I's canalization of 5 km of the river Clwyd and the construction of a harbour to serve the new castle of Rhuddlan were only feasible because of centuries of experience in water works for agrarian purposes (Morris, J. E., 1901, 145). The building of dykes, the digging of channels and the diversion of rivers and streams had enabled the draining and cultivation of large areas of wetlands, above all around the Wash, in the twelfth and thirteenth centuries. Drainage projects revived, after a lull, at the end of the fifteenth century with such works as Morton's Leam in Cambridgeshire (Darby 1940, 167–8). The techniques were so accomplished that some original drainage channels (after numerous scourings) are still in use today. As well as skill in calculating levels, forward planning, and a huge amount of spadework, the construction of dykes needed foundations of timber, brushwood and stones. The works received constant renewal and maintenance from those living in the nearby villages, the tasks and costs being allocated according to local custom. The system was strengthened from the late thirteenth century onwards by the royal appointment of commissions of sewers, whose job was to hear from local juries on the deficiencies of the dykes and drains, and then to order the necessary work. Such improvements could entail major projects, like that recommended when a Norfolk jury reported to the commissioners in 1320 that 'a causeway ought to be made in Wiggenhall next to the Newelonddich on the south side . . . ten feet wide at the bottom, six feet wide at the top, six feet high . . .' (Owen 1981, 34).

On a more modest scale medieval skill in water control was directed towards providing a power source for mills, which required the building of dams and the cutting of leats. Much of this construction had been done before the Conquest, but the old works needed constant repair and refinement, and some new mills were constructed. Improvements to the mill at Mildenhall (Suffolk) in 1323–4 cost 39s 2d to pay for 188 men for a day digging earth, ramming timber, and scouring a leat two furlongs (400 m) in length. In 1335 a new leat was made across land claimed by the neighbouring vill of Lakenheath; the annoyed Lakenheath jury complained that the work was one and a half leagues (4 km) long and a perch (5 m) wide (Bodl. Lib. Suffolk rolls, no. 21; C.U.L., EDC 7/15/11/2/15). Ponds for freshwater fish also involved a formidable amount of earth moving and skilled carpentry.

In arable farming, livestock management and hydraulic engineering time-honoured practices were combined with gradual innovation. Technical change in the middle ages tended to occur slowly, emerging from practical experience and trial and error. Walter of Henley, although mainly concerned with passing on to his readers the accumulated wisdom of authority, was capable of suggesting a modest experiment to prove the advantages of using seed from outside the manor: 'Cause two ridges (selions) to be ploughed in one day, and sow the one with the bought seed and the other with the seed which grew on your own, and at harvest you will see that I tell you the truth' (Oschinsky 1971, 324–5).

Despite this practical and rational approach, agricultural production had many faults. Over most of England demesne cereal yields remained well below 2 hectolitres per ha (15 bushels per acre), or six times the seed planted. The speculation that the peasants did better because of their higher input of labour and superior motivation is not supported by the rare examples of peasant yields revealed when a departed tenant's crops were harvested by the lord's officials (Hilton 1975, 201–2). The main disadvantage for the peasant cultivator lay in the imbalance between arable and pasture. All of our evidence for peasant animals, deriving from tax records, accusations of trespass or confiscated stock, suggest that animals were very unevenly distributed among the peasants, with many having no more than a cow or two. Only a minority of wealthy people owned large enough sheep flocks – more than two or three per ha – to fertilise the arable adequately (Postan 1973, 214–48). Villages set limits to the numbers of animals that could be kept on the common pastures, like Croxton Kerrial (Leics.) in the thirteenth century, where yardlanders (those with *c.* 12 ha) were allowed to have no more than 40 adult sheep, two oxen, a cow and two pigs (VCH 1954, 164). Such stints were designed to prevent individuals from overstocking, but many peasants owned much smaller numbers of animals, and their arable must have been under-manured.

Specific areas of weakness in medieval agriculture can be indicated by comparisons both with the continent, especially the intensive and progressive rural economy of Flanders (Tits-Dieuaide 1981; 1984), and with the new developments in England in the post-medieval centuries (Kerridge 1967; Thirsk 1978). Horticulture seems to have been underdeveloped: gardens occupied small areas of land, less than 2 per cent of the total, and they produced a very limited range of vegetables and fruit, for the most part apples, pears, cabbages, onions, leeks and garlic. Industrial crops, mainly flax and hemp, and a little madder, were cultivated on a small scale also (p. 122, 124). An evident reluctance to specialize led to the production of crops for which the soils and climate seem not to have been best suited, hence the peasants of the Peak District of Derbyshire, who were no doubt anxious to provide as much of their cereal needs as possible, grew oats on bleak hillsides more appropriately used for grazing. Shortages of animal feed did not stimulate the improvement of the natural meadows, and although the acreage under legumes increased in the thirteenth and fourteenth centuries, no other specialised fodder crops were grown.

Exchange

Medieval peasants and lords alike often used the produce of their lands in their own households. It can reasonably be estimated from our knowledge of the size of holdings that half of the English population in the thirteenth century could provide for the bulk of their food needs themselves. However, the extent of self-sufficiency should not be exaggerated. From very early times lords had been involved in exchange of a non-commercial type, achieved by grouping into estates manors with greatly varied economies. Household accounts demonstrate the prevalence of gift-giving among the aristocracy, especially of scarce and high status foodstuffs such as venison. Households also practised hospitality towards social equals, and granted charity to inferiors. Before 1200 large households lived off their manors, either by travelling over the estate, eating produce as they went, or in the case of monasteries by arranging for food to be transported to the house from each manor on a rota. Already by 1086 the existence of large demesne sheep flocks (whose wool was presumably sold) and the confident assumption of

Domesday Book that every manor could be assigned a cash value, points to some production for the market (Sawyer 1965, 145–64). By the thirteenth century it was not unknown for both monastic and lay estates to sell the grain from their manors, and to buy supplies at their convenience in markets near to the household. We should be wary of thinking of the growth of the market as a simple, progressive development, because in the late fourteenth century some lords reverted to direct provisioning of their households from their manors (Harvey, B. 1977, 135–40). After 1400 the purchase of foodstuffs became a normal way of aristocratic life, with the important exception of the gentry who retained direct supplies from a home farm.

The peasantry had also developed a strong market orientation by the late thirteenth century. They had to raise cash by produce sales in order to pay rents and taxes. Many dues were determined by ancient custom, but obligations increased because of such variable payments as entry fines needed to acquire land. A customary yardland in the midlands with annual rents fixed at £1, might command a fine of £5 or £10 when it changed hands. Scarce assart land being rented for the first time in 1308–9 could cost as much as 10s 0d per acre (VCH 1979, 36). Increasingly, former demesne land was being let on leasehold terms with rents fixed in relation to market forces. The land market is attested by the numerous transfers of customary land found in manorial court rolls, and the many deeds by which free tenants bought and sold their property. It may sometimes, especially in periods of low commercial activity, have been a 'natural' market which allowed those with growing families to acquire extra resources as their needs increased, and to shed land as the children left home, and the tenants grew older and less active (Dyer 1980, 301–12). In buoyant commercial circumstances, such as in East Anglia around 1300, the land market allowed 'kulaks' (thriving, prosperous peasants) to build up larger and more profitable holdings, though these accumulations of land tended to be fragile and to be broken up soon after their creation (Smith, R. M. 1984b, 135–45).

Every type of produce was sold, from the obvious cash crops such as grain, wool and dairy produce, to such byproducts as straw and manure, and the furze, bracken, rushes and reeds that could be gathered from commons. Even rights – to fold animals on arable or to pasture animals on commons – might be traded, leading to the anguish of fellow villagers who complained that the common was being 'overburdened with the beasts of strangers'. Peasants often sold their goods in processed form, deriving extra profit from trade in ale, bread and candles. Middlemen gained a living from buying from peasant producers for resale, such as the cornmongers who make a shadowy appearance in the documents, notably when the central government attempted to regulate their activities (Hilton 1975, 89).

As well as the sale and purchase of agricultural produce carried out within the village, a great deal of long-distance trade helped to redress imbalances between the resources of different regions. This helps to explain the location of many towns on or near the frontier between farming regions. Through the funnel of the town's market the timber and cattle of a wood pasture district would be exchanged for the grain of a champion or mixed farming area. The peasants of pastoral districts were especially dependent on long-distance contacts, for otherwise they could not have exchanged their surpluses of animal produce for cereals. The inhabitants of champion countries had often cleared so many of their woods that they were dependent on trade for supplies of timber and fuel. East Anglia obtained much of its timber from Scandinavia, and ports like King's Lynn in turn exported the region's surplus of grain (Carus-Wilson 1962–3). The aristocracy's taste for wine had been partly satisfied by English vineyards in the early middle ages. The abandonment of these vineyards in the thirteenth and later centuries may be connected with a climatic change, but is more likely to be a further example of specialization created by market forces, because Gascon wine was cheaper, better and more reliable in supply. The towns themselves provided a large market for agricultural produce, as they contained concentrations of people who had little or no access to agricultural land. They accounted for one-eighth or more of the population, and London, with its 80,000 or more inhabitants in *c.*1300, drew into itself the agricultural surpluses of a wide hinterland.

The market in agricultural produce influenced the development of the countryside. The intensity of production in East Anglia arose from the pull of both the urban market within the region, and the export trade. Higher prices prevailed in the vicinity of London, and helped to stimulate wheat production (Gras 1915, 42–55). Urban butchers were prominent figures in villages near the larger towns where they rented pastures and bought animals from the local peasantry. Above all, sheep farming in many regions was encouraged by the high international demand for wool which reached a peak around 1300.

Neither aristocratic nor peasant households can be regarded as fully self-sufficient. For the higher nobility, from the thirteenth century not just exotic luxuries but also basic necessities were purchased. The better-off peasants, those with more than 6 ha of arable, produced for the market, spending the cash not only on the compulsory charges of rents and taxes, but also on cloth and the services of building workers. Poorer peasants needed to sell their own labour, or the products of part-time industrial work (spinning, for example), or ale, to supplement the income from their holdings.

Conclusion: Change

Documents, especially those in long series, provide us with ample evidence for change. The previous sections on hierarchy, efficiency and exchange are mainly concerned with the decades around 1300, which marked a turning point between centuries of growth and a succeeding period of contraction. One way of explaining the long-term changes is to see them as simple reflections of shifts in supply and demand. Let us take as an illustration the price of wheat. A quarter (enough grain to keep an adult alive for a year) cost 2s 0d in the twelfth century, increased to 6s 0d by 1300, and then fell to about 5s 0d in the fifteenth century, only to rise again after about 1520. To express these sums in real terms, an unskilled worker in the late thirteenth century had to work for 48 days to earn enough money to buy a quarter of wheat, but his successor in the fifteenth could buy the same quantity from only 15 days' earnings. It might be said that the price moved simply in response to increased demand because of a growth in population up to *c.*1300, and then in the opposite direction because of reduced numbers of people. The explanation must be much more complicated. For example, the supply of money had an influence on prices. But let us confine ourselves to the internal history of the countryside, continuing to use as a framework the factors of hierarchy, efficiency and exchange.

Firstly the social hierarchy, though not transformed by the upheavals of the fourteenth century, had its balance tipped in favour of the lower orders. This did not happen 'naturally'; wage-earners and peasants had to challenge the authority of their lords, and to escape such restrictions as serfdom by migrating from their native manors. In consequence of their resistance peasants paid less in rents and dues, and were therefore able to consume more of their own produce. Individual peasants acquired larger holdings, both because of reduced demand for land, and also because of the lords' policy of leasing out demesnes. Peasants continued to compete for the use of commons, but the village community gradually weakened, and could no longer prevent a selfish minority from taking more than their fair share.

Secondly agricultural methods were adapted to meet new circumstances. This required new attitudes and initiatives, to make the best use of larger holdings. The widespread trend from arable to pasture farming resulted from positive decisions to invest in stock and in such facilities as buildings and fencing. The consolidation of holdings that often accompanied increases in grazing land was achieved by strategic purchases and negotiations for exchanges of land. We cannot be sure that such changes led to an increase in productivity of land per acre, though the productive capacity of each worker rose as holdings grew in size.

Thirdly, the total volume of goods exchanged may have dwindled with the reduced population, but the market influenced the countryside still. The increased demand for meat helped to shift farming into the pastoral sector. The growth in real specialization in pastoral agriculture followed from the decision of some upland and woodland producers to abandon cultivation. And the land market allowed the accumulation of yeomen's holdings which in the decades around 1500 tended to remain intact over a number of generations. The growth of rural industries was partly encouraged by the consumer demand from the rural population for metals and clothing.

Confident in the achievements of modern technology, we are often tempted to picture the medieval past as simple and static. All sources of evidence refute the view, and the documents demonstrate conclusively the complex and evolving character of the medieval countryside.

3

Rural Settlement: the Toft and the Croft

Grenville Astill

The New Medieval Countryside

Twenty years can be a long time in the study of medieval rural settlement, and this is particularly true of the last twenty. Students of the medieval countryside in the 1960s might now feel that they have lost their bearings in the terrain they thought they knew so well. The old landmarks do not seem so prominent – villages, particularly deserted ones, do not dominate the scene. The 'new' medieval countryside is a landscape: the settlements are still there, in a variety of forms – farms, hamlets and villages – but the fields which surround them, the tracks which join them and the buildings within them are as much in focus. This dramatic change has occurred since the writing of that influential book on medieval settlement, *Deserted Medieval Villages* (Beresford and Hurst 1971); it has come about as a result of increased cooperation between archaeologists, documentary historians and historical geographers.

It is worth reviewing briefly the major elements of this new perspective and the extent to which it reconciles different views of rural society. Firstly, the concern with the landscape is part and parcel of the general reorientation of archaeological fieldwork away from the study of individual sites and towards the study of a block of countryside and the inter-relationship between the human and animal populations, settlements, fields and the environment and how that relationship changes through time. So far, work has concentrated on establishing elements of the landscape and often the sense of the dynamic is missing, or the economic implications absent.

Secondly, the status of the medieval village has changed. The village was regarded as the epitome of rural settlement in the lowland areas of England; dispersed forms, solitary building groups or hamlets, were typical only of the highland zone. Now the division is not so clear-cut. In lowland England the village coexisted with other, non-nucleated settlement forms by the twelfth century; but it may well have been the most recent addition. Taking a long perspective, the nucleated settlement was a short and aberrant episode in the long history of dispersed settlement which characterized all of this country (Taylor 1983, 12, 125–8).

Explaining why people chose to live in villages during the medieval period is difficult. The closest we have come is the observation that the process of nucleation coincides with the creation of common fields, and therefore these two might be a reflection of a single general circumstance. Some of the resources essential to the survival of rural communities were coming under sufficient pressure to warrant a greater degree of cooperation, and this was easier to achieve with a village/common field arrangement. This invites us to consider the basic relationship between settlement form and the character of the rural economy. While historians of field systems have embarked on this quest, archaeologists have not: it is something to consider below.

Evidence for the new view comes from several disciplines. Firstly, the cumulative results from excavations of Saxon settlements have failed to show signs of nucleation (Taylor 1983, 116–20). Few sites, however, have been investigated extensively and, therefore, this view might be challenged as reflecting merely the small scale of excavation were it not for evidence from other quarters. The portrayal of lowland England as a landscape of villages in Domesday Book is now recognized to be a distortion; most of the country supported a much more dispersed settlement pattern (Sawyer 1979, 1–8). The absence of pre-twelfth-century material from excavations of deserted medieval villages has also been used to show the 'late' appearance of villages. However the lack of early material might merely demonstrate settlement shift rather than settlement absence; the few cases where 'absence' has been convincingly demonstrated are those where recently ploughed villages have been fieldwalked. Yet is is difficult to demonstrate early medieval settlement: extensive excavation of Barton Blount and Goltho has shown that late Saxon structures within crofts can be associated with very little pottery (Beresford, G. 1975, 21).

The case for a transition from dispersed settlement to villages is strengthened by an analysis of plans. Research pioneered by historical geographers has shifted from deserted villages to the spatial arrangements of existing settlements. Two models are favoured for the origin of nucleated settlement. The first appears to be a conscious replanning of existing settlements so that a regularly disposed village is created. At present most examples come from the north which reflects the greater amount of work there. The second process involves the gradual coming together of several small settlements, the end result being the village which betrays its origins in its 'polyfocal' character (Roberts 1977, 117–58; Taylor 1983, 131–4).

An increasing number of planned medieval villages is being identified and, indeed, in some parts of the country it is argued that this was the most common village form. Less progress has been made however in finding a suitable date or context for such replanning. The change seems so dramatic and thoroughgoing to us that there is a tendency to find an equally dramatic explanation, nearly always from the documentation. The most common and accepted contexts for such a reorganization of the landscape in the north are either the Scandinavian colonization or William I's 'Harrying of the North' (for example Hurst 1984, 85–6). Leaving aside the problems of associating specific documentary references with landscape changes, difficulties still remain, for areas of planned settlements do not always coincide with those of colonization or devastation. While accepting that the eleventh century is still the most likely date for village reorganization, Sheppard (1975) has suggested that the decision to carry out such measures could have rested with the manorial lord and that there may be a correlation between particular lords and particular types of village plan.

This, then, is the stage that research on medieval rural settlement has reached. Scholars have encouraged a landscape approach, but most work in any one geographical area has concentrated on one element of that landscape. In order to explain that particular element, reference is not made to other constituents of the same landscape but rather to extraneous stimuli such as invaders, a marauding army or landlords. Another line of enquiry might be to consider whether the particular local economic conditions necessitated a reorganization in the way farmers chose to live and work together. Such an approach would allow change to occur at different times in different parts of the country, but it is not being actively pursued, although Roberts has begun an investigation into the regional character of particular village plans (Roberts 1985).

While the extent of reorganization into villages was unforeseen by Beresford and Hurst, they did identify two other kinds of change, the character and degree of which have been subsequently questioned. Firstly is the extent to which the basic element of the village, the toft or farmyard, was modified. When houses were replaced, they were frequently built away from, or only partially overlapping, the site of their predecessor. The best example of this comes from Wharram Percy where in the course of about three centuries four buildings were built on different alignments on the same toft (Hurst 1979, 26–41). More recent results have shown that such realignments occurred less frequently elsewhere, and usually in the course of the complete reorganization of the holding (Austin forthcoming).

Beresford and Hurst also discussed cases of a more substantial change in the village fabric such as the rerouting of streets and the amalgamation of tofts. It is often difficult to know how much these changes affected the whole village, for the excavations were at best confined to one toft. In one case, however, they were able to show that such a change was extensive, and in doing so they foreshadowed subsequent work on the 'shifting village'. The deserted village at Wawne in Yorkshire originally consisted of a rather haphazard collection of timber buildings and yards which were occupied between the twelfth and fourteenth centuries. In the course of the fourteenth century the settlement was apparently deserted in favour of a new planned block of stone houses and streets built *c*.100 m to the south (Beresford and Hurst 1971, 125–6).

Village settlement in the medieval period was, it seems, considerably more fluid than was thought possible some twenty years ago. The complete desertion of settlements rarely happened, but there is increasing evidence to suggest modification of existing villages. The shrunken village is an extremely common feature of what survives of the medieval landscape. It used to be argued that the shrinkage was a result of depopulation, but more recently the idea of the village shifting has gained acceptance. In Northamptonshire there are many examples of extensive earthworks of streets and house plots on the boundary of the present-day village, testifying to the mobility of the local population (Taylor 1978).

The shifting village then has taken its place alongside the planned settlement as further evidence for dramatic change in the medieval countryside. But evidence for change has to be reconciled with the existence of common fields round most villages, and these must have had a limiting effect on a settlement's mobility. There was of course change within fields. Ridge and furrow over- or underlies house plots in many parts of the country, but the small scale of such movement cannot be evidence of the shift of a whole village. It is interesting therefore to note Hayfield's reinterpretation of the Wawne sequence. The later, planned, block was not so much a fourteenth-century creation as a rearrangement of a part of the village which had been contemporary with the twelfth- to fourteenth-century houses and streets to the north. The 'shift' was therefore not a movement of population from an old to a new site, but a contraction in the extent of the village, coupled with a consequent reorganization of that part which remained occupied. Wawne was thus a polyfocal settlement which lost one of its foci (figure 3.2; Hayfield 1984, 41–67). This sequence could be relevant for other cases of village shift.

The achievements of rural studies over the past twenty years might be summarized by saying that the importance of the concept of fluidity in assessing the countryside has been confirmed, but the emphasis on where change took place has altered. Recent work has chosen to focus on the evolution of villages and the fact that they rarely remained in the same place, rather than on smaller-scale changes within the framework of the settlement.

Regionalism

Whereas the 'regional' approach may have been missing from explanations of large-scale changes in the settlement pattern, it could be argued that regionalism has been too prominent in the interpretation of rural standards of living or the 'quality' of rural life.

Archaeologists have always had a low opinion of the conditions under which the medieval peasant lived. This in part stems from a confusion between the level at which life was actually conducted and the remains which survive for the archaeologist to recover. While most archaeologists accept that the quality and range of small finds from a rural site are unlikely to reflect the standard of living of the occupants accurately, they do not apply the same criteria when assessing the remains of structures. It seems that medieval archaeologists refuse to learn from the mistakes of their colleagues working in the Saxon period. Not so very long ago the houses in which Saxons lived were regarded as hovels which indicated their low level of life. More recently the archaeological evidence has been reassessed, and it has been found that the remains are commensurate with sophisticated, often timber-framed, buildings (Rahtz 1976).

Recent statements about medieval peasant housing emphasize the apparently low-level achievement of those who built them. It is as though there had been a decline in the ability to construct houses after the Norman Conquest. Buildings are referred to as 'flimsy' and 'impermanent' and it has been claimed that this was one of the major reasons for the repeated reconstruction of houses (Hurst 1986, 206). Indeed, the assumed impermanence of houses has often been used to provide a chronology in the absence of dated archaeological material. Some assume that most houses could not have lasted for more than twenty years. This minimalist view of the peasant house has been compounded by the reluctance of vernacular architectural historians to accept that fully framed timber buildings existed before *c*.1400 (Beresford, G. 1975, 19–43).

The change from entirely timber buildings to those with dwarf stone walls has usually been interpreted as indicating a decline in the availability of timber as a result of the expansion of arable land at the expense of woodland and pasture (Beresford and Hurst 1971, 93). Thus the change is seen as a means of preserving the existing 'low-level' form of housing rather than heralding an improvement. Advances were not possible because the size of the available timber remained the same or even decreased. This view is extremely 'regionalist' because it assumes that all the resources for housing had to come from the immediate area, an interpretation which verges on regarding the medieval economy as essentially 'natural'.

Dyer has cogently argued for a high standard of construction and durability in most peasant housing. From the thirteenth century houses were constructed by professional carpenters and he argues that the introduction of dwarf stone walls is to be associated with the widespread use of timber framing. This is a very different view of peasant society, and one it must be said that chimes with documentary evidence – a society that is much more 'open', relying on the market for materials that cannot be obtained from the immediate vicinity. Viewed in this light, the introduction of framed buildings is not a consequence of materials being close to hand, but of the availability of money to employ the expertise of the professional carpenter: access to the market remains fundamental (Dyer 1986).

Discussion has concentrated on those areas of the country where stone was freely available, but similar evidence exists for the claylands. This raises the problem of the degree to which peasant culture in medieval England was homogeneous. In many respects – inheritance customs, dialect, field systems – there were enormous differences, but the fact of this variation is not taken into account when discussing changes that apparently affected the whole country. The dating of sequences from excavations of medieval villages is notoriously difficult and this latitude in dating compounds the problem by making it easier to fit individual site chronologies into a broad documentary framework. The danger is that the most obvious indications of change are taken out of context to provide evidence of a 'national' trend, whether it be for climatic or demographic change, while their real significance can only be appreciated in the context of the locality.

It is necessary therefore to try to disentangle the causes of the various changes that have been identified in rural society in different parts of the country. This is a formidable task, and one that must be for the future. An alternative would be to estimate the extent to which regional considerations determined an apparently country-wide trend. To do so it is necessary to establish which parts of the archaeological record betray regional differences. Such an approach recalls some of the early work on medieval settlement (for example Jope 1963).

The present chapter will review the archaeology of the peasant holding and explore the possibility of a regional approach. Where regional variation might, and might not, be expected will be shown by the topics considered: the extent to which the form of peasant settlement was influenced by local characteristics of the agrarian economy; the use of the croft; the toft and the activities which took place there, both inside and outside buildings. Information has been drawn from 35 sites where buildings survived sufficiently well to reconstruct the plan, producing details for some 162 buildings. A more exhaustive search would produce further cases, but this represents a healthy increase on the 91 structures Hurst reviewed in 1971 (Beresford and Hurst 1971, 147). However it is still a small sample for many purposes. The 35 sites have been grouped into four major geographical areas and these form the basis of our 'regions' (figure 3.1). These regions are therefore to some extent arbitrarily determined by where archaeologists have chosen to excavate; and they also cut across some major geological boundaries. However, there is a general correspondence with Thirsk's farming regions: for example, Region 1 lies within an 'open pasture' area of cattle and sheep rearing, 2 is largely a mixed farming area of sheep and corn, as is Region 3; Region 4 is mainly within a 'corn and stock variously combined' area (figure 2.3; Thirsk 1967a, 4).

Region 1 covers the south-west and is geographically the most coherent. Excavations have been conducted on a series of small sites and provide the best information we have for what is now appreciated as the 'typical' English medieval

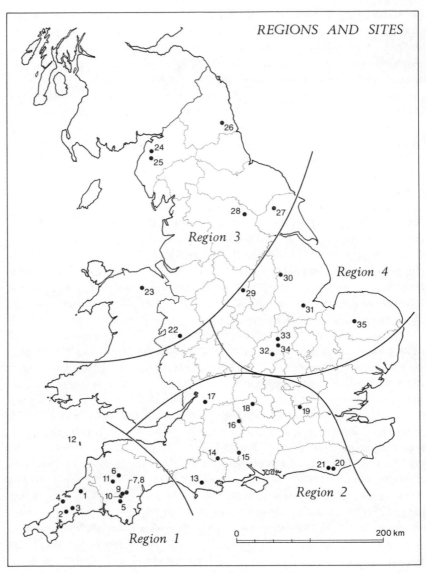

3.1 *Regions and sites (see p. 41).*

Region 1: *1. Garrow Tor; 2. Treworld; 3. Tresmorn; 4. Mawgan Porth; 5. Dean Moor;*
6. Beere; 7. Houndtor 1; 8. Houndtor 2; 9. Hutholes; 10. Dinna Clerks; 11.
Okehampton 59; 12. Lundy.

Region 2: *13. Holworth; 14. Wroughton Copse; 15. Gomeldon; 16. Littlecote; 17. Upton;*
18. Seacourt; 19. Caldecote; 20. Bullock Down; 21. Hangleton.

Region 3: *22. Abdon; 23. Brenig; 24. King's Stables; 25. Millhouse; 26. West Hartburn;*
27. Wharram Percy; 28. Riplingham.

Region 4: *29. Barton Blount; 30. Goltho; 31. Riseholme; 32. Wythemail; 33. Lyveden;*
34. Faxton; 35. Grenstein.

settlement — the hamlet. It is unfortunate that the sites themselves were anything but typical, even for the south-west. Most were sited on the higher land, on areas traditionally regarded as marginal, and are interpreted as settlements with a limited life, created in the twelfth or thirteenth century in response to an increase in population and deserted when that pressure had eased (Austin 1985, 75).

Pre-twelfth-century hamlets, comprising turf buildings, have been claimed on some of these sites, but this has been challenged largely on the grounds that the character of the occupation is unsuitable for an agricultural settlement like a hamlet (Beresford, G. 1979, 112–24; Austin 1985, 71–3). Another possibility is that the earlier occupation may reflect a less intense form of farming, and may represent shielings (seasonally occupied settlements associated with transhumance) converted later into permanently occupied hamlets. Most of the later buildings are of stone and are thus well preserved and provide information about internal arrangements. Unfortunately, the acid nature of the soils means that the archaeological assemblage lacks metal finds and bones.

Region 2 covers southern central England and includes a range of geologies: the sites occur on the Cotswold limestones, the chalk of the south Chilterns and the Wiltshire and Sussex downland as well as on the clays in the Kennet and Thames valleys. Despite this variety, the sites show similarities in building type and materials. Most demonstrate a progression from early timber (earthfast) buildings to stone buildings or to timber framing resting on dwarf stone walls. The majority of excavations have been located within village sites. Two, however — Wroughton Copse (Wilts.) and Bullock Down (Sussex) — are interpreted as smaller, shorter lived settlements on the higher parts of the downs (Fowler 1963; Drewett 1982).

A small number of sites in the north represent Region 3. The majority are villages on the Yorkshire Wolds, the rest shielings on the Cumbrian Fells. By contrast Region 4 has a variety of geologies and the greatest range of building types of all the regions. It embraces the claylands of Derbyshire, Lincolnshire and Norfolk as well as the (clay-capped) limestones of Northamptonshire. Excavations here have demonstrated the many ways earth, timber and stone could be combined to build houses, from those based on earthfast timber posts, through walls made of timber and clay resting on the ground surface, or timbers resting on padstones, or clay walls (cob), or cob on stone foundations, to stone walls.

Various attributes of the excavated buildings, for example dimensions, area, shape, material, function, supplemented by more qualitative information from excavation and field survey, have been analysed according to date and region.

Regional Differences in Settlement Form

Recent discussions about buildings and their arrangements have considered whether it is possible to detect regional differences. In their survey of medieval building types Chapelot and Fossier noted the limited distribution of the longhouse, where people and animals lived under the same roof, and not only equated this building type with an economy that had a high pastoral element, but thought it a comment on the state of that economy. The longhouse thus 'survived in the Highland Zone of the British Isles because a relatively poor form of peasant agriculture predominated there, based on grain production and a backward form of stockraising'. The longhouse then was 'the type of dwelling best adapted to this type of farming' (Chapelot and Fossier 1985, 228).

In the report of his excavations at the clayland villages of Barton Blount and Goltho, Beresford presented strong evidence for the reorganization of village tenements in order to create yards. He attributed this change to the reorientation of the regional economy in the mid-fourteenth century and later when there was a greater emphasis on stock rearing. The yards enabled large numbers of cattle to be overwintered without damaging the pasture during wet weather (Beresford, G. 1975, 13–18).

Both these explanations for particular regional differences emphasize the economy as the determining factor, and crucial to each is the relative importance of crop and animal production. This is not surprising; similar arguments are used to explain variations within field arrangements. For example, the tightly regulated midland field system occurred where a shortage of pasture necessitated restrictions on the grazing of animals (p. 68). Is it possible then to recognize in the archaeological record evidence for a change in the balance of the agrarian economy?

One approach might be to identify settlements known to be primarily concerned with the management of stock and isolate distinctive attributes which might be recognized at other sites. A brief review of shielings, followed by sites in areas known to be primarily concerned with animal husbandry, mainly regions 1 and 3, might help us to appreciate the way villages, and then the house plots within them, were organized.

Many shielings have been identified through fieldwork, particularly in Cumberland and Westmorland (RCHM 1970a), but our information is biassed towards seasonal settlements located on the uplands. Very little work has been done on shielings associated with low-lying pasture areas, and few have been excavated. Most shielings are defined by an enclosure, often ovoid, and set in areas of rough pasture without any trackways leading to them. The enclosure consists of either a dry stone wall or a bank with an internal ditch which betrays its stock-keeping purpose; often there is only one entrance. Within the enclosure there was only one building, the seasonal residence, made of either cob, turf or stone, with a thatched roof. As in all other medieval rural houses, there was a central hearth, although often the interior does not seem to have been partitioned and many had unusually wide doorways.

Another common feature within the enclosure was the midden, rarely encountered on agricultural settlements. The layering of those at Brenig demonstrated that they remained untouched and were added to season after season (Allen 1979, 5, 11). These were settlements with no need of manure, a testimony to their seasonal and pastoral character. The collection of finds from shielings, mainly from middens, can usefully be compared with those from a permanently occupied site. The range of metalwork is remarkably similar – the spurs, arrowheads, padlocks, knives, horseshoes and buckles could be found on any medieval rural site; but there is a notable absence of ironwork associated with more permanently occupied buildings – hasps, swivel hooks, door pivots and hinges. There was a similar bias in the range of pottery, for drinking vessels and jugs predominated on most sites (Allen 1979, 34–41; Richardson 1979, 26; Lowndes 1967, 35–50). Somewhat incongruously, some shieling sites have produced evidence of iron smelting; it is difficult to imagine a more inconvenient location for such an activity (Coggins et al. 1983, 12–14).

The only other type of site specifically associated with stock management during the medieval period was the vaccary, and recent work in the Lancashire uplands has identified such a settlement form. It had a distinctive arrangement of a single group of buildings, associated with two banked and hedged oval enclosures for stock, set within what may have been contemporary fields. The trackways which led through the fields were constricted at certain points in order better to control herding and prevent the cattle damaging the fields (Atkin 1985, 171–7).

Similar kinds of arrangements can be found on other sites where animal husbandry was important, but where there was also some evidence of crop production. In the eleventh and twelfth centuries at Lawrence Field, 290 m up in the Peak District, there was a small settlement consisting of two bow-sided stone buildings. Both were protected by, and connected to, a small square enclosure which was a garden. Beyond was a larger enclosure divided into strips for ploughing. This field was protected from the stock which grazed the rough pasture beyond by a stone wall with an external ditch (figure 3.2; Hart 1981, 132–4). At Dean Moor on Dartmoor there were several large ditched and walled enclosures for stock. At their centre was another enclosure within which there were two buildings connected by walls to form a small yard. Access to the residential building could only be obtained via the yard and the other building which was clearly a byre (Fox, A. 1958, 144–8). Again some precautions were taken to restrict animal damage.

This sample would suggest that small settlements within a largely pastoral area had certain features that aided animal management, but at the same time measures were taken to exclude stock from gardens or fields. The clutch of larger settlements excavated on the fringes of Dartmoor show the same features, but in a more developed way. The south-west has always been regarded as a pastoral region, but there is increasing evidence for crop cultivation from both fieldwork

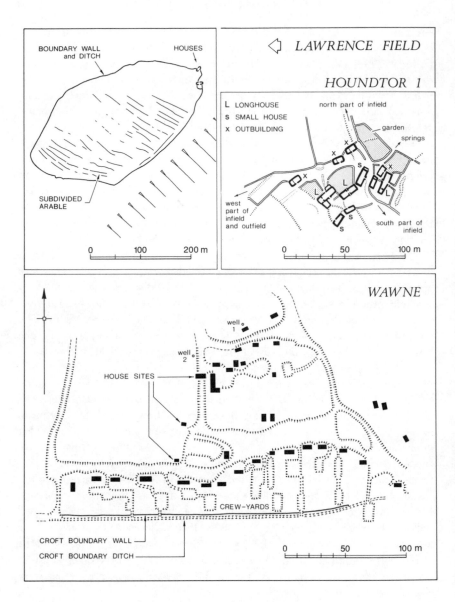

3.2   *Plans of Lawrence Field, Houndtor and Wawne showing different arrangements of*
buildings, enclosures and tracks
(source: Hart 1981; Aston 1985; Hayfield 1984).

and pollen analysis (Austin and Walker 1985). Most of the settlements are surrounded by the earthworks of fields – Houndtor, Garrow Tor, Okehampton 59, Holne Moor – but these fields are defined by substantial boundaries of bank, wall and ditch, the 'corn ditches' (Beresford, G. 1979, 150–3; Dudley and Minter 1962–3, 273; Austin 1978, 197–9; Fleming and Ralph 1982, 107–9). Threading through the fields were wide tracks, lined by stone walls, which led from the settlements to the areas of rough pasture beyond the fields. It is interesting that there has been little discussion about which animals were bred and reared in these areas. The fact that longhouses occur predisposes commentators to emphasize the importance of cattle, but the byres in the houses may only have been used to overwinter plough animals. Indeed the byres probably served as stables, for horses require more shelter than oxen. Sheep may have been much more important: the lack of faunal assemblages deprives us of a critical source of evidence, but some have argued that the funnelling of tracks is most appropriate to sheep management (Fleming and Ralph 1982, 132). There was often a constriction in the droveways at the point of entry, which was to aid stock management (for example, Houndtor I, figure 3.2; Beresford, G. 1979, 103).

The tracks led into the settlement area. There was a clear demarcation between fields and settlement, usually by a stone wall. Compared with village sites the living area appears to be unstructured. On some sites, for example Okehampton 59 and Hutholes, there were no property divisions within the settlement area. It has been suggested that the two building groups at Okehampton may have belonged to the same extended family and therefore boundaries were unnecessary (Austin 1978, 220). At Houndtor the settlement area was much more carefully arranged. Each major residence had a walled enclosure attached to it. There was only one entry into these gardens, for that is what they must have been – with entrances only 0.30 m wide they could not have been paddocks. A further reason why these areas were not meant for animals is that the walls of houses, tracks and enclosures were built with the specific intention of guiding those animals which did enter the settlement directly into the byres of the longhouses, thus avoiding the risk of stock wandering around the houses (figure 3.2). This settlement arrangement is similar to that of early medieval highland sites in Scandinavia, especially south-west Norway (Myhre 1982).

The integral connection between buildings and enclosures in settlements in the south-west (Region 1) would militate against the alterations in the positions of houses which were common on village sites elsewhere. Indeed it is noticeable that throughout Region 1 there is very little evidence of settlement change. Perhaps one reason for this is that in the south-west there was no clearly defined plot on which the house stood. Often the house backed on to the public areas of the settlement and there was little room for manoeuvre. In addition, the absence from all these sites of the 'croft', a close attached to the building plot and lying between the plot and the fields, may be another reflection of the varied resources which were available to the inhabitants of the uplands. One view of the function of the croft is that it provided pasture which was not subject to common grazing rights. If this were the case elsewhere, there was little need for specific pastures when there was easy and unpressured access to moorland.

It is worth looking at the house plot and croft arrangement in other areas of the country, and this involves shifting our attention from dispersed settlements to villages. Little systematic work has been done on the croft and toft arrangement; a partial explanation for this is that we are dependent on earthwork evidence and, while it is possible to be reasonably certain whether crofts as well as tofts existed in stone-using areas, there is a much greater margin for error in, for example, the claylands. Excavation has shown that the boundaries of individual properties remained remarkably stable. The disposition and size of the croft and toft probably reflect the original perception by the villagers of what resources were needed close to the home. At Goltho, Barton Blount and Caldecote properties were demarcated in the late eleventh, and at Holworth in the early thirteenth century (Beresford, G. 1975, 12–13; Beresford, G. 1978, 5–10; Rahtz 1959, 133).

There was a great variety of size and shape among crofts. For example, in Region 2 (south and central England) most of the sites had well-defined earthworks and in some areas it is possible to point to a degree of consistency in toft and croft size and arrangement, for example in the Winterbourne and Milbourne valleys in central Dorset (RCHM 1970b, lxvii). Yet there are also cases where the house plot and the croft were ill-defined, as in the case of Upton (Glos.), or sites where they were absent, as at Bullock Down in Sussex (figure 3.3; Hilton and Rahtz 1966, 87; Drewett 1982, 143, 164). The same is true in Region 3 where well-defined crofts and tofts could be found at Wharram and Thrislington, but apparently merged at West Hartburn (Hurst 1984, 82–7; Austin forthcoming; Still and Pallister 1967, 140).

Less variation occurs within Region 4, the east midlands and East Anglia. Here there did not seem to be a separation between the house site and the croft; buildings were usually set within enclosures which were squarer than in the rest of the country, and were of a size which fell in between that of the toft and the croft elsewhere. At Goltho, Barton Blount, Grenstein and Riseholme the buildings stood within a close which fronted the village street and backed on to the open fields (figure 3.3; Beresford, G. 1975, 7–11; Wade-Martins 1980, 102–7; Thompson 1960, 96–7).

An explanation for this variation will require much further work, but it is tempting to connect the various dispositions with the strategy of animal management, which in turn is a reflection of the range of resources available and the extent to which they were under pressure. The absence of crofts in the upland sites at Upton and Bullock Down may testify to a practice of keeping animals, in these cases sheep, away from the core of the settlement. In Region 4, there may

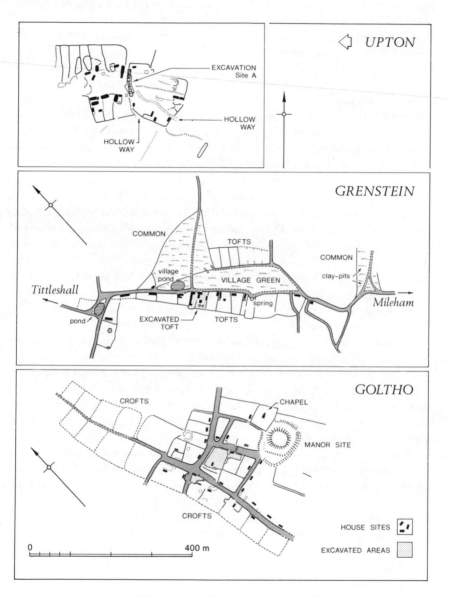

3.3   *Village plans of Upton, Grenstein and Goltho*
(source: Watts and Rahtz 1984; Wade-Martins 1980; Beresford, G. 1975).

have been no need of crofts for extra pasture because the existing grassland was adequate and did not even warrant grazing regulations (Campbell 1981b, 113–19). This of course begs the question of the croft and toft, and it is this that we should now try to answer.

The Croft

Crofts are usually interpreted as gardens, or paddocks, depending on their size. To judge from the ridge and furrow which survives within some, crofts could be large enough to be worth ploughing, presumably allowing peasant families to supplement the harvest that came from their share of the common fields. At Holworth village in Dorset there is a ramp in the north-west corner of each croft which may have allowed a plough team access to the common fields; these ramps resemble those which occur at the end of strip lynchets (RCHM 1970c, 36). Some crofts however were never cultivated. At Wharram Percy, for example, excavation of one croft has shown that underlying the turf and topsoil were the remains of middle Saxon middens and late Saxon rubbish pits. The fact that these features remained undisturbed suggests that the crofts were unploughed and were treated as paddocks, perhaps for the horses for which Wharram has provided so much evidence (Ryder 1974). Crofts may have been a way of overwintering animals without risking the trampling of young grass in the larger pastures in wet spring weather.

Whereas villages with crofts had a certain flexibility which allowed the occupants to respond to changes in the economic climate, those without engineered alterations on their plots. For example, at Barton Blount and Goltho in the later fourteenth century several of the tenements were reorganized into crew yards which allowed cattle to be overwintered (figure 3.4; Beresford, G. 1975, 13–18). The same is true at Wawne, another site without well-defined crofts: in the later fourteenth century sunken cobbled 'fold yards' were created behind a row of houses; apparently there was no connection between the tofts and the yards. Sunken tracks ran from the yards to the street and avoided the tofts: there appears to have been a strict separation between animal and residential areas (Hayfield 1984, 41–67).

These arrangements allowed for no gardens, and the same appears to have been true on other sites in Region 4 (Grenstein, Thuxton, Faxton: Wade-Martins 1980, 118–24; Wilson and Hurst 1965, 214; 1969, 279). Excavation here however has shown that in the latest stages of the villages not all the crofts were occupied. At Goltho a complete row of crofts had been deserted and incorporated into the open fields (Beresford, G. 1975, 7–11). At other sites the crofts were turned over to paddocks or gardens, for example at Grenstein (Wade-Martins 1980, 114). A household could extend its activities beyond its own croft: the late medieval reduction in population enabled specialization to take place in neighbouring vacant holdings.

Other regions have more limited evidence. In some settlements there was a clear provision for gardens, as at Thrislington (Region 3), but in others a process similar to that experienced by the Region 4 sites may have taken place. Clear examples of the late medieval amalgamation of tofts exist at Hangleton and Caldecote (Region 2) but this was to create a collection of buildings arranged around a cobbled yard (Austin forthcoming; Hurst and Hurst 1964, 96; Beresford, G. 1978, 5–10). This courtyard arrangement also occurred on single tofts at Gomeldon (figure 3.4; Musty and Algar 1986, 133–6, 142–4). In all these cases, part of the crofts may have been set aside for gardens or, in the fourteenth century and later, vacant tofts taken over and used. No definite garden soil has been identified over an excavated house site, but 'gardening' might explain the poor preservation of some of the buildings that have been discovered.

The Toft

The toft, the medieval farmyard including the buildings, has received more archaeological attention. While acknowledging that the individual living areas within villages had always been defined by banks or ditches, some have remarked upon the increase in size of the boundaries in the late thirteenth and fourteenth centuries, and taken this to indicate either a deterioration in the climate or a statement of ownership at a time when there was an increased pressure on land (Beresford and Hurst 1971, 121–2; Beresford, G. 1975, 50–2; Stamper 1983, 43–6). Two points need to be considered here: the general character of toft boundaries and whether or not there was a marked change in the later medieval period.

Since Beresford and Hurst wrote their review, much new information about toft boundaries has been generated. It seems that we have underestimated the extent to which tofts were defined *throughout* medieval England. While the evidence for clear demarcations of areas around buildings has been accepted for the south-west, it comes as a shock to realize the same was true of other parts of England.

Neither aerial photography, which emphasizes the unity of the village, nor topographic work, which has identified planned settlements, has made us appreciate how separate the tofts were. For example, a common type of village plan consisted of a street with tofts arranged on either side. Yet excavations show that there was a clear, deep boundary between toft and street and access to the tofts was restricted. One toft at Grenstein was separated from the cobbled street by a ditch 1.2 m deep and cleaned out regulary; access was gained via a bridge (figure 3.4; Wade-Martins 1980, 114–16). At Riplingham (Yorks.) there was an almost 1.5 m drop and an intervening ditch between a toft and the street (Wacher 1966, 620–2).

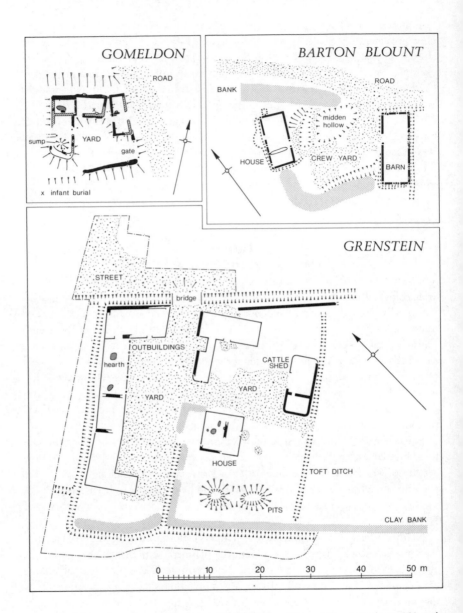

3.4 *Building arrangements. 'Farms' at Gomeldon (area 7) and Grenstein (area 10) and a crewyard at Barton Blount (area 4)*
(source: Musty and Algar 1986; Wade-Martins 1980; Beresford, G. 1975).

Not only was there a division between toft and street, but also between neighbouring tofts. The ditches that surrounded the tofts on all sides at Grenstein were accompanied by banks with hedges on top (figure 3.4). These not only provided a more effective barrier, but also a supply of small wood and faggots. At other settlements banks were raised without ditches, but were topped by stone walls, as at Thrislington. In some cases the sides of buildings were incorporated into these boundary walls – Riseholme, Hangleton and Seacourt (Austin forthcoming; Thompson 1960, 101; Holden 1963, 72–94; Biddle 1961–2, 92–3). In chalk areas some tofts must have resembled stockades; at Hangleton and Bullock Down they were defined by palisades of closely spaced upright timbers (Holden 1963, 85, 97; Drewett 1982, 149). At Gomeldon one toft was bounded by a dry-stone wall and could only be entered by a strongly built gate 3 m wide (figure 3.4; Musty and Algar 1986, 142–4). The separateness of each toft in stone areas would have been emphasized by terracing, as at Wythemail, Hangleton and Gomeldon (Hurst and Hurst 1969, 173–5; Holden 1963, 85; Musty and Algar 1986, 141–2). So far all this evidence comes from thirteenth- and early fourteenth-century contexts which pushes back into the thirteenth century the construction of these deep ditches and banks. The impression is that walking down the main village street it would have been difficult to see into the individual tofts, for most of the banks, walls or hedges would have been at head height.

There appear to have been no widespread innovative changes in the arrangement of tofts in the fourteenth century. Where neighbouring tofts were amalgamated, access was made by slighting the banks and filling the ditches, as at Grenstein; nevertheless, the integrity of each toft remained. Massive banks, over 1.8 m high, were associated with the crew yards at Goltho and Barton Blount, and perhaps at Wharram Percy and Wawne (figure 3.4; Beresford, G. 1975, 13–18; Hurst 1979, 51–4; Hayfield 1984, 41–67). These banks did not follow the toft boundaries exactly, but were built to help manage the cattle.

Why do these holdings seem so private? They stand in stark contrast to some arrangements in Europe where houses were built side by side (Demians D'Archimbaud 1981, 127–224; Pesez 1975). One explanation may be that these were precautions taken to exclude animals. All the examples come from areas which had a mixed economy and include instances where crofts were present as well as absent. Another possibility is that the boundaries were intended as some kind of defence against human interference. Hurst (1984, 98) has commented on the prolific evidence for locks and bolts which came from village sites, and suggests that precautions had to be taken to protect moveable property when the whole family was absent. The boundaries might have been intended to guard against crimes of entry which are well documented. They may also have a symbolic significance in emphasizing the importance of the family group and its right to that particular piece of land in the village. The well-defined tofts, from the thirteenth century at least, might reflect a mixed economy where animals were brought into the main residential area, in which case the arrangement of the buildings might be distinctive (see below); but equally they could reflect a desire to be separate from the rest of the village in a society where agricultural routine depended to such a great extent on cooperation.

Activities within the Toft

Buildings dominated the toft, and it is on these that most archaeological effort has been concentrated, not only in terms of their construction, but also the way they were arranged. Discussion about building types and materials has centred on the apparently widespread change from timber buildings to those which incorporated stone, either as foundations or as wall material. Although mainly seen in stone-producing areas, similar shifts in building construction are apparent in most areas of Britain and are usually related to a decreasing availability of timber (Beresford and Hurst 1971, 73). The construction of dwarf stone walls, or of timber buildings resting on the ground or padstones, are all interpreted as measures to prolong the life of wood at a time when the resource was becoming scarce.

If this were the case it was not reflected in the size of the buildings. The vast majority had a roof supported by trusses whose weight was taken by the walls without the need of internal posts. The internal breadth of all buildings in all four regions shows little change over time, including Region 4 where there was the greatest variety of building materials. The longest timbers needed for the construction of a house were for the tie beams, and the width they spanned did not decrease. Presumably, therefore, there was little shortage of large timber, whether it was obtained on the market or from the locality, or had been reused from older buildings. There was some variation from region to region. In the south-west (Region 1) the average internal breadth was 3.7 m; this is to be compared with the 3.9 m from Region 4. In Region 2 the average breadth in the twelfth and thirteenth centuries was just under 4.2 m, but there was an increase from the fourteenth century onwards to an average of 4.7 m – a clear indication that substantial timbers were still available in the later medieval period, despite an apparent shortage of woodland.

Excavation has located buildings of various function within tofts. The most commonly found were houses, outbuildings, barns or byres. Often the interpretation of function is dependent on internal arrangements; for example, a hearth is regarded as indicating a house, a building with wide doors a barn. Most structures, however, produce no evidence of internal features and so it is difficult even to suggest a primary purpose, let alone to confront the problem of changing function.

One possibility is to consider the shape of a building, that is the relationship between length and breadth. A 'shape index' can be compiled by calculating the breadth of a building as a percentage of its length. The most significant result of this exercise is that, in all regions and at all times between the eleventh and fifteenth centuries, the shape of buildings did not vary according to their function. The range of shape within the group of structures interpreted as houses, for example, was the same and of the same order as that of buildings assigned a different function, say outhouses. This allowed a certain flexibility where structures could be put to several uses, as indeed excavations have shown.

In some areas however the form of buildings did change. The longhouse has, for example, attracted much discussion. An essentially architectural definition of this building type emphasizes that humans and animals lived under the same roof, but each had a specific area which was often separated by the doors and passageway situated in the middle of the long walls. This definition has proved difficult for the archaeologist because evidence for animal, rather than human, occupation is often very difficult to find (Alcock and Smith 1972, 145–6; Meirion-Jones 1973, 135–7). Archaeological evidence for the use of buildings has been found in the south-west, for example in the presence of a central drain, subdivision of the area into stalls or provision of mangers; all these fittings survived well because they were of stone. Such evidence is more difficult to find elsewhere and the term longhouse has been used to describe any building that has two parts separated by a passage (Beresford and Hurst 1971, 113). Thus a longhouse had a residential area with a second space which could have been devoted to a function that leaves no archaeological trace – storerooms and cloth fulling have both been suggested; and it is also possible that both rooms may have had a human, residential function.

Given this, it is perhaps best to separate buildings where there was definite provision for animals, from those structures where there may have been a range of possible functions additional to human occupation. Hurst has argued that the longhouse was a common building type in west and central England, which was replaced by the 'farm' where animal and human shelter was segregated in different buildings arranged around a courtyard (Beresford and Hurst 1971, 104–13). While some examples of the farm can be dated to the twelfth or early thirteenth century, most are later. This development seems clear in Region 2, whichever definition of longhouse is used. But again there are regional variations. The longhouse remained a popular building form in the north until the fifteenth century and there is little sign here of farm arrangements. Region 4 is even more interesting: this area is said to have produced few longhouses (Beresford, G. 1975, 12–13), but examples of 'non-animal' longhouses exist, and apparently increase in the fourteenth and fifteenth centuries. Nor is there much evidence of farms until the fifteenth century. In contrast to Regions 1 and 2, both Regions 3 and 4 show a noticeable absence of outbuildings or barns. Such variation may be the result of archaeological visibility but it could reflect the different ways the toft was used. For example, activities that required outhouses or barns took place in the toft in some areas (Region 2), whereas elsewhere the same activities were conducted in another part of the village, or in the fields. The earthworks of structures within fields have been interpreted as barns and sheepfolds, and platforms recognized as stack stands (Steane 1984, 187; Gingell and Gingell 1981, 67). Just as it is possible that the majority of animals were excluded from the toft, could it be that so too were other agricultural activities? It is noticeable that the areas where there was a general lack of outbuildings were also those where the division between toft and croft was least marked.

In some areas, then, there was provision for storage of equipment and the sheltering of animals within the toft but separate from the house; in others there was a similar provision, but usually small-scale, and incorporated into the main residential building. This difference may be due to region rather than status, for there are a number of sites where a consistent arrangement has been found on more than one croft. Hurst's farm arrangement has been identified on three tofts at Gomeldon in the thirteenth century, while between the twelfth and fourteenth centuries at Barton Blount, Goltho and Wharram Percy on two or more tofts in each village there were either longhouses or purely residential buildings with few outbuildings or barns (Musty and Algar 1986, 145–6; Beresford, G. 1975, 12–47; Hurst 1979, 26–45).

Whereas the type of accommodation for humans, livestock and equipment varied according to region, the size of area devoted to particular activities showed a similar pattern throughout the country. The size of the human living area can be measured, whether it was located within a longhouse or in a separate building. The average living area, in square metres, in the thirteenth and early fourteenth century was 30.5 in Region 1, 34.1 in Region 2 and 37.3 in Region 4. In Regions 2 and 4 there was a large increase in area during the fourteenth and fifteenth centuries – to 50.2 (Region 2) and 46.7 (Region 4). An average increase of 60 per cent in area is also apparent in the case of outbuildings in Region 2. The documented shift from arable to pasture in the late medieval period would have meant that there was less equipment to store, but perhaps more animals to shelter. Large barns have also been noted on some late medieval tofts and interpreted as a means of storing grain so that it could be released on to the market at profitable times (Astill 1983, 232–5). These increases in area seem to suggest that there was a continued improvement in standards of living during the fourteenth and fifteenth centuries. This evidence should be set beside the apparent improvement in building construction in the late twelfth and thirteenth centuries.

The interior of a medieval peasant house is difficult to reconstruct, although there is more information for the fifteenth century and later (Field 1965; Barley 1961). The most common feature was the central hearth, sometimes with an associated firepit for baking or holding ashes. In some cases the remains of collapsed fire canopies have been found (Houndtor, Garrow, Goltho), while in others screens may have been placed around the hearth. Stone fire screens were peculiar to the south-west. The room where the hearth was located was for both living and sleeping. On south-west sites benches and perhaps recesses for beds were found within the thickness of the walls, and the same was true of Wroughton Copse in Wiltshire (Beresford, G. 1979, 129–35; Dudley and Minter 1962–3, 273–7; Beresford, G. 1979, 23; Fowler 1963, 110).

The few surviving examples of vernacular architecture (Alcock and Laithwaite 1973, 100–25) suggest that buildings could be higher than a single storey, but there are only hints of this in the archaeological record. At Upton a stair pit gave access to an upper room, while the 'inn' at Seacourt was thought to have another storey, as indeed were the later fifteenth-century houses in Caldecote (Rahtz 1969, 86–9; Biddle 1961–2, 109–11; Beresford, G. 1978, 4–6). This dearth of evidence is curiously at odds with that from documents which suggests that such buildings were common.

Medieval housing was poorly lit: there would have been few windows, and none would have been glazed; instead they probably had shutters. Internal lighting is well attested by the candle holder, a common find from house sites; few however have produced pottery lamps. Finds give some insight into the quality of life. House fittings, such as door and window pivots, emphasize the solidity of the peasant house. The frequent occurrence of padlocks and keys as well as chest fittings points not only to the need for security, but also to the desirability of storing items in order to create space in the one room where most of the family lived. Some of the most frequent finds are weapons, especially arrowheads, and items associated with horses – spurs, stirrups, shoes and horse furniture. These are two aspects of peasant life which are often underrated: access to hunting areas is usually supposed to have been limited and the ownership of horses confined to the upper echelons of peasant society.

The toft was sometimes the source of building materials. At Wharram Percy and Bullock Down quarries dug within the toft had been allowed to fill naturally (Hurst 1979, 32–7; Drewett 1982, 176). At Caldecote, Brenig and Grenstein pits were dug to obtain wall material and afterwards they were used as water holes. Indeed many tofts had their own water supply (Riseholme, Barton Blount, Bullock Down and Wroughton Copse – Beresford, G. 1978, 4–6; Allen 1979, 25; Wade-Martins 1980, 116–17; Thompson 1960, 104–5; Beresford, G. 1975, 44; Fowler 1963, 342–4).

Most attention has been paid to buildings within the toft. The degree of detachment from village life that the toft provided may have meant that its open areas were just as important as the buildings. However the picture of the toft with much empty space within it may be exaggerated because some buildings may have left no trace in the ground; in the west midlands, for example, we have references to 'helms', that is, barns which rested on staddle stones (Dyer 1984).

Yet some household activities clearly took place out of doors: external hearths have been found, particularly on shieling sites but also at the hamlets of Houndtor and Tresmorn (Beresford, G. 1979, 121; Beresford, G. 1971, 57–9). External ovens were also found at Wroughton Copse and Beere (Fowler 1963, 345; Jope and Threlfall 1958, 123). Ovens and drying kilns sometimes occur in separate buildings; many have been found on upland sites in the south-west and here were perhaps used for drying crops, but they commonly occur in all regions (Upton, Wroughton Copse, Hangleton, Gomeldon in Region 2, West Hartburn in Region 3, Faxton in Region 4), and could have been used for malting barley.

The attachment of the peasant family to the toft is suggested by its use for infant burials. These were located sometimes inside buildings (Upton, Gomeldon, Riplingham) but also in the toft, as for example in the top fill of a well at Thrislington. These were hardly attempts to conceal the birth of a child – the Upton baby was at least six months old at death (Rahtz 1969, 86–8, 123; Musty and Algar 1986, 142–3; Wacher 1966, 622; Austin forthcoming).

The toft was sometimes used for agricultural purposes. A cobbled surface at Tetsworth, associated with storage vessels, was interpreted as a threshing floor; at Grenstein a stack yard was identified (Robinson 1973, 71–4; Wade-Martins 1980, 114). Pens for animals have been suggested at Bullock Down, Gomeldon and Okehampton and such features may in fact be quite common – posts located outside buildings and previously interpreted as earlier structures in some cases might be reinterpreted as pens (Drewett 1982, 176; Austin 1978, 217).

One of the most striking aspects (with the exception perhaps of the late fourteenth and fifteenth centuries) of this evidence from excavated structures in tofts is the lack of specialization in building design. This may be a comment on the low level of efficiency of medieval agriculture, but there were advantages: the most important was that a collection of similar buildings allowed a great deal of flexibility to cope not only with major shifts in the economy but also changes in the composition of the family. Recently archaeological evidence has been interpreted in the light of documentary work which demonstrates that the family holding had to provide for a fluctuating number of people, and often elderly parents were retired and settled in separate accommodation in the same toft (Smith, R.M. 1982). For example, at both Upton and Gomeldon there were two living units on the same toft in the late thirteenth century (Rahtz 1969, 97; Musty and Algar 1986, 145–8). At Hutholes and Okehampton a similar arrangement can be seen (Beresford, G. 1979, 106–9; Austin 1978, 213–14). There are also examples of extensions added to residential buildings. These had hearths but no connection with the main part of the house and often had independent doorways, as at Okehampton. An increase in family size could also be accommodated by changing the use of some subsidiary buildings. Barns were changed to longhouses at Upton, while at Houndtor a corn-drying oven was converted into a house and a barn into a longhouse (Hilton and Rahtz 1966, 103–4; Beresford, G. 1979, 133–4). Some writers have also suggested that the 'inner room' in some houses may have sheltered additional families (Beresford and Hurst 1971, 112–13).

Problems of temporary accommodation may have existed when houses were rebuilt. Much emphasis has been placed on the reorientation of houses within tofts, but there has been little consideration of the implications of this movement. Most rebuildings overlie old house sites, so that shelter would not have been possible during building works, and in cases where rebuildings on different orientations can be demonstrated, there were few buildings in the toft which could have acted as temporary houses. Only at Gomeldon was there significant change on a toft which ensured that the old house could be occupied while its replacement was built. It was not, of course, necessary to change the location of a house if it needed rebuilding. Archaeologists have noticed that the walls of some

3.5   *Cowlam deserted village, Yorkshire. A regularly arranged village with a broad street in the middle of the photograph. The house sites and tofts overlook the street, and the crofts are the long rectangular enclosures behind. The ridge and furrow of the field runs up to the croft boundary on the right. A modern track cuts across the site*
(photo: Cambridge Committee for Aerial Photography).

structures show signs that stretches were rebuilt suggesting that dwarf stone walls could have been replaced while the superstructure remained in place (Hurst 1979, 54). One excavator has even suggested that a byre wall of a longhouse at Wroughton Copse was demolished every time it was mucked out (Fowler 1963, 110).

As a review of the archaeological evidence for the peasant household, this chapter is short on explanation: that must remain on the agenda. It has shown however that regional variation should be expected within, and not just between, settlements. The most striking instance of this is the range of building types. Geographical differences, giving rise to the particular character of local economies, were no doubt responsible for some of this regional variation. Another factor deserving of more emphasis is the extent to which the resources of a locality were exploited; and this of course would change through time. At the moment it is only possible to see the way resources were used over the whole country by looking at the relative importance of cereal production and animal husbandry: hence the crude picture presented here. Further environmental work should allow of a more satisfactory assessment where regional variation might be related to the different types of crop grown or the range of animals reared.

Any tendency to geographical determinism that this view might imply should be balanced by the evidence we have for the overriding of regional differences by major shifts in the medieval economy. One case is the shift from arable to pasture in the later middle ages, best illustrated in the claylands of the east midlands. Here is an area where the results of the change were obvious and dramatic with the construction of crew yards. Future work should be directed towards establishing what were the effects in other parts of the country.

The recent emphasis on the difference between villages and farms or hamlets has caused us rather to lose sight of the individual families which were the basic living unit in both forms of settlement. The way house plots were arranged restates for us the importance of the family unit; the need for the family to be consciously and physically separated from the rest of the community has not received sufficient attention.

Two of medieval archaeology's critical concerns – its relationship with documentary history and the reliability of its chronology – are highlighted by the interesting evidence for the continuous improvement of peasant standards of living, as reflected in buildings. Increasing sophistication in the construction of houses is well known and its early beginnings have given some historians cause for concern. Recent evidence may also suggest that this improvement continues, not in terms of construction, but rather in terms of size. From the fourteenth century there was an increase generally in the size of the living area available to the peasant family. Chronology however remains imprecise and so this development cannot be compared to documented changes in family structure or standards of living. While this may be frustrating now, the refinements in medieval chronology coming from urban excavations, together with more detailed environmental work, should allow future archaeological investigations to result in a much better assessment of rural living conditions in medieval England.

4

Fields

Grenville Astill

Fields lie at the heart of any discussion about the medieval economy, for they were the units in which England's greatest resource, land, was exploited. Just as the arrangement of settlements and the tofts and crofts within, provides much information about the peasant household, so the fields give insights into the foundations of peasant life, showing the extent to which this was based on an exploitation of naturally occurring resources. While the emphasis in what follows is on arable, we should not forget the critical importance of fields of meadow and woodland pasture (p. 119–21, 133–5). The role fields have in any reconstruction of the medieval economy is reflected in the length of time during which they have been studied, their vast bibliography, and not least by the number of controversies they have engendered.

The way in which fields have been studied has also had a profound influence on approaches to other aspects of medieval life. For example, the previous chapter was concerned with how the concept of regional variation had been used in the study of settlements. This approach has been fundamental to research into fields from the beginning and is particularly prominent in the work of pioneers like Seebohm (1905), Vinogradoff (1892) and Gray (1915). Identifying differences in the way fields were arranged and worked was one thing, but explaining them was another and here scholars parted company. For Gray, variations in field systems were best explained by the ethnic differences of the Germanic tribes which settled in Britain in the fifth century. The Anglo-Saxons introduced not only open field systems, but also villages. Gray may have thus proposed the idea of a link between open fields and nucleated settlements which has been a leitmotiv in field studies and is now receiving much attention. The Orwins were also concerned with explaining the origin of open fields. For them, the open field arrangement was a commonsense solution for immigrants faced with a landscape which was either virgin forest or old abandoned fields supporting regenerated woodland (Orwin and Orwin 1967).

Recent work has tended to emphasize that a number of influences might have been responsible for regional differences, and that different combinations at different times were decisive. Four major determinants have been favoured and these reflect the wide-ranging nature of the enquiry which researchers are pursuing. The physical conditions are clearly decisive: soil type and topography are going to determine not only the kind of farming but also which land can be farmed. Next comes the way the land had been used in the past, a factor that has only become important since the Orwins wrote. By the eleventh century Britain was clearly 'an old country' which had been extensively farmed since prehistoric times. The way it had been farmed in the past may well have influenced the medieval peasant's agricultural strategy. The third factor is the way the land was distributed within families. Rules of inheritance varied a great deal around the country and this should be taken into account (p. 205). Last are the socioeconomic influences which at some times have reinforced the physical influences on farming but at others may have run counter to them. A rise in the population, for example, or an increased desire to participate in the market could dramatically affect the agrarian regime of a region (Taylor 1975, 72–4).

For some writers it is the variety of influences that determined the character of fields in any one region; for others it is the variety of response to what were essentially similar influences that is critical (Dodgshon 1980). Both views incorporate a sense of the dynamic which was missing to some extent from earlier discussions. Recent work has been concerned not only with the origins of medieval fields, but also how they changed.

This approach is partly the result of more dialogue between those studying fields and those looking at settlements, a corollary of 'landscape studies'; there has also been more cooperation between historical geographers, documentary historians and archaeologists. One outcome of this cooperation is that the problems of the origins of villages and of the origins of open fields have become intertwined. The medieval village is now seen as a particular settlement form which only developed in some areas of medieval England, whereas the more dispersed types of settlement, such as the farm or hamlet, were more typical of the whole country. Most hamlets did not have the communal form of agriculture necessary for an open field system; instead there was an infield–outfield system, where the infield, the land close to the settlement, was intensively cultivated while the wider expanses of outfield were used for pasture and occasionally brought into short-term cultivation. Just as the village developed out of a dispersed settlement structure, so it is argued the open fields evolved from an infield–outfield system (Baker and Butlin 1973, 655–6). While there is a small amount of evidence to substantiate the sequence for settlements, there is little to support it for fields. Most infield–outfield arrangements exist in upland areas, but the occasional survival of the system in areas where open fields predominate, such as Carburton in Nottinghamshire, might suggest that they were originally more widespread (Beresford and St Joseph 1979, 45–6).

The review of field studies which follows will attempt to consider what the available information can tell us about how fields were worked, how particular types may have originated, and what the implications are of their physical layout.

At the outset it is important to realize that there are two distinct sources which give us totally different information. Firstly, documentary work provides the only information about how the farming of the fields was organized, how the blocks of land within the fields were held, what crops were grown, and what the harvests were like. In other words it can tell us how the fields fitted into a farming system. But such information only survives for particular times in the medieval period. So we have a better idea of how field systems functioned in the thirteenth and fourteenth centuries than in the eleventh, twelfth or fifteenth centuries. There is valuable evidence, especially maps, from the sixteenth century onwards, but it is difficult to assess the extent to which the sixteenth-century or later situation can be projected back into the medieval period; this will be considered later.

The second source is the physical evidence for what some fields looked like, how they changed and why they had a particular form. This information comes from the interpretation of maps, usually of seventeenth-century date or later, by historical geographers and the examination or excavation of surviving traces of fields by archaeologists. Again the problem is deciding the extent to which this information is relevant for the medieval period. While the archaeological information might establish the physical character of a field, it cannot tell us whether that field was cultivated within a communal system of agriculture or as a separate piece of land.

Field Systems

The available documentry evidence regarding medieval fields is weighted heavily towards those arranged in an open field system; there is thus a danger of gaining the (false) impression that all fields in England were worked in this way. Open field systems were most often associated with nucleated settlements and were only as typical of fields as villages were of settlements in general.

The essence of an open field system was that the resources of the manor were distributed among the inhabitants in a way which necessitated cooperation. The amount of cooperation inherent in any particular field system was to a certain extent indicative of the degree to which critical resources were under pressure. Perhaps the most important factor that determined the nature of the field system was the ratio between arable and pasture. Another governing consideration was the need to ensure that the level of soil fertility was maintained. The usual way of doing this was to have periods of fallow for some land and to create opportunities for animals to manure the fields. The most common response to these various

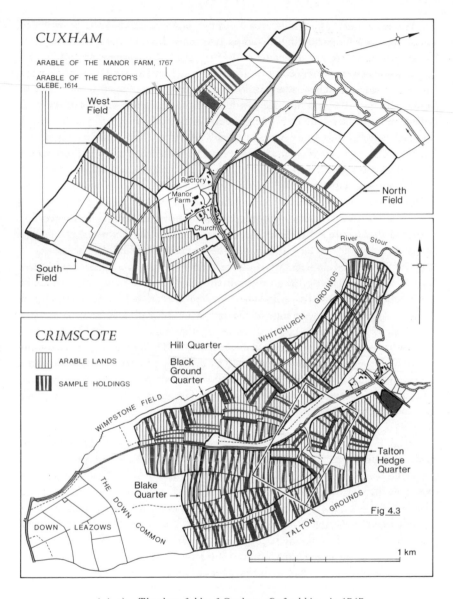

4.1 a) *The three fields of Cuxham, Oxfordshire, in 1767*
(source: Harvey 1965).

4.1 b) *The four fields of Crimscote, Warwickshire, in 1844. The arrangements of the furlongs suggest that there could originally have been just two fields, separated by the stream running down the middle*
(source: Roberts 1973).

needs was to divide the arable areas into two or three 'fields' in each of which every villager had his holdings distributed as individual, long plots (figure 4.1). These holdings were sometimes arranged in a very precise way so that, although a peasant's plots were widely scattered in the fields, he often had the same people's land on either side. This pattern, known as solskifte, was sometimes a reflection of the way the tofts were arranged in the village. A peasant's neighbours in the village were thus likely to be his neighbours in the fields. It is difficult to know if this pattern was general in the medieval period, or how frequently it represented a later rationalization of a more complicated situation; there are cases which demonstrate that both happened.

This dispersed pattern has been used not only to demonstrate the general inefficiency of the open field method of farming, but also to explain its demise in the face of enclosure. However, economists, impressed by the resilience and longevity of the open fields, have argued that in the circumstances the system was an efficient way to exploit resources. The scattering of land can be seen as a precaution against complete crop failure, a form of risk avoidance (McCloskey 1976). Dahlman has applied an economic interpretation to the whole method of open field farming and has found that the combination of private ownership of arable and collective ownership of the scarce resource of pasture worked very efficiently (1980, 93–145). Often the key to the smooth running of the system was the appointment of 'resource managers' who made sure that a farmer took his collective responsibilities seriously, often by upholding by-laws. Officials like the reeve, herdsman, hayward and warden were responsible for ensuring that, for example, harvesting was carried out fairly, that the commons were not overstocked, and that crops were protected from animals (Ault 1972, 18–72).

Variability in the pressure on pasture resources and the need for fallowing, then, were probably responsible for the different types of field arrangements that could be seen throughout medieval England. Gray identified various systems which he thought were dominant in some areas of the country (1915, 272–354). While his scheme is still generally accepted, it is now felt that particular areas included more variation in the way fields were laid out, and that these variations were a reflection of local, often geographical, differences (figure 4.2).

Gray's 'midland system' has attracted the most attention: it has been regarded by some as the ultimate stage in the long process of the evolution of field systems; and it was certainly the most enduring and the best-documented system in the post-medieval period. It had four distinctive features. Firstly, the plots or strips were unfenced and grouped in interlocking bundles, usually called furlongs, which were sometimes used as a cropping unit; the furlongs in turn were grouped into two or three great sectors, the 'fields'. Secondly, each year one field was set aside as fallow where all the cultivators were allowed to graze their animals. Thirdly, there was common grazing on the marginal areas or 'waste'. Fourthly,

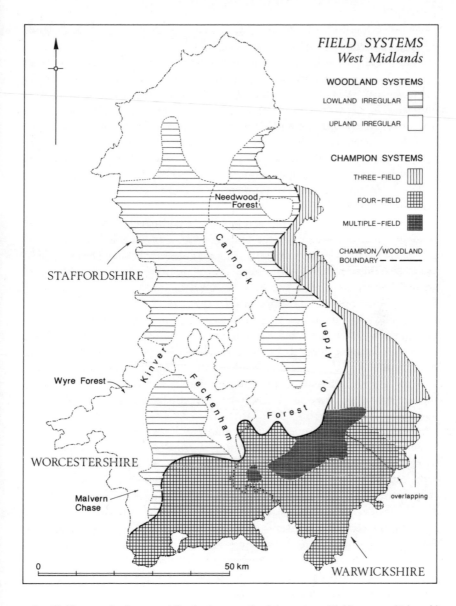

4.2 *Field systems in the west midlands. An example of the variety of field systems which could*
coexist in a region
(source: Roberts 1973).

all activities concerned with farming were regulated communally by an assembly of all those involved or by the manor court.

Most of the other field systems had some subdivision of arable into strips and a degree of communal regulation, but the division of the arable into two or three roughly equal fields and the setting aside of one for communal grazing were unusual. The need for such careful regulation of grazing might point to the scarcity of pasture, perhaps a result of having to extend the arable to support an increased population (Thirsk 1964). Others have argued that such a system represents a rationalization of earlier practices and could only have been achieved when there was no demographic pressure (Campbell 1981b, 119–21).

The other types of field arrangement do not have such a large element of communal participation, and probably reflect the greater amount of waste and pasture that was available for grazing. This would have allowed much more flexibility than was possible in the midland system and enabled an increase in population to be absorbed more easily. In some areas, such as east Devon, no field was left to fallow and no provision made for communal grazing on the uncropped arable. Neither were there two or three great blocks of arable, but rather a variable number of fields of different sizes (Fox, H. S. A. 1981, 92). In other areas, for example the Lincolnshire fens or Kent, common rights only extended to the grazing of the waste and the arable was cropped and grazed separately (in severalty) (Campbell 1981b, 114–15). These 'irregular multifield' systems could be found on the edge of the midland field belt in for example Shropshire, Herefordshire, Derbyshire and Nottinghamshire and in areas where there was a higher proportion of pasture and woodland (figure 4.2; Fox, H. S. A. 1981, 91–5).

Thirsk (1964) has argued that the midland system evolved as late as the thirteenth century as a result of increased pressure on land due to population growth. The common field system of farming developed slowly out of individually owned and farmed holdings, which with subdivision through inheritance became increasingly difficult to farm. Cooperation was thus necessary for the efficient exploitation of peasant holdings. This scheme has been generally accepted, but recently the date of the reorganization into the midland system has been challenged. Fox places the advent of the communal system in the late Saxon period, when he sees as present many of the characteristics which Thirsk identified in the thirteenth century. The earlier date seems to accord with recent archaeological evidence that nucleation of settlements, and perhaps reorganization of fields, was taking place in some parts of the country from the ninth century (Fox, H. S. A. 1981).

The Archaeological Dimension

It is appropriate to consider what new information about fields archaeological work has generated. The hypothesis that common fields developed from individual holdings (or even from an infield–outfield system) which were reorganized, perhaps on several occasions, implies that the present-day remains of fields are a palimpsest. Fieldwork and excavation have produced examples of fields which have been modified and have also given us some indications of how fields were organized at particular times.

Fieldwork has concentrated on examining the earthwork remains of field systems. Much of this work has formed part of the county-wide surveys of monuments carried out by the Royal Commission on Historical Monuments and by organizations such as archaeological units. There is a geographical bias in this work towards the midlands and so the results mainly relate to fields in a 'midland system'. The fieldwork consists essentially of a combination of surveying and interpreting surviving earthworks in conjunction with the study of aerial photographs and early maps. In many areas the earthworks have been ploughed out and only the more prominent ridges survive as breaks in slope. Aerial photographs however often show soil marks which represent the vestiges of ploughed-out earthworks. It should be emphasized that most of this work can only tell us about the state of the fields at the time they were last ploughed and therefore gives more information perhaps about post-medieval than medieval fields. However study of soil marks can discover features which run under the latest field systems and give us information about field changes, some of which must be medieval.

The second source of information is from excavation, and the evidence is much more fragmented. Archaeological research programmes have rarely been designed to excavate field systems, so most of our evidence is incidental. For example, there has been much excavation of settlement sites on the river gravels of the major midland rivers such as the Thames, Avon, Welland and Trent. Most of these sites were of prehistoric or Roman date, and were ploughed over in the medieval period. This activity partially destroyed the earlier occupation, but in the process scored the gravel surface, giving us some very basic information about medieval fields. Given that the priorities of the rescue projects were to excavate settlement sites, little time could be spent on the evidence for ploughing; however, it should be said that in many cases there was little scope for more detailed investigation because of modern farming practices.

Working the Fields

The remains of fields are the most common surviving feature of the medieval landscape. Because there was no consistent way for the arable to be organized over the whole country, a great variety of field shape and arrangement is apparent. It was, however, the way the soil was prepared for crops that has given us the most ubiquitous and characteristic earthworks – the method of ploughing determined the appearance of a field more than any of the subsequent operations such as harrowing.

By the eleventh century a plough with a coulter and a mouldboard (as well as a share) was in use over most of England (p. 89). This type of plough can break up the ground more thoroughly than earlier light versions, but in order to be effective it has to be drawn by a team of, traditionally six or eight, oxen or horses. As the plough was drawn through the ground the coulter and then the share sliced the earth and the mouldboard turned the sod over to one side. When the team had been turned, a second furrow was cut parallel to the first, but the sod that was turned this time rested against the first thus creating a small ridge. The plough team then ploughed round and round this ridge, throwing the soil in the same direction and creating a bank until the 'travelling time', that is the distance over which the plough was idle when it was being turned, was regarded as too great. A new furrow would then be cut at some distance from the ploughed area, and the process repeated. The width of these ridges, as well as their length, would also be determined by local conditions – the type of soil, how well it drained, and the topography.

This is the Orwins' 'commonsense' explanation of the corrugations known as ridge and furrow which can still be seen over large areas of the countryside (1967, 30–3). Earthworks of ridge and furrow type can, however, only be produced by ploughing in exactly the same way over a prolonged period. For this to have happened, medieval farmers must have appreciated that there was a definite advantage in having their land corrugated in this way. It was after all relatively easy to avoid the ridging by alternating the positions of the ridges and furrows, and indeed there are areas of the country where these earthworks are rarely found, for example the light soils of the Norfolk and Suffolk breckland or south Devon. The usual explanations for ridging are that it improved drainage and was a convenient way of defining an individual's land without the need for boundary markers. However it is difficult even to estimate how much of the ridge and furrow we see today is of medieval date. Ridges are simply the product of a plough with a mouldboard and therefore can date to any time after the introduction of that kind of plough, that is, after the later prehistoric period. Ridge and furrow has, for example, been identified on Roman sites (Gillam et al. 1973, 84–5). What is distinctively medieval however is the way that the ridging was maintained, but this field arrangement continued as long as it was perceived as being advantageous, and so at the other end of the time scale this meant in many cases its use extended into the seventeenth and eighteenth centuries. Therefore much ridge and furrow could be of post-medieval date, but it may be assumed that it perpetuates a medieval arrangement (figure 4.3).

This method of ploughing produces other earthwork features. It was impossible to plough furrows up to the field edge because it was necessary to leave a wide margin to allow the plough team to turn. At this margin a pronounced linear earthwork formed across the heads of the ridges, the result it is claimed of soil being deposited when the plough was lifted from the furrow prior to being turned. These 'headlands' were often ploughed separately or sometimes left as pasture. Because of their size, headlands are often the last vestiges of medieval fields to survive modern ploughing (figure 4.3).

Another characteristic feature is that the ridges are often not straight but are curved or have a reversed 'S' shape. This has been interpreted as a way of coping with the problem of turning a long team without having to leave an excessively wide headland: the team is prepared for the turn in the course of ploughing the furrow (figure 4.3). Some writers have regarded this device as particularly necessary when oxen are used as draught animals, because they are less manoeuvrable than horses: indeed the change from a sinuous line to a straight one, observed in some fields, has been seen as indicative of the changeover from oxen to horses. It may however be more complicated than this. Langdon has pointed out that, although the cost of feeding was greater, it was more economical for some medieval peasants to use horses as draught animals, though the demesne plough teams were often composed of oxen. However, in the upland areas the choice did not exist for oxen were often the only beasts capable of pulling a plough up steep slopes (Langdon 1982). Given this explanation of the curving ridges, one would expect a proportionate increase in the occurrence of sinuous ridges in upland areas but there is little sign of such a correlation.

The strip lynchet is another characteristic earthwork, a step-like feature seen on hillsides. The terrace-like appearance is produced by ploughing in one direction only. Lynchets are interpreted as having been created at times when the need for crops was such that it could not be satisfied by the more intensive cultivation of existing fields (Taylor 1966; 1975, 88–92).

Aerial photographs show that ridge and furrow often varied in width within the same field system. Surveys in Northamptonshire, Cambridgeshire and Buckinghamshire, for example, show that while the most common width between ridges is 7 to 9 m, the range is often between 3 and 16 m (RCHM 1975, xliii; RCHM 1968, lxvi–lxvii; Mead 1954). Such a large difference might be explained by fields being ploughed differently at certain periods. For example, a narrow form of ridging was produced by steam ploughing in the later eighteenth and nineteenth centuries. Yet there are places where a great range of widths exists and it is known that the fields were turned over permanently to pasture from the sixteenth century. The Orwins argued that the differences could be explained by different soil types, and that the narrowest widths were used on the heaviest soils: by increasing the number of furrows the drainage was improved (1967, 33–4). Clark, however, found there was little relationship between the shape of strips, or indeed shape of the furlong and soil type (1960). More recently, on the basis of surveys in Cambridgeshire and Buckinghamshire and an excavated case in Essex, Drury has argued the opposite, that broad

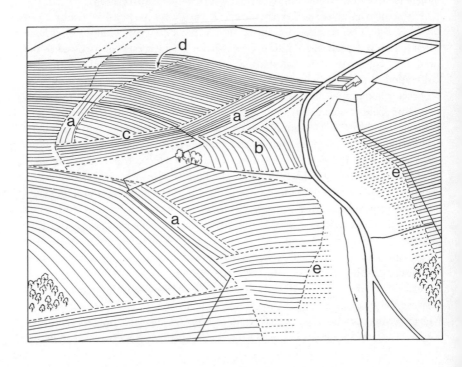

ridging was associated with heavy soils. He also thought that broad ridging was more likely to be found in known areas of common field because it could have been made to correspond with individuals' strips and thus the furrows could perform a secondary function as boundaries (1981).

Drury's view cannot be reconciled with the other excavated examples of ridge and furrow. A preliminary search has found 18 cases of excavated ridge and furrow, and of these it is possible to date roughly 10. Of the 10 dated examples, seven are before the thirteenth century. We can be confident that this dating relates to the period when the fields were actually being worked because the fields were subsequently abandoned, either when built over by earthworks – whether castles (Hen Domen: Barker and Lawson 1971; Sandal: Mayes and Butler 1983, 30, 70–2), moated sites (Walsall: Wrathmell and Wrathmell 1974–5, 52) or abbey precincts (Bordesley: Rahtz and Hirst 1976, 128–9) – or when rendered impossible to cultivate because of extensive sand invasion, as at Gwithian and West Stow (Fowler and Thomas 1962; West 1985, 10). The broadest ridging (and it must be said the most difficult to date) occurred on the light soils overlying the gravels of our midland river valleys where a width of between 9 and 14 m was common. Table 4.1 illustrates some widths found.

These examples suggest that the narrowest ridging occurred most frequently on the heavier soils, especially clays, which may support the Orwins' views. There is however a hint that the width of ridge and furrow might have a chronological significance.

The width of the ridge and furrow from these seven pre-1200 cases ranges between 2.4 and 4.5 m. The earlier, tenth- or eleventh-century, examples from Gwithian and Sandal were also the narrowest. All seven cases had been produced by ploughing rather than hand digging, although the excavators thought the Gwithian field may have been partly hand dug. These tentative findings do find support from Denmark, where the early ridge and furrow from Lindholm, dated to *c.* 1000, was only 1.25 m wide, while at Borup the strips cultivated between 1000 and 1200 were up to 10 m wide (Ramskou 1957,193–201; Steensberg 1983, 184–92).

This argument relies on negative evidence because no examples of ridge and furrow that can be confidently dated to the thirteenth century or later exist. Narrow ridging which contains pottery from the entire medieval period, as at

---

4.3   *Crimscote, looking south-west, showing the common earthworks of a medieval open field*
(see figure 4.1)
(photo: Crown Copyright reserved).

Key: a)   *interlocking furlongs with ridge and furrow; b) reversed 'S' ridge and furrow; c)*
headlands; d) overploughed headlands; e) contraction of cultivated area; new headland formed
over abandoned ridge and furrow.

Table 4.1 *Excavated ridge and furrow*

Site	Subsoil	Century	Average Width (m)
Gwithian	sand	10–11	2.4
Sandal	clay	10–11	2.7
Hen Domen	clay	11	4.0
Bordesley	clay	12	4.5
Walsall	clay	12	4.0
West Stow	sand	12–13	4.2
Hill Hall	clay	12–13	4.0
Chelmsford	clay	12–15	3.3
Maxey I	gravel	12–15	14.0
Briar Hill	sand	13	8.5
Maxey II	gravel		8.0
Farmoor	gravel		9.0
Lechlade	gravel		9.0
Radford	gravel		8.8
Stretton	gravel		8.5
Kettering	gravel		4.5
Eynsham	gravel		9.0
Maxey III	gravel		16.0

Source: Fowler and Thomas 1962; Mayes and Butler 1983, 30, 70–2; Barker and Lawson 1971; Rahtz and Hirst 1976, 218–19; Wrathmell and Wrathmell 1974–5, 52; West, S., 1985; P. Drury and D. Gadd pers. comm.; Drury 1981; Addyman 1964, 23; Bamford 1985, 55–7; Simpson 1981, 37–40; Lambrick and Robinson 1979, 76; Wilson and Hurst 1964, 292; Haigh et al. 1976–7, 114–17; Gardner et al. 1980, 1–35; Jackson 1976, 75; Hawkes and Gray 1969, 1–4; Pryor et al. 1985, 39–40.

Chelmsford, may merely demonstrate that once a pattern was established it was maintained. If the narrowest ridges, found mostly on heavy soils, are indeed the earliest, then perhaps cultivation of the river valleys may be later than that of the heavy soils, a curious inversion of traditional reasoning (Rowley 1982, 48). That there was indeed a significant change in the character of some fields during the thirteenth century is suggested from work at Frocester in Gloucestershire. Fieldwork has demonstrated that there was a narrow form of ridging and a headland up to the thirteenth century. The arrangement was then changed: the headland was moved and the ridges became wider and more prominent (Aston 1985, 122–4). Changes such as this are clearly significant for the way the field was worked; however it cannot as yet be used to document a change in the type of field system. Indeed, there is no guarantee that any of the examples discussed came from within a common field.

Adaptation and Change

The common field system of agriculture allowed a certain flexibility which could alleviate pressure on particular resources. Sometimes this flexibility involved a reorganization which left physical traces and this evidence can be grouped into two categories: firstly, that for a thoroughgoing re-ordering of the landscape of a medieval parish and secondly, evidence for piecemeal change.

One example of a major rearrangement of the landscape has come from Holderness, a part of Yorkshire which was ill-drained in the medieval period. Here Harvey has reconstructed from maps the pre-enclosure field pattern and found it to be unusual in three respects. Firstly, most of the arable dependent on a settlement was arranged in two fields. Secondly, individual strips within fields were often extremely long, sometimes extending to a kilometre. Thirdly, the majority of the strips ran parallel, and furlongs, subdivisions of the fields, were few. The uniform way in which land in Holderness was partitioned has been taken as evidence of massive planning which affected the whole of a settlement's landed resources. Such a widespread event could, it is argued, only be achieved by the exercise of strong political power. This assumption, together with the idea that such a phenomenon would not be associated with an initial phase of settlement and colonization because the size of population would be too low to justify, or achieve, such a reorganization, has more than anything else influenced the dating of the field pattern. Harvey has noted that during the eleventh century there was a dramatic fall in the value of Holderness manors and this, along with their tenurial complexity which could have made the earlier system of agriculture cumbersome, may provide a time and an explanation for these large-scale changes (Harvey, M. 1981).

Until recently these 'long-stripped' fields were assumed to be specific to badly drained areas because a similar pattern had been established for the Fens (Hall, D. 1981b). However the same arrangement has also been found on the Yorkshire Wolds where strips were long and arranged in a way that ignored the topography (Harvey, M. 1982; Hurst 1984, 85). Sheppard had identified planned settlements in Yorkshire which she associated with the reorganization necessary after William I's 'Harrying of the North'; perhaps this entailed a rearrangement of fields as well as settlements (1975). More recently there has been a tendency to emphasize the Scandinavian characteristics of the territorial pattern and thus a date in the ninth century has been mooted. Yet we should be aware that we are merely matching an undated pattern with a few likely events for which we have documentation. If, for example, we countenance the idea that widespread change in rural society can be affected by the rural population acting in concert (as they had to do when farming) then we are not tied by major political events; we could then consider the conditions in the locality which could prompt such a great change. Just because a similar pattern has been identified in several places it does not mean that it was produced under the same conditions or for the same reasons.

Problems of origin are compounded by a lack of fieldwork. We do not know how such long strips were managed – the very length of the strips would preclude using them as suitable ploughing units. Is there evidence of headlands in these strips? Would a lack of headlands suggest that the field pattern was relatively recent? Another problem of management is considering how much of the land divided into strips was actually farmed at any one time, or in a communal way. In some cases this pattern of long-stripped fields has been interpreted as evidence that the entire landed resources of a settlement were in use at an early date – in one case by the eighth century, a view which tallies with that of those historians who see the later Saxon countryside as being fully exploited (Hall, D. 1982, 48–55; Sawyer 1979). If this had been the case those same resources would have come under increasing pressure in the twelfth and thirteenth centuries, the time for which there is clear evidence for extensive colonization. Would the response have been to change this field pattern, and to change it sufficiently to leave some physical mark? Clearly we must not confuse the evidence for land allotment with that for land use. One possibility might be that, in the face of an increasing need to produce food, an infield–outfield system was replaced by an arrangement approximating to a two field system. Hall has seen a change from a long-strip field pattern to an interlocking furlong arrangement in some Northamptonshire parishes, but neither the dating nor sequence is clear (Hall, D. 1982, 45–55).

The second type of evidence for reorganization is mainly concerned with minor changes within field systems, and largely comes from the midlands. Most midland fields were composed either of interlocking furlongs or furlongs that were arranged end-on with a large headland or baulk in between (figure 4.3). Surveys have found a predominance of one or the other within a parish. The disposition of the furlongs is assumed to take advantage of the lie of the land so that, for example, the furrows straddle the contours in order to aid drainage. A further assumption is that the interlocking pattern in particular was produced by the piecemeal absorption of land into the common fields, so that colonization proceeded outwards from the core where the settlement and original fields were located. Hall, however, has argued that the midland furlong arrangement represented a reorganization of an earlier long-stripped field system, and therefore cannot be associated with colonization. He has produced cases where original long field strips had been divided by medieval roads or by furlongs running in different directions (Hall, D. 1981a). The topographic evidence used – for example furrows that ran under a (later) headland – does not necessarily demonstrate Hall's thesis: it merely shows that a field was cultivated in shorter stretches (Hall, D. 1982, 44–55). Indeed in some cases it is possible to show that the interlocking pattern was the original pattern – as in Addyman's excavations at Maxey (1964, 23). Furthermore while cases of long strips are numerous in Northamptonshire, it is clear that they were produced by overploughing the headlands separating end-on furlongs (RCHM 1975, 27; 1982, 95).

A further fundamental consideration must be the extent to which the layout of the medieval fields was conditioned by the way the land had been used at an earlier time. The Orwins assumed that the common field system had been devised to cope with the process of colonization, of wresting arable land from scrub and woodland. One of the major contributions of field archaeology has been to demonstrate that by the medieval period there was very little of this country which had not at some time been exploited and that this process had left features in the landscape which influenced the way later generations used the land.

Not surprisingly the upland areas produce cases where prehistoric features have been incorporated into medieval fields. In northern Cumbria, areas of ridge and furrow were set within banks which were part of an earlier Celtic field system (Higham 1980, 142–52). Similarly on the chalk downlands the more prominent banks of a Celtic field system were often used to define medieval fields while the subsidiary boundaries were ploughed over, as at Fyfield Down in Wiltshire (Bowen and Fowler 1962, 104–8). The medieval phase of farming in these areas has been assumed to be short-lived, associated with the period of colonization in the twelfth and thirteenth centuries, and therefore not sufficiently intense to reorganize the landscape.

Earlier field arrangements would have been mostly obliterated by total reoganization of the field patterns, but more fieldwork is necessary. This kind of reorganization may have taken place at Wharram Percy, a planned settlement which has a long-strip field arrangement, but evidence survived to show that the boundaries separating the tofts from the fields followed the alignment of prehistoric and Roman ditches (Hurst 1984, 77–87).

Taylor and Fowler considered the evidence for earlier land use in other parts of the country in 1978. Cuts through headlands in Cambridgeshire had shown underlying ditches, some of which contained abraded late Roman pottery. In Northamptonshire there were cases of ditches underlying, and on the same alignment as, headlands which defined furlongs. At Barton Court Farm a lynchet with associated ridge and furrow followed the course of a late Roman ditch. Taylor suggested that these ditches originally defined Roman field enclosures which were subsequently incorporated into the medieval field systems (1978, 159–60). Since 1978 further scraps of evidence have been forthcoming. At Lechlade furrow ends were defined by ditches which underlay headlands, and at

Beckford an area of ridge and furrow had been created within a pre-existing ditch system (Wilson and Hurst 1964, 292; Britnell 1965). At Berinsfield, Oxfordshire, a headland appeared to follow the line of successive Iron Age and Roman ditches (Lambrick forthcoming). The dating of these examples is extremely difficult, and in the Cambridgeshire cases the Roman pottery merely gives a *terminus post quem*. It is possible, for example, that the ditches were dug by hand to act as boundaries before the headlands had developed. A tantalizing piece of evidence comes from Banbury where ridge and furrow overlay a ditch containing late Saxon pottery (Youngs et al. 1984, 235). The accumulation of such scraps of information may eventually help us to appreciate the complex origins of the patchwork configuration of many medieval fields. It should however be said that often divisions between furlongs were not marked by any ditches, as in Bardyke field at Maxey, and at Walsall (Pryor et al. 1985, 247–64; Wrathmell and Wrathmell 1974–5), and moreover that in some cases neither prehistoric nor Roman sites had much effect on the shape of ridge and furrow (Pryor et al. 1985, 14–15; Bamford 1985, 55–57).

However much earlier features determined the shape of medieval fields, the earthwork evidence shows that considerable alterations took place within the fields. Most common appears to be the joining up of adjacent furlongs, particularly when they were end-on. The overploughed headlands can often be seen as ephemeral banks in the middle of ridge and furrow (figure 4.3). Sometimes the ridging kinks at the abandoned headlands in order to join up the ridges of the two different furlongs. In Northamptonshire furlongs of over 400 m have been produced by absorption, and sometimes this is betrayed by a furlong having a triple reversed S shape in its ridging (RCHM 1975, 25; 1982, 95).

Sometimes headlands had been overploughed in order to increase the area under cultivation, a feature which is most obvious on the steeper valley slopes. Presumably this was part of an attempt to colonize marginal land; it is shown dramatically at Great Houghton where, although the steepness of the slopes had caused landslips, nevertheless the slips themselves were overploughed. Less frequently, signs of contraction can be seen, where ridging (again most commonly on slopes) has been shortened and new headlands formed (RCHM 1975, 84, 123–5, 147–8). In other cases contraction in the fields may mark a change in land use. For example, in both Northamptonshire and Wiltshire there are cases of later medieval stock enclosures and sheep folds that overlie ridge and furrow on the higher valley sides (Gingell and Gingell 1981; RCHM 1975, 112).

The intimate connection between the village and its fields is shown in those cases where the shape of the settlement altered and there were consequent field changes. Long gardens, or paddocks, behind the houses at Harrowden and Harrington were incorporated into the open field, perhaps reflecting a time when there was a greater need for arable than pasture (RCHM 1975, 4, 67).

The shifting of a settlement, or its contraction, often left crofts uninhabited: these too were incorporated into the fields (Barton Blount; Goltho: Beresford, G. 1975, 7, 9), just as in areas where the village expanded crofts were built over ridge and furrow. In the later medieval period there are even some examples of complete settlements being overploughed, as at Glassthorpe and Woodend (RCHM 1975, 93–4; 1982, 173). At Charlock we have an example of the reverse process where a hamlet, consisting of at least three buildings and crofts and small fields, was built on top of a furlong which was within, but on the periphery of, the fields of the main settlement (figure 4.4; RCHM 1982, 3–6).

Traces of other earthworks within the village and its fields demonstrate aspects of the agricultural cycle. Fishponds, for example, frequently occur as earthworks near medieval villages and it is clear from the ridge and furrow in the bottom of these ponds that they were periodically drained, ploughed and a crop taken (RCHM 1982, 115). Isolated platforms surrounded by the ridge and furrow of an open field have been interpreted as areas for rick stands (RCHM 1981, 5).

The fertility of the open fields was maintained principally by leaving one field fallow for a year and allowing the communal grazing of animals. Other measures were the substitution of fodder crops, particularly legumes, for bare fallow, an emphasis on spring-sown crops, and the ploughing in of manure from stall-fed livestock. From an archaeological point of view the latter is susceptible of enquiry. Rubbish pits or middens have rarely been found on excavations of medieval villges. Even when quarries or storage pits went out of use they were not filled with rubbish but were allowed to silt up (Hurst 1979, 32–7). Refuse was regarded as too important to be put into holes: the assumption is that it was used to manure the fields.

Fieldwalking (the collection of archaeological material from the surface of cultivated fields) around medieval settlements has produced an even, low scatter of pottery which is regarded as the result of manuring. Such a scatter however is not to be found over all the arable belonging to the settlement. At Wharram Percy pottery was found over the fields immediately to the north, west and east of the village, but not beyond. This might suggest that rubbish was carted out to the nearest fields and the land beyond was manured by animals, or that a kind of infield–outfield system was practised (Hurst 1984, 99). The fields around Thrislington produced a similar pattern (Austin forthcoming). In contrast, at Beedon in Berkshire a scatter of thirteenth-century pottery, interpreted as manuring, was found high up on the chalk downs on the parish boundary, as though the least fertile fields were being fertilized (Richards 1978, 75–80). In other parts of the downland the reverse seems to be true. Archaeologists have commented on the lack of pottery from open fields, and excavation through a section of ridge and furrow at Fyfield produced no medieval pottery (Fowler et al. 1965, 67, 73). A similar lack of pottery from strip lynchets has helped to fuel the debate about their date (Taylor 1966; Woods 1962, 163–71). More

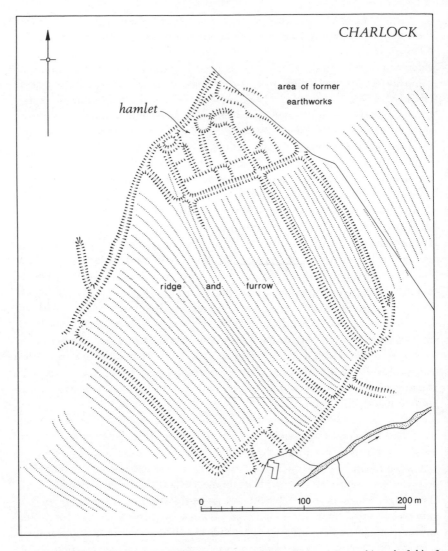

4.4   *The deserted hamlet of Charlock, Northamptonshire, which was inserted into the fields of*
Abthorpe
(source: RCHM 1982).

fieldwork needs to be done before we can explain these divergent patterns, but
there are at least two possibilities. Firstly, that the downs were peripheral to the
main core of fields which were spread with rubbish or, secondly, that the
arable–pasture ratio may have been favourable to the keeping of animals, and
this livestock was folded on the downland.

Woodland and Upland – Regions of Enclosure

Most of the comments so far relate to those parts of medieval England where the majority of arable, and perhaps pasture, was communally regulated. There were, however, large areas where the exercise of communal control over some of the landed resources was much less pronounced and there was instead a consequent emphasis on individual ownership. This pattern was particularly noticeable in two types of region, both of which appear to have supported a dispersed form of settlement.

Firstly, there were those areas, usually of heavy soils, which still supported woodland and which appear to have had a thin population. In the course of the twelfth century and later, colonization (assarting) was carried out on an individual basis. Fields were enclosed by hedges and ditches, and the characteristic settlement form was either a single group of buildings, occasionally within a moat, or the hamlet. The opportunity or need for communal regulation in these circumstances was very limited. North Warwickshire (Arden) and Worcestershire, Essex and the Wealden areas of Kent and Sussex would have been typical of this landscape, but it is unfortunate that fieldwork is at such a rudimentary stage (Roberts 1973; Britnell 1983). It is however noticeable that the process of enclosure gathered momentum during the later middle ages. Enclosure was often the natural response of a farmer who had succeeded in consolidating his land, and this can be seen increasingly after the mid-fourteenth century, a trend that was accentuated with the increase in the size of some holdings, and by the increasing shift from arable to pastoral farming in many parts of the country (Dyer 1981).

The second regional type is associated with the upland zones of Britain, such as the south-west. Here easy access to the high slopes leading to moorland meant that there was no pressure on pasture and there was also the possibility of bringing into temporary cultivation the valley slopes. Yet, despite the abundant pasture, these were essentially areas of mixed farming and the arable of individual farmers was often held in subdivided fields which were subject to some communal regulation in the more fertile areas like east Devon and the southern border between the coast and Dartmoor. The arrangements were, however, much more haphazard than in the midlands. In central and northern Devon the fields may have always been enclosed (Fox, H. S. A. 1975). Here the necessary fieldwork has not been carried out to try and trace the apparently complicated progress towards enclosure, but there has been much high quality survey work on the fringes of the moors. It is unfortunate that our view of agriculture in the upland regions is biased towards those parts which are located at the very limit of where farming was possible.

A combination of archaeological survey and documentary evidence has produced a sequence of medieval fields at Holne Moor on the east side of Dartmoor (figure 4.5). The earliest evidence can probably be dated between the tenth and eleventh centuries, when there were three areas of fields enclosed by hedges and block walls (lobes). These are interpreted as the sheltered fields of people living in farms in the valley of the Venford Brook. The enclosed lobe fields were divided into strips and each lobe seems also to have been partitioned into three, perhaps to allow for some element of crop rotation as well as an area of good pasture. Associated with these fields were trackways which gave access to adjacent moorland, and their pronounced hollowing implies heavy use. In the thirteenth century, following a period when this area was declared to be under forest law and the fields were protected by 'corn ditches', small-scale field extensions were followed by a further large enclosure and new tracks leading to the moor. In about 1300 an even larger extension was made which was briefly cultivated before reverting to moorland. In this later period the other extensions and even parts of the original lobes were turned over to pasture, and remained as such (Fleming and Ralph 1982).

This sequence, and a less detailed one for Houndtor (Aston 1985, 130–1), are interesting because they demonstrate how upland areas were brought into greater use during periods of increased pressure on existing resources (figure 4.5). It also shows the value of what is frequently called marginal land and the variety of ways it could be exploited. Similar, but less complete, evidence has come from the southern parts of Dartmoor and from Bodmin Moor (Collis 1983; Brisbane and Clews 1979). In these cases ridging has been observed within enclosed fields, but because of the steepness of the land and the narrowness of the ridges they are assumed to have been dug by hand.

Work in Okehampton Park, on the north fringes of Dartmoor, has located small settlements, one of which is dated to the thirteenth century, and associated fields. There was a variety of ridge and furrow which was thought to reflect the long history of cultivation in the area, but one particular type was related to the medieval settlements. This consisted of narrow ridge and furrow grouped into long units and separated by low banks. In has been suggested that areas were demarcated for arable, but the strips within were farmed individually (Austin et al. 1980). Pollen sequences from both Okehampton and Houndtor suggest that intensive cultivation began in the late twelfth or thirteenth century and that, while barley was the main crop, rye and possibly oats and wheat were also grown. There was, however, a percentage of grassland which emphasizes the mixed character of the farming in these upland zones (Austin et al. 1980; Austin and Walker 1985).

The evidence from the upland zone reminds us that there was a variety of ways to cultivate fields, and that while the mouldboard plough was predominant hand digging was also possible in some circumstances. It is interesting to note that evidence for cross-ploughing within a ditched enclosure, associated with

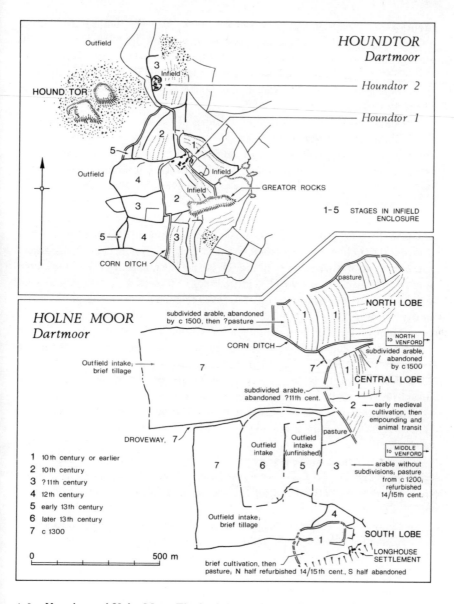

HOUNDTOR
Dartmoor

Outfield

HOUND TOR

3
Infield

———— Houndtor 2

———— Houndtor 1

2

5

1

4
Outfield

Infield

3

2
Infield

GREATOR ROCKS

5   4   3

1–5 STAGES IN INFIELD ENCLOSURE

CORN DITCH

HOLNE MOOR
Dartmoor

subdivided arable, abandoned
by c 1500, then ?pasture

pasture

NORTH LOBE

1   1

CORN DITCH

to NORTH VENFORD

subdivided arable,
abandoned
by c 1500

Outfield intake;
brief tillage

7

7

1

CENTRAL LOBE

subdivided arable,
abandoned ?11th cent.

2 ← early medieval
cultivation, then
empounding and
animal transit

DROVEWAY, 7

pasture

Outfield
intake

Outfield
intake
(unfinished)

to MIDDLE VENFORD

1 10th century or earlier
2 10th century
3 ? 11th century
4 12th century
5 early 13th century
6 later 13th century
7 c 1300

7   6   5   3

arable without
subdivisions, pasture
from c 1200;
refurbished
14/15th cent.

4

Outfield intake;
brief tillage

1

SOUTH LOBE

LONGHOUSE
SETTLEMENT

0   500 m

brief cultivation, then
pasture; N half refurbished 14/15th cent., S half abandoned

4.5 *Houndtor and Holne Moor. The development of two upland field systems on Dartmoor
(source: Fleming and Ralph 1982; Aston 1985).*

twelfth-century pottery, has been reported from Surrey (Webster and Cherry 1972, 205). The long strips separated by low banks found in Okehampton Park are reminiscent of the long thin fields separated by unploughed baulks that were excavated above the west wing of the Roman palace at Fishbourne; these were associated with twelfth- to fourteenth-century pottery (Cunliffe 1971, 194).

The importance of the archaeological evidence lies in its ability to demonstrate the flexibility of field systems; changes identified within the earthworks of fields show the adjustments that were made, but within a framework which may often betray the origins of the arrangement. In this respect the archaeology parallels the documentary evidence which indicates a similarly flexible approach towards the management of the fields and cropping. The visible traces of medieval fields are therefore a palimpsest, and we need to become more proficient at reading it.

Given this plentiful evidence for change within some field systems we have to confront the problem of why others retained their original pristine and planned appearance, as in Yorkshire, even though the fields had been worked in the same way since perhaps at least the eleventh century. Much of the problem may stem from a difficulty in dating features and, given that the fields have been constantly in use, this is unlikely to improve. Even if land has been fertilized with rubbish containing pottery, this does not give a strict guide to the period over which the field has been cultivated. Phases of expansion can be identified within a settlement's fields, but when and why did these take place? At present we can only relate them tentatively to the major economic trends outlined by historians. But the uplands of the south-west should remind us that while there is archaeological evidence for the documented expansion of arable in the late twelfth and thirteenth centuries, it is only part of a long sequence of colonization which started in the tenth century.

The reasons for change also need to be considered. At present there is an emphasis on geographical and economic factors to explain regional variation, but these factors are not considered sufficient in themselves to cause the alterations in many fields. There also appears to be a trend towards minimizing the power of rural communities to change their environment. Often the changes are seen to be so dramatic that only the lords could have had sufficient power to achieve them. This view is apparent throughout the whole of medieval rural settlement studies – it was the lords who replanned settlements, as they did field systems, and even the evidence for the expansion of settlement and fields on to uplands is interpreted as extensions of the lord's demesne (Austin 1978, 195–6, 220–1). To see the lord as an agent of change within medieval rural society is of course correct, but he was not the only stimulus and it is curious that archaeologists are choosing to champion the lord when some historians are starting to produce evidence of the power of rural communities when acting in concert (Dyer 1985).

The study of fields, then, is in the same healthy state as it was at the beginning of the century in the sense that progress is accompanied by controversy. The difference is that with more sophisticated topographical and archaeological techniques there will be a more accurate, reliable and substantial data base from which to reconstruct the agrarian system of medieval England.

5

Agricultural Equipment

John Langdon

The various pieces of equipment with which medieval English farmers had to work were often crude and cheaply constructed, yet they were a vital element in the production, consumption and marketing of agricultural produce. Tools formed extensions of the farmer's body and enabled him to perform tasks with an efficiency far beyond the capabilities of an unequipped man. Moreover, many tools could be applied to other power sources, particularly that of animals, and this access to energy sources other than manpower multiplied many times over the effectiveness of agricultural work.

None of this was particularly new to England at the turn of the first millenium. Tools for farming had already existed in Britain and elsewhere for many thousands of years, and by AD 1000 horses, mules, donkeys, oxen and various other animals were already being used for agricultural tasks. Water power was also exploited for milling and wind power for such tasks as winnowing threshed corn (and eventually for milling also). Yet England was not a society that had settled irrevocably into a routine pattern in its application of tools. The development in the creation, construction and use of equipment was a continuing process and it would be hard to pinpoint any era or place in historical time where some overall progress in the use of tools was not evident. Yet this progress often tended to be fitful, and periods of stagnation or perhaps even regression are by no means unknown. This chapter will explore, inter alia, whether the development of tool technology in English agriculture was progressive, moderate, or stagnant between the eleventh and sixteenth centuries, and how much of an impact, if any, it had upon English society.

Sources

The study of agricultural tools in England during this period relies on the three main categories of documentary, iconographic and archaeological evidence.

The documentary evidence is discussed in chapter 2, so little will be added here, except to say that, as a source of information or agricultural equipment, it is voluminous; details of the construction, maintenance, purchase or simple existence of tools are found regularly in records such as manorial accounts and court rolls. Used with care – the translation and interpretation of written sources are a continual problem – such records can be immensely revealing. In addition, of particular interest for tools and their use, are the agricultural treatises written for the instruction of farmers and estate managers. These begin in the early eleventh century with the treatise *Gerefa* (Cunningham 1905), and then surface again in the thirteenth century with the production of such works as Bishop Grosseteste's *Rules*, Walter of Henley's *Husbandry*, and a number of anonymous works including *Seneschaucy*, *Husbandry* and *Fleta* (Oschinsky 1971; Richardson and Sayles 1953). Finally, after another gap of 200 years or so, there was a new efflorescence in English agricultural writing with the publication of Fitzherbert's *Book of Husbandry* in 1523 (Skeat 1882), which initiated a tradition of agricultural writing that has continued until our own time. A tendency to be noted in the early treatises, however, was that they were very backward-looking, emphasizing and advocating practices which were already very ancient. Only towards the end of the sixteenth century can a greater emphasis on innovation and improvement be seen.

The second main source – iconographic evidence – includes pictures of tools from illuminated manuscripts, tapestries, printed books, wall paintings, stained glass and also carved and sculpted figures. This evidence must be used very carefully, since medieval artists in particular were often careless in depicting the details of tools and implements, or simply copied a tool or implement from an earlier manuscript, often one from several centuries before (for example, Passmore 1930, plate I). None the less, at their best, iconographic representations of tools are immensely valuable and, for hand tools in particular, still a largely unexplored area.

The third main source, archaeological evidence, has the great advantage of having the actual implement to hand. Unfortunately, tools surviving intact are an extreme rarity; generally we are left with only parts of the tool, particularly those elements made of metal, although wood will sometimes survive in certain conditions. Dating of these fragments is often a problem, as is even the recognition of a piece of iron or wood as being from a particular tool. For many tools, too, the archaeological finds to date have been disappointing; the remains of medieval vehicles, for instance, are virtually non-existent, and the same applies for any tool which had relatively little metal in its construction.

None the less, the sum of documentary, iconographic and archaeological evidence is considerable, and much more will undoubtedly come to light in the future. The aim of the rest of this chapter will be to review the current evidence relating to the various items of agricultural equipment found and then to consider what this range of tools and implements tells us about English agriculture of the time. Discussion will be mainly limited to those tools and implements associated with the growing of crops since, for most of the period under consideration, England was predominantly a grain-growing country. In addition, some reference will be made to tools associated specifically with animal husbandry, forest clearance and other activities, but general household tools, such as knives, will be excluded.

Large Implements – Ploughs, Harrows and Vehicles

Since it was essential to bury the seed for the crops, ground-breaking tools were the most important implements in the medieval agrarian economy, particularly on land already cleared. The plough, as the most efficient of these ground-breaking tools, was pre-eminent in the medieval period. Although the breaking of the ground by men alone, using either spades or proto-ploughs such as the caschrom or the later breast or push plough would continue to play a subsidiary role (Passmore 1930, 2; Fussell 1933, 109–14; 1952, 67), the plough hauled by animals quickly dominated the farming scene and was unquestionably the prime means of soil breaking during the medieval period. Virtually all farms over about 4 ha were equipped with ploughs and animals, and smaller holdings may also have been ploughed with teams hired, borrowed or shared with others (Langdon 1986a, 235–44). Although it can be little more than a guess, it seems likely that a good 90 per cent of land was cultivated using animal-drawn ploughs, with very small holdings and garden plots being the main exceptions.

What did these ploughs look like? The transition from the ard or scratch plough to the heavy mouldboard plough has been seen as one of the most important of agricultural developments in pre-industrial Europe (Gimpel 1977, 40–3; White 1962, 41–57). The mouldboard plough (figure 5.1) allowed the turning of the sod and a much more efficient covering of the seed and tearing up of weeds than the scratch-ploughing performed by the ard. Just when this transition took place in England, however, is very much a point of controversy. Pieces of equipment that would be associated with mouldboard ploughs later in the middle ages, such as coulters and asymmetrical shares, were used in the Roman period (Rees 1979, 48–61), but the crucial element of a mouldboard, necessary for the effective lifting up and turning over of the soil, is not found conclusively in iconographic and documentary evidence until the eleventh or twelfth centuries (Singer et al. 1956, 89; Steensberg 1936, 262–71; Langdon 1986a, 75–6; Haudricourt and Delamarre 1955, 357–66). None the less, ploughs capable of turning soil in this way were in existence before the Norman Conquest, judging both from early signs of ridge and furrow and from an Anglo-Saxon riddle which suggests that ploughs did turn over the soil (Fowler

5.1   *An ox-drawn mouldboard plough from the fourteenth-century Luttrell Psalter*
(*Brit. Lib. Add. MS 42130, fo. 170*).

1976, 28–9; Whitman 1982, 177–8; Harvey, N. 1972, 223; 1980, 95). As a result, it seems that by *c*.1000 ploughs capable of producing a substantial furrow were already in existence and that further changes involved creating varieties of these mouldboard ploughs rather than radical new plough types.

By the thirteenth century three main varieties of ploughs were in evidence: wheeled, foot and swing (for examples of which, see Singer et al. 1956, 88–91; figures 5.1 shows a swing plough). The differences amongst them were based on the extent to which ploughing depth could be controlled. Wheeled ploughs were best because the setting of the plough body in relation to the wheels at the front provided a constant depth of ploughing. However, in wet weather the wheels on these ploughs tended to clog up and become inoperable. In the foot plough the wheels were replaced by a piece of wood or iron, the 'foot', set into the front of the plough-beam. This foot rested upon the ground and again helped to control ploughing depth. In many instances, however, even the plough foot was dispensed with, as it was felt better to leave all the depth control in the hands of the ploughmen. The term 'swing plough' reflects the versatility that the implement had in the hands of a ploughman. It thus had to be handled with considerable skill but in the hands of a competent ploughmen would result in a quality of ploughing at least equal to that produced by other varieties of ploughs (Handley 1840, 142, 144–5). Manorial accounts provide some indication as to the distribution of these ploughs types on demesnes – that is, the lord's farm as opposed to those lands held by his tenants – as shown on figure 5.2. Wheeled ploughs are found essentially only in the south and east of the country, foot ploughs to the west and some in the north, and swing ploughs mostly in the east midlands and together with foot ploughs in the north. It is not known whether peasant ploughs followed the same pattern, although occasional references from sixteenth-century probate inventories suggest that a similar pattern may have existed among lesser farms. A more detailed analysis of these plough type distributions elsewhere has shown how slowly the distribution of wheeled, foot and swing ploughs changed over the medieval period (Langdon 1986a, 132–41,

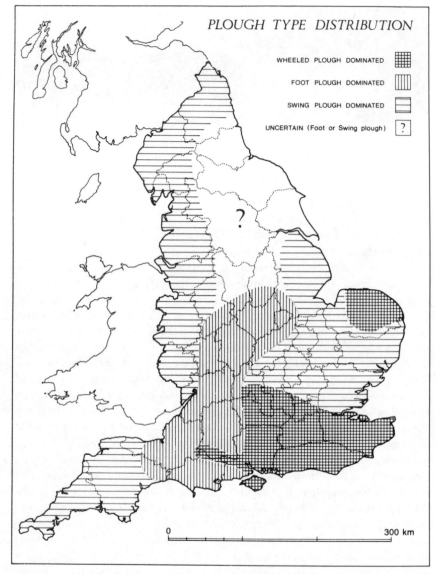

5.2   *Plough type distribution in the thirteenth and fourteenth centuries*
(source: Langdon 1986a, 134–9).

291). Even so, within this tripartite division, the variation in plough types was likely to be complicated, with many different forms of wheeled, foot and swing ploughs evident, as, for example, the 'one-way' plough, usually wheeled, found particularly in Kent (Skeat 1882, 9; Nightingale 1953, 21–3).

Harrows are frequently featured in medieval illustrations and manorial records, the first illustration being found in the Bayeux Tapestry (Stenton 1957, pl. 12). In England they were generally rectangular in shape; none of the triangular or trapezoidal harrows that were popular on the continent were in evidence in England before the end of the sixteenth century (Singer et al. 1956, 94; Parain 1966, 154; Langdon 1986a, 141). Their construction was fairly straightforward with four, five or six wooden beams, called 'bulls', into which were set iron or wooden teeth; the bulls were joined together by wooden cross-members to give the harrow its characteristic rectangular shape. Harrows were most often pulled by horses, although larger, heavier versions were drawn by oxen in cases where the ground needed a particularly rigorous treatment (Skeat 1882, 24). Although their presence in the evidence is very elusive, it is probable that bush harrows were also used and were the likely predecessors of the wooden-frame harrows (Parain 1966, 153–4). As described in the seventeenth century, these were simply thornbushes weighted down by logs and dragged after the horse (Markham 1649, 70–1; Whitaker 1958, 149, 155; Fussell 1952, 68). Finally, during the sixteenth century rollers were beginning to be used as an adjunct or alternative to harrows (Skeat 1882, 25; Grigson 1984, 87, 94).

Carts or other forms of vehicle transport were possessed by farmers of virtually all social levels in medieval England (Langdon 1986a, 221–5). In hilly areas, like Devon and Cornwall or Cumberland, slide cars or sledges rather than wheeled vehicles may have been popular (e.g., Singer et al. 1957, 139–41), but wheeled vehicles seem to have predominated, especially in the south and east of the country (Langdon 1986a, 78, 154). As for ploughs, there were many varieties of carts, as indicated by the number of terms used to describe them: *carecta*, *carrus*, *plaustrum*, *curtena*, *quadriga*, *biga*, *tumberellus*, *rheda* (Langdon 1986a, 76–8, 142–54, 246–50). Many of the vehicles represented by these terms probably had quite diverse features, but the most useful distinction for our purposes is simply to divide them into those pulled by horses and those by oxen. The twelfth and thirteenth centuries saw a very marked increase in the use of horses for hauling. In the eleventh century virtually all farm hauling was performed by oxen, but by the end of the thirteenth something like three-quarters of farm hauling was done by horses (Langdon 1984). In general, farm hauling by horses predominated in the south-east and became less common towards the north and west, as shown in figure 5.3, which depicts the situation at about the end of the thirteenth century. The position effectively stabilized so that the distribution of horse versus ox hauling remained essentially the same until the end of the sixteenth century (Langdon 1984, 58).

The vehicles associated with each animal tended to have certain similar characteristics. According to manorial surveys, the horse-hauled vehicles – for example the cart (*carecta*) and tumbrel (*tumberellus*) – were small vehicles, with about half the capacity of the ox-hauled versions (Langdon 1986a, 151–3, 247).

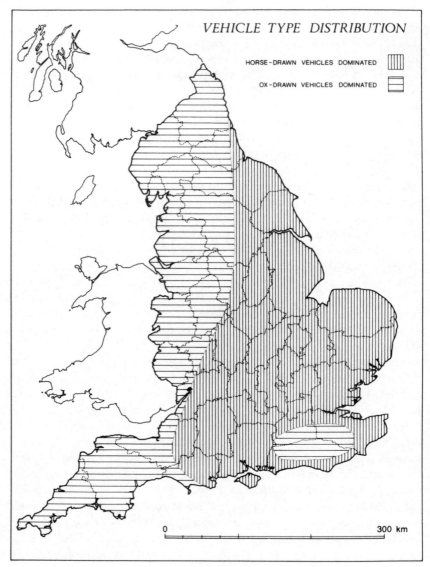

5.3   *Vehicle type distribution at the end of the thirteenth century*
(*source: Langdon 1986a, 144–9*).

They were often double shafted to accommodate a single horse or a line in
tandem, as shown in figure 5.4. These vehicles have been characterized as box-
carts (Jenkins 1961; Fenton 1976, 2), although the sides of the vehicles were
often rudimentary, sometimes made up of simple rails or wickerwork, as shown

in the figure. Documentary, and to a certain extent iconographic, evidence shows that these horse-drawn vehicles were most often hauled by only one animal (Langdon 1986a, 224–5), which further supports the belief that they were fairly light vehicles. None the less, in at least one instance, they were allegedly capable of hauling five quarters of wheat, which implies a carrying capacity of about a tonne (Langdon 1986a, 116n).

5.4   A horse-drawn cart from the fourteenth-century Luttrell Psalter. The horses are shoed and are harnessed with padded collars
(Brit. Lib. Add. MS 42130, fo. 162).

If this was the case, then ox-drawn vehicles, such as the *plaustrum*, similar to the post-medieval wain, could haul well over a ton, and ox-hauled *plaustra* hauling wood and even coal are well documented (Langdon 1986a, 156, 224). They were much preferred for this sort of heavy-duty work, although they were also used in the fields and elsewhere in the same way as carts (Langdon 1986a, 151, 154). The construction of these ox-hauled vehicles must have been robust. One reference from Knowle, Warwickshire, in 1293–4 indicates that the wheels for a *plaustrum* cost two and a half times those for a cart (*carecta*) (Langdon 1986a, 151). This might suggest that the wheels were very heavy and solidly built, perhaps even of the block variety, since the post-medieval experience of Portugal and Czechoslovakia suggests that the distinction between horse- and ox-hauled vehicles was also accompanied by a distinction between spoked and solid wheels (Fenton 1976, 5–7). None the less, iconographic evidence suggests that ox-hauled wains or carts in England from Anglo-Saxon times onwards probably had spoked wheels in the majority of cases. Fitzherbert, for instance, in his general description of a wain, indicates that the wheels were made of 'nathes, spokes, fellyes, and dowles' and were 'well fettred with wood or yren' (Skeat 1882, 14). Altogether Fitzherbert's description of the wain is of a very solidly built and imposing vehicle, largely made of oak. In contrast, he suggests that a cart should be built of ash because the low density of the wood suited that type of vehicle (p. 138). For both carts and wains Fitzherbert advises the use of cart-ladders to extend the effective length of the vehicle behind or in front, as shown in somewhat attentuated form in figure 5.4.

Ox-hauled and horse-hauled vehicles both generally had two wheels. Although some four-wheeled wagons were in use during the medieval period, they were mostly employed for road transport, particularly for moving the itinerant households of wealthy personages (Langdon 1986a, 152; Jenkins 1961, 6–7). Wagons had no place on the farm until the seventeenth century (Porter 1983; Jenkins 1961, 10), probably because the moveable forecarriage, or pivoted front axles, of wagons had not been sufficiently developed to allow a turning arc that was practicable for normal farm work (Langdon 1986a, 155).

The general trend during the middle ages was towards lighter horse-hauled vehicles, which could move much more swiftly than the old ox-hauled versions. It seems doubtful, however, that medieval farmers had to make substantial adjustments to their vehicles to accommodate this shift to horses.

Yokes and harness for these vehicles formed an integral part of farming equipment for the period and are frequently found in equipment lists in accounts, probate inventories, and so on. The padded horse collar with which we are familiar today was introduced by at least the twelfth century and was one of several elements – including horseshoeing, harnessing in file, whippletrees and traces – that effectively revolutionized horse traction from the end of the Roman period (Langdon 1986a, 8 ff). By the thirteenth and fourteenth centuries the harnessing of horses had more or less attained its modern form (see figure 5.4). Yokes and other equipment for ox traction, on the other hand, showed little change throughout the period and were still essentially the same as in ancient times (see figure 5.1).

Of all of these improvements in horse and ox traction, shoeing is the easiest to follow, since it has left plenty of traces in both the documentary and archaeological records. The shoeing of horses seems to have been a continuing practice right through our period, although manorial accounts show that it was common to shoe ploughing horses on the front feet only. The horseshoes themselves went through a transition from a rather crude, wavey-edged form, caused by extension of the iron when the nails were hammered into the shoe, to a heavier, more competently manufactured shoe later in the middle ages. The transition period between the two forms occurred roughly in the thirteenth century (Sparke 1976, 10; Goodall 1980, 180–1; 1981, 61) and may reflect a more liberal use of iron. The practice of ox-shoeing gradually increased during the period, so that by the end of the fourteenth century a quarter or so of demesnes were shoeing their oxen as well as their horses (Langdon 1986b, 173–9; and see figure 8.3).

Hand Tools

Hand tools, although less impressive and cheaper than plough or carts, were by no means less important. If anything, hand tools might be seen as even more crucial to the medieval agrarian situation, as they were used by all levels of rural society. The poorest farmer may not have had a plough or cart, but even he would have been able to afford, or make, a small selection of hand tools. Indeed, one of the striking features about medieval hand tools is how few of them seem to have been required. Fitzherbert, whose account at the beginning of the sixteenth century probably gives us a good idea of the situation existing earlier, lists the necessary hand tools for a farmer as an axe, a hatchet, a hedging bill, augers, a flail, a spade, a shovel and a pitchfork (Skeat 1882, 14–15). He omits a number of important items, such as a seedlip, that is, a seed basket, a sickle, a scythe, a rake, although he mentions these elsewhere in his account. In general, his list agrees well with those occasionally given in manorial records. For instance, a fine set of *principalia* lists survives from the court rolls of a number of Worcestershire manors from the late fourteenth and early fifteenth century (Field 1965). These lists, drawn up for the lord, were descriptions of holdings and possessions of servile tenants, the rationale being that these goods belonged – in theory at least – to the lord and that he was ensuring that they passed intact to the next tenant. These lists are very useful in itemizing the farm equipment, including hand tools, of a substantial number of tenants. For example, in 1374 John Baker of Himbleton was recorded as having a plough, cart, harrow and various pieces of yokes and harness, as well as the following hand tools: a sickle or scythe, an axe or hatchet, a bush-hook (or billhook), a shovel or spade, a flail, a pitchfork, a fork 'for lifting sheaves' (*pro garbis sublevendis*), and a pair of shears. Items contained in other lists were three-tined forks, mattocks, seedlips, sieves, riddles, bushel measures, sacks, hoes, gimlets (a type of small boring tool), various combs for cleaning or dressing hemp or flax and a selection of buckets, vats and other containers for dairying or brewing (Field 1965, 137–45).

The range of tools on demesnes was often of a similar nature to, although, as expected, of a greater variety than, that on a peasant holding. A very full list of demesne tools, excluding the larger implements such as ploughs and vehicles, is provided for the demesne at Cuxham (Oxon.) in 1349, which mentions virtually all the tools given above, and such things as a winnowing fan (*vannus*), a 'furrowing shovel' (*forewynschovele*), parts of a cider press, a balance, a kneading trough and a mortar and pestle (Harvey, P. D. A. 1976, 151–2). Nor was this solely a feature of the later middle ages, since the early eleventh-century *Gerefa* gives a tool list of similar length and complexity (Cunningham 1905, 575).

Altogether the information from these and other sources allows us to build up a

picture of what might have been a fairly complete set of hand tools for the
medieval English farmer, as shown by the following list.

Activity	*Tools Involved*
ground clearance, drainage and preparation	axe, hatchet, shovel, spade, fork, mattock, hoe, pickaxe, mallet
seeding	seedlip or cloth bag
weeding	weeding hook and stick, spud, tongs?
haymaking	scythe, rake and fork
harvesting	sickle or reaping hook, scythes, fork (for raising sheaves), rake
threshing, winnowing and storing	flail, winnowing sheet, sieves, riddle, bushel measure, sacks
processing	handmill or quern, mortar and pestle
hedging	billhook
wool clipping	shears, combs
flax and hemp processing	combs
milking, butter and cheesemaking	milk pails or buckets, cheese press, jars to mould cheese, jugs, etc.
wood collecting	axe, hatchet, hooks
slaughtering	axe, knives, cleavers, meat hooks
others	wheelbarrow, shovels, augers, gimlets, saws, hammers, chisels, ladders, traps and nets (for fish, vermin or game), tripod, balance, whetstone.

The above would equate to a very well-equipped farm during the medieval
period, and in fact there must have been very few places that had all of these.
Judging from the Worcesterhire *principalia* lists, most peasants had only a few,
and we must presume that either many were simply not recorded or peasants
made do with what they had or borrowed from neighbours. Even demesnes
seldom had anything like the above collection, although it may be that in many
cases they expected their tenants to bring their own tools with them in order to
perform the various labour services that they owed.

Tools used in the preparation of the fields for sowing are the most numerous
and include axes and hatchets for clearing ground, spades, forks, mattocks and
hoes for preparing the ground itself (particularly in garden plots), and mallets
for breaking up the clods of earth that the ploughs and harrows left behind. Axes
are portrayed in many medieval illustrations (for example, figure 5.5; Wormald
1960, pl. 13; Sandler 1974, 19; Stenton 1957, pl. 38) and axe blades are
frequently found on archaeological sites (Wheeler, R. E. M. 1954, 55–7;
Holden 1963, 170–1; Morris, C. A. 1983, 71). In general, axes used on the

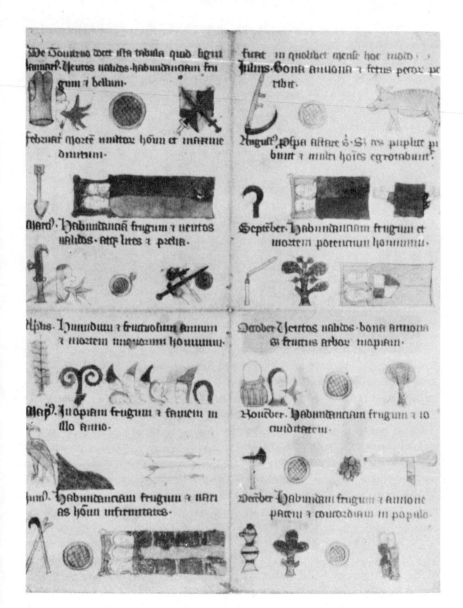

5.5 *Hand tools illustrated in a late fourteenth-century set of calendarial and astrological pieces. The tools include riddles, a glove, a two barred scythe, a one-sided iron 'shoed' spade, a sickle, a billhook, a flail, a pail, an axe and a weeding hook and forked stick (Bod. Lib. MS Rawl. D. 939/3).*

farm were made of iron and had flat, broad heads with flared cutting edges (figure 10.2; Singer et al. 1956, 100; Goodall 1981, fig. 51, nos. 2, 4). In addition, a farm might have had a number of carpenter's axes, with different shapes of blades depending on the job required (Singer et al. 1956, 100, 389–90). Axes were also used to slaughter pigs or other animals: the animal's head was struck with the heel of the axe in order to stun it before bleeding (figure 10.2). Shorter-handled axes or hatchets are also evident from tool lists (e.g. Harvey, P. D. A. 1976, 152; Havinden 1965, 46, 47, 50; Kennedy 1963, 9, 18, 22), although in many cases the billhook performed the same sort of close chopping work.

Spades, forks, mattocks, hoes and pickaxes could all be used for preparing the soil in addition to the plough. Spades came in several varieties and were often one-sided (figure 5.5; Sandler 1974, 17, 26; Higgs 1977, pls 12a, 12b). These spades were mostly made of oak (Morris, C. A. 1984, 8), and, as shown by many archaeological finds (Goodall 1981, 55–6; 1980, 64–7), were often fitted with iron 'shoes' to protect them from wearing out, a practice carried over from Roman times (Rees 1979, 322–6). All-iron spade blades were rare and probably used only on industrial sites, where great heat was expected, as in iron- or glassmaking (Goodall 1980, 67–8). There are frequent references to 'iron spades' (*vange ferrata*; Page 1936, 10) in the records, but it is likely that they referred to the 'shod' variety. Forks (*furcae* and possibly *tribulae*) are also frequently recorded and often seen in medieval illustrations. These seem to be of straightforward construction with two, or even three, prongs and are often referred to as being 'ironed'. This is borne out by archaeological evidence, where the iron tines from a number of two- or three-pronged forks have been found (Goodall 1981, 54–5; 1980, 68, 75–6). As in the Roman period, though, it seems likely that most pitchforks were made of wood, possibly with the tines sleeved in iron (Rees 1979, 483; Morris, C. A. 1984, 25–6). These forks were used not only for ground preparation but also in the harvest and for haymaking. The iron heads of mattocks, hoes and pickaxes for grubbing up the ground and digging out roots and stumps are also found on archaeological sites and the same tools are frequently depicted in manuscripts (Goodall 1981, 55–6; 1980, 43, 42–3, 69; Wormald 1960, pl. 12). An interesting piece of equipment that seems to have had its origins in medieval times was the long-handled clodding mallet or beetle for breaking down lumps of earth left over from the ploughing and harrowing (Millar 1932, fo. 171b; Skeat 1882, 25). These tools remained in existence until animal-drawn rollers became predominant about 1800 (Fussell 1952, 67).

English farmers before 1600 seem to have had relatively few implements for drainage work. The practice of 'furrowing', of course, was a ubiquitous feature of the agriculture of the time (Oschinsky 1971, 323), and 'furrowing shovels' are by no means unknown (p. 95). However, specialized trenching tools only begin to appear in the seventeenth century (Blith, 1653, 69), and it seems likely that their development was connected with the introduction of water meadows from the late sixteenth century onwards and in general reflected the new wave of drainage techniques at this time (Fussell 1952, 18; 1959, 363–4; Kerridge 1967, 251–67).

Once the ground was prepared, it was ready for seeding. Until the introduction of seed drilling from the seventeenth century onwards, broadcast sowing for virtually all crops was universal, although dibbling is occasionally indicated for such crops as beans or woad (Cunningham 1905, 575). In broadcast sowing the seed was distributed by the sower from a seedlip or a cloth bag, more usually the former in England. These seedlips were usually baskets with wickerwork sides, sometimes kidney-shaped to fit the contour of the sower's body, and they are evident from at least the tenth century (Wright 1970, 84–8; Singer et al. 1956, 100). The technique for sowing was more important than the equipment for it, since it required a very deliberate and rhythmic series of movements so that the seed was spread evenly over the ground, a procedure that seems deceptively easy when described in agricultural treatises (for example, Skeat 1882, 19) but was probably difficult to do well.

Once the seed was put down and perhaps covered by a harrowing, there followed a time of waiting until the crop was ready for harvesting. During this interval a principal activity, apart from keeping animals and other intruders off the fields, was weeding. Judging from documentary evidence weeding was a relatively neglected activity. The thirteenth-century agricultural treatise, *Fleta*, indicated that less than 2 per cent of the total cost of bringing in a crop should be spent on weeding, and manorial accounts suggest that this parsimonious attitude was more or less followed in practice (Richardson and Sayles 1953, 256; Langdon 1986a, 267). Such weeding as occurred was most often carried out using a distinctively medieval innovation, the long-handled weeding hook and forked stick, show in in many illuminated manuscripts (figures 2.4 and 5.5; Millar 1932, fo. 172; Sandler 1974, 18). Here the weed was pinched between the hook and fork and its stem was severed as close to the ground as possible. To facilitate the cutting of the weed the hook normally had a metal edge (Goodall 1981, 54–5; 1980, 70–3), and in some cases the hook may have simply consisted of a sickle attached to a pole (Daumas 1969, 465). The chief advantage of the technique, as Fitzherbert indicates, is that the person weeding did not have to stoop (Skeat 1882, 31). An alternative was to use a hoe-like tool called a spud which had been in use since Roman times (Rees 1979, 330–1); judging from the number found on archaeological sites (Goodall 1980, 70–3), they seem to have been less popular than the weeding hook and fork. For wet ground Fitzherbert, and later Markham, suggested a pair of wooden tongs or nippers so that the weeds could be pulled up by the roots rather than simply cut off at the base (Skeat 1882, 31; Markham 1649, 25), although this technique does not seem to appear in earlier sources.

The other key agricultural activity between sowing and harvesting was haymaking. Here the important tools were scythes, rakes and forks. Scythes are common in the archaeological record (for example Goodall 1981, 54–5; 1980, 75), and by the beginning of the second millenium had developed the distinctive short bar, or bars, on the shaft which would assist in the handling of the implement (figures 5.5 and 6.3). This type remained in use throughout the medieval period. Rakes were essential for haymaking, being used for spreading the grass and taking it up after drying. Although some may have had iron prongs (Goodall 1980, 69), they were normally made of wood, as witnessed by Fitzherberts's description of their construction (see p. 103). Forks were used for spreading or tedding hay after it had been cut and for picking up the haycocks for their trip to the barn (Skeat 1882, 33–4).

When the harvesting season arrived in the late summer, a new set of hand tools came into prominence, in particular sickles or reaping hooks for cutting the corn. These implements have a long history in Britain (Fowler 1983, 178–9; Rees 1979, 438 ff.) and by the start of the second millenium AD were predominantly in the 'balanced sickle' form with the iron blade angled backward from the handle to allow a smooth cutting motion, as shown in figures 5.5 and 5.7. Sickles could be either saw-toothed or smooth-edged (Parain 1966, 155–6; Higgs 1977, pls 18b and 18c; Goodall, 1980, 74–5), and both types were probably in use in England. Although scythes were occasionally used for harvesting crops, especially barley and oats (Skeat 1882, 36; Grigson 1984, 118, 123), sickles normally held sway for harvest work until the eighteenth century (Perkins 1977–8, 88; Fenton 1973–4, 35). Other tools used at the harvest were rakes for gathering up stray ears of corn and forks for lifting sheaves.

With the harvest in the barn, there began a long and gradual process of processing the crops. Threshing was of primary concern. It was a tedious job, but could be made to fit into periods of slack time or inclement weather. In the Roman period, the *tribulum* or threshing sledge pulled by oxen or other animals may have been used in Britain, particularly for larger farms (Rees 1979, 485–6; Applebaum 1972, 81, 238; White, K. D. 1967, 154–6), but by the medieval period the flail had taken over completely, and indeed is included among the tools listed in the *Gerefa* (Cunningham 1905, 575). Some regional variations in flails were evident, particularly in the way in which the two wooden pieces of the flail – the handle and the striker – were joined together (Allison 1904, 96–110), but in general the construction and form of the implement were consistent throughout the British Isles, with a long handle and a somewhat shorter striker, as shown in figure 5.5. Why the threshing sledge should apparently have been discontinued, particularly when animals were commonly used for other tasks, is difficult to say, but it seems likely that threshing by flails was more efficient, and with the spare-time nature of the task perhaps it was not so vital to find ways of saving labour. Winnowing – the separation of the corn kernels from the outer husks or chaff – followed naturally upon threshing and was often done by throwing the threshed corn up from a special winnowing basket. A breeze, artifically created by a winnowing fan (*vannus*) or sheet or naturally available by doing the winnowing out of doors, provided the mechanism by which the lighter chaff was blown away from the heavier kernels, which fell back into the basket of the winnower. Rakes, sieves, riddles (figure 5.5), and sacks were also necessary for gathering up the threshed or winnowed grain, sorting it out, and storing it away. All these pieces of equipment are well documented (Field 1965, 137–45; Page 1936, 3, 10; Lee et al. 1976, 52). It is possible that in some cases corn would be prepared for consumption using a handmill or quern (for example, DeWindt 1976, 53, 108, 175) or possibly even in a mortar and pestle, but in most cases it probably went to the lord's mill for grinding.

Apart from the growing or processing of crops, a vital task was the collection of fuel, particularly wood. Axes and hatchets were essential, but other tools were useful as well. Hooks, pieces of wood with a curve at the end, were employed for knocking down the lower branches of trees and acorns for swine (Morgan 1984, pl. facing 161). Another very useful tool was the billhook, as shown in several medieval illustrations and found on many archaeological sites (figure 5.5; Lee et al. 1976, 52; Morgan 1984, pl. facing 161; Rahtz 1969, 108–9; Goodall 1980, 70). This cutting and slashing tool, which could take on many shapes ranging from a heavy curved knife to something like a butcher's cleaver, was useful for a multitude of chores, from cutting off boughs and branches for fuel to constructing and trimming hedges (Rees 1981a, 26). Billhooks have had a very long history in England. Although many varieties of the tool existed, including smaller pruning knives or hooks (Wheeler, R. E. M. 1954, 124), in general their form changed little from Roman times to the present century (Rees 1981a, 26, 27; Sayce 1936, 68; Rees 1981b, 67–8).

The pastoral side of the rural economy also generated its own tools. Apart from grain growing the raising of sheep for wool and meat was the most important component of the medieval agrarian economy. Tools for the sheep industry, however, were rather limited. Shepherds had crooks, but these may often have been simply clubs or sticks curved at one end that only slowly evolved into the more stylized crooks of later times (Salzman 1957, 91–2; Ingram 1977, 7–11). Spring-tined shears for removing the wool from sheep, as well as performing a multitude of other chores such as cloth cutting, showed a remarkable consistency in their design over the medieval period (figure 5.6; Wheeler, R. E. M. 1954, 153–8; Beresford, G. 1975, 80, 82; 1977, 257, 273; Goodall 1981, 56–9), and there seems to have been little attempt to improve the efficiency of this operation until very recent times. In dairying, too, there was little change and little needed

5.6 *A man using a pair of hand shears to shear a sheep, from a twelfth-century calendar illustrating the occupations of the months. The monogram is for June and July (Bod. Lib. MS Auct. D. 2.6 (S.C. 3636), fo. 4).*

beyond buckets, jars for moulding cheese, cheese presses, jugs and churns (figures 5.5 and 8.3; Page 1936, 3, 10; Singer et al. 1956, 100, 255; Morris, C. A. 1984, 93–5, 138–42, fig. 79).

There were also a number of what might be called miscellaneous implements. Shovels were required for a great number of chores, from spreading dung to shifting sand and gravel or generally clearing up messes around the farm. Some at least of these shovels had detachable wooden blades which could be replaced when they broke or split (Morris, C. A. 1980; 1981). Wheelbarrows were common and appear to have been a medieval innovation; they also came in several designs, judging from medieval illustrations (Singer et al. 1956, 546–7, 641). Wooden ladders are frequently mentioned in medieval and early modern documentation and must have been a common piece of equipment (Singer et al. 1956, 100; Page 1936, 3, 10; Havinden 1965, 51). Traps and nets for catching fish and game were also an integral part of the range of farming equipment and are shown on several medieval illustrations (figure 8.5; Peate 1934, 153–4; Trevelyan 1942, pls 30–3). Tripods, balances and whetstones are again fairly common pieces of equipment (Harvey, P. D. A. 1976, 151–2; Wheeler, R. E. M. 1954, 293–4). Finally, tools that occurred with considerable frequency on medieval farms were augers, gimlets and related boring tools, as well as other carpentry tools such as bits, saws and chisels (Goodall 1980, ch. 3; 1981, 52–3) Beresford, G. 1975, 87–8, 97; Hilton and Rahtz 1966, 119–20; see also pp. 95–6). These were obviously very important for making other tools and illustrate quite forcibly the general sentiment among medieval farmers that the good husbandman made some at least of his own tools and implements. Hammers and nails are evident from archaeological sites (Goodall 1980, 34–5), but were not always necessary, as indicated by Fitzherbert's instructions for making rakes and forks (Skeat 1882, 33):

> And whan the housbande sytteth by the fyre, and hath nothynge to do, than maye he make theym [rakes and forks] redye, and tothe the rakes with drye wethywode, and bore the holes with his wymble, bothe aboue and vnder, and driue the tethe vpwarde faste and harde, and than wedge them aboue with drye woode of oke, for that is hard, and wil driue and neuer come out.

From this passage medieval rural people were clearly expected to have some carpentry skills, but there was undoubtedly some scope for the professional toolmaker (Morris 1984, 28, 237–40; Birrell 1969, 94–5). Some items were traditionally left to specialized craftsmen, such as wheels to the wheelwright, while iron fittings were almost certainly fabricated by a smith. Nevertheless, it would seem that one of the hallmarks of a competent farmer or farm employee was not only the ability to use his tools efficiently but to make at least some of them as well.

Conclusions

The importance of a farmer's tools and implements as a factor in his ability to make a living – and indeed simply to survive – is amply evident. The course of development that these tools followed had important repercussions on the development and effectiveness of agriculture as a whole, and over the centuries a range of tools was developed to fit as well as possible into the existing environmental and social realities of the English countryside. Some adjustments had obviously to be made. For example, the decline of viticulture in the later middle ages, whether due to climate or other causes (pp. 33, 233), led to the abandonment of the range of pruning and cutting tools that accompanied that particular crop production (Daumas 1969, 466).

The list of tools available to, and used by, medieval English farmers was lengthy. Those we have discussed in this chapter give some indication of the variety available, and there were more for which we have little evidence or simply do not have enough space to itemize here. None the less the range of tools available to the medieval farming community was still very limited compared to later periods. By the nineteenth century it is estimated that the number of different agricultural tools reached into the thousands (Harvey, N. 1980, 92). It seems very unlikely, even including varieties of tools that we may have excluded, that the range of such tools during our period was anything of that order. A good example of this concerns the development of hand tools for drainage, which only began to spread in the seventeenth century and after.

Part of this relative lack of variety in hand tools and implements can be laid at the door of a lack of technical expertise. This is particularly so in the case of four-wheeled wagons versus two-wheeled wains, where the problem of the movable forecarriage had probably not been solved during our period in a way that would make four-wheeled wagons useful for farm work. But this lack of technical expertise is relevant for only a few implements. After all, many tools – such as rakes, spades, hoes, mattocks, pickaxes – have changed little from ancient times. Admittedly the increased use of iron may have improved the effectiveness, and certainly increased the life, of these tools. It has been claimed that the increasing use of iron for tools was one of the important technical innovations of medieval period (White 1962, 40–1; Gimpel 1977, 64–6; Duby 1968, 108–9), and certainly there are signs that the use of iron was becoming more prevalent in medieval English agriculture (see p. 94; Mate 1980, 329–30). This was probably given impetus as the iron-making industry in England became more important at the end of the medieval period. It is, however, all too easy to exaggerate this. The use of iron during the medieval period seems to have been no more extensive than during the Roman period, where iron was used on a similar range of tools and perhaps even to a greater extent, judging from the rather more extensive finds of iron in some tools such as rakes and possibly spades (Rees 1979, 484–5, 326–9; 1981a, 28–9; cf. Goodall 1980, 69, 67–8). Even the Anglo-Saxon period, especially its later phase, may not have been so far behind in its use of iron for tools (Wilson 1981, 80–5; 1976, 255–6; Addyman 1964, 60–1). Also, as Fitzherbert pointed out in relation to harrows, iron was not necessarily the most sensible choice for a given tool; wood in certain circumstances might be much more economical (Skeat 1882, 25). Indeed the widespread use of iron in agricultural tools often had to be accompanied by significant changes in the design of these tools, as exemplified by the eighteenth-century development of all-iron ploughs (Fussell 1966, 183–6; Partridge 1973, 39–42; 1969, 3).

Perhaps the most important factor affecting the proliferation of varieties of tools was the gradual growth in the complexity of the agrarian and market economy. In many ways the rural economy of England up to the middle of the fourteenth century was considerably simpler – or at least showed less variation – than that which followed. For instance, there was a great emphasis, virtually countrywide, upon the mixing of arable and pastoral elements, a philosophy, perhaps based upon a desire for self-sufficiency, that characterized even large estates (pp. 16–18; Dahlman 1980, 104–8; Kerridge 1967, 182). Accompanying this was the emphasis, not to say obsession, upon the growing of crops (figure 5.7), with the pastoral economy by and large performing a secondary role (p. 18). Agrarian technique also tended to be more uniform across the country than it came to be later (Langdon 1986a, 273–4; Mate 1985, 31). With the decline of population in the later fourteenth century and afterwards, however, the pressure on arable farming was no longer so acute. Some regions could and did change to pastoral activities while others remained in their arable mode (Thirsk 1967a, 110; Dyer 1981, 18). The result was to accentuate the differences among areas, a feature that was made increasingly possible by the growing influence of market forces, particularly in the specialization of these markets, as in the horse trade (Langdon 1986a, 287–8). This was emphasized by an upsurge in enclosure, which reflected the reality that it was no longer necessary or sensible to be as self-sufficient in both grain and livestock as before (Dahlman 1980, 153–69; Thirsk 1967a, 3–5). This differentiation was further reflected in a marked polarization in the practices of one region versus another, such as in the use of horses and oxen (Langdon 1986a, 288). As a result, most of the complexity of farming regions evident in figure 2.3 seems to have stemmed from this later period. All of this impinged upon the use of tools. Towards the end of the sixteenth century and afterwards, specialization in regional economies seems to have been followed in many cases by regional specializations in techniques and equipment (for example, in the use of horses and oxen; Langdon 1986a, 273–6),

5.7 *A harvesting scene from the fourteenth-century Luttrell Psalter. The women are using 'balanced sickles'*
(Brit. Lib. Add. MS 42130, fo. 172b).

accompanied – it appears – by acceleration in the adoption of ideas from overseas (for example, the Dutch plough: Thirsk 1967b, 164; Fussell 1966,185).

This increase in the degree of regionalism, however, was a feature that became evident only towards the closing centuries of our period. Before then, the range of tool types and their design tended to remain rather static. Only in a few instances (mouldboard ploughs, horse harness, wheelbarrows, flails, seedlips, clodding mallets, weeding hooks and forks) is much in the way of change evident between the Roman period and the seventeenth century. In most of these cases, too, the development of the pertinent tool did not take place during the period under consideration. The form of the mouldboard plough, for instance, had essentially been completed by *c.*1000, while the development of the movable forecarriage for wagons, although under way, was only essentially complete after 1600. Perhaps the most important development in agricultural equipment during the medieval period was the introduction of the modern horse harness, which, as we have already indicated, led to the much increased use of horses in farm work, particularly for hauling. But it is unlikely that this impinged much on the design of other implements. There was no doubt a substantial move to lighter vehicles in the wake of the adoption of the horse for hauling in the twelfth and thirteenth centuries, but it seems that these vehicles – or something very like them – were already available, judging from early medieval illustrations (Langdon 1986a, 25).

This relative conservatism in tool development was paralleled, among the farming elite at least, by a growth in a common pool of ideas concerning farming, particularly as evidenced by the great agrarian treatises of the thirteenth century. On one level the appearance of these treatises was highly innovative, but on another these works may conversely have fostered a very conservative attitude among medieval farmers of the time – an attitude that stressed consistency and continuity of farming practice (Mate 1985, 31) and the application of existing ideas and equipment to their maximum potential, but did little to encourage new practices accompanied by new pieces of equipment. This convervatism was evident as late as the beginning of the sixteenth century with works like those of Fitzherbert and Tusser which, by and large, were very backward-looking in their view of agriculture. Only by the end of the sixteenth century and afterwards did the mood become more progressive, as indicated by the emphasis on improvement in such works as Hugh Plat's and Walter Blith's (Plat 1601; Blith 1653), and the interest in new tools and techniques quickened accordingly (Fussell 1952, 218–22). It should be said that some exceptions to this archetypal conservatism in agrarian practices did exist, such as the proliferation of windmills. Nor was this conservatism necessarily shared by the lower orders in the agrarian society. Peasants in the medieval period, for instance, seem to have shown considerably more innovation – in such areas as the introduction of horses to farming and possibly the use of legumes – than did their social superiors (Langdon 1986a, 291–2; 1982).

Whether or not there were changes in tool design, they certainly seem to have had a limited effect on agrarian productivity. There was probably some increase in total production from the land in England, particularly during the twelfth and thirteenth centuries because of land clearance, but the increase in productivity (per unit of land) was marginal at best from *c.*1000 up until the middle of the fourteenth century and even beyond (Postan 1966, 556–9, 600–2; 1975; Titow 1972; Grigg 1980, 91–2), although the last word on this question has yet to be delivered (Campbell 1983b). This is the area where significant changes in tool types might have had an effect, but little change is evident. The improvement in the population-to-land ratio in the latter part of the middle ages may have led to some improvement in productivity but, if so, this was probably due more to beneficial changes in the balance between grain and grass than improvements in tools (Bolton 1980, 242–5).

In summary, tool development during the middle ages tended to stagnate, at least in relation to the periods which preceded or followed. This was not necessarily a bad thing, since the range of tools may well have been sufficient for the times, and in any case traditional methods of agriculture could often prove to be very adaptable in certain circumstances (Campbell 1983a; Havinden 1968). Nevertheless, eventually improvements in tool development would have to take place as an essential part of the improvement of agriculture as a whole. Some of this was starting to happen at the end of the sixteenth century, but it was only a tentative beginning. Otherwise, there seems to have been a feeling of satisfaction if not complacency on the part of medieval English farmers concerning the tools and implements they were using.

6

Plant Resources

James Greig

This chapter contains the botanist's tale of medieval plant resources. The historical evidence is compared with the more modest data so far available from archaeobotanical work on plant remains (see p. 5; figure 6.1).

Feeding People: the Staple Foods

The grain crops wheat, barley, oats and rye were clearly the most imporant foodplant resource for the people. Some parts of the country had an economy based mainly upon arable crops, and even where stock-raising was more important, grain had to be grown or brought in to feed people and animals. Wheat seems to have been the preferred food grain, and amounted to half the food in 83 late medieval maintenance agreements studied by Dyer (1983, 201). The names in documents usually refer only to the general kind of grain such as the wheat mentioned above, barley, oats or rye, or just grain, 'ble' (Oschinsky 1971, 330–1). Fitzherbert's 'Book of Husbandry', written around 1534, names seven kinds of wheat, although they cannot all be recognised in modern terms (Skeat 1882, 40–1).

The archaeobotanical evidence for wheat is widespread, in the form of charred remains of grains, chaff and straw which are ubiquitous on archaeological sites, as are those from the other cereals. The grains themselves cannot usually be identified more exactly than to genus (*Triticum* sp.). Wheat was the main charred cereal found in medieval pits in Winchester, for example, followed by barley, then by oats. These scattered finds could be from tail grain and weed seeds and were probably domestic waste which was discarded into domestic firesides and there charred, then thrown with other rubbish into pits. This evidence seems to show that wheat was the main food grain grown around Winchester in the medieval period, although it could merely demonstrate that wheat had a greater chance of being charred than the other cereals, perhaps because its straw was

6.1   *Preserved plant remains. Sloe, plum and cherry stones from twelfth-century deposits at 16–22 Coppergate, York. The diameter of the dish is 100 mm*
(photo: R. Hunter).

more generally used and then burnt. Such finds are, however, far less likely to show the relative importance of the various foodstuffs than the rare finds of grain stores such as those from burnt houses (Green 1982; 1984). Remains from other parts of Britain such as the midlands, show a somewhat different pattern of cereal abundance (Moffet in preparation a; b; c). Grain remains are also found in waterlogged deposits, either whole or as bran fragments (Hall, A. R. et al. 1983; Hillman in press), desiccated in daub and other building material, or mineralized especially in a lime-rich soil, as at Winchester (Green 1979a). Cereal pollen is also found (Greig 1982).

The most important wheats were bread wheat (*Triticum aestivum*) and rivet wheat (*Triticum turgidum*). Compact wheat (*Triticum compactum*) and spelt wheat

(*Triticum spelta*) do not seem to have been significant. Although many of the wheat remains which are identifiable to species are of bread wheat, it is becoming apparent that rivet wheat was also widely grown in the medieval period (Moffet in preparation d). Rivet wheat, also known as pollard or cone wheat, seems to have been well known when Fitzherbert and Tusser were writing in the sixteenth century, and probably before, although none of the many names of wheat used in the thirteenth-century *Walter of Henley* are recognisable as this (Skeat 1882, 40; Grigson 1984, 43; Oschinsky 1971, 330–1). It is most often recognised from rachises (chaff fragments), which are identified as *Triticum turgidum/durum* (rivet or macaroni wheat) although in all likelihood it was the former that grew in Britain. Thus a significant proportion of the wheat finds from medieval Stafford have been identified as probable rivet wheat, for instance those in a pit dated to the twelfth century, in which bread and compact wheats were the majority of the chaff and grain, but about 15 per cent were rivet wheat. There were also traces of rye, barley, oat, pea and bean, and weed seeds (Moffet in preparation b). Rivet wheat has also been found at a *c*.eleventh-century manor site, North Shoebury, Essex, in early thirteenth-century charred rubbish at Taunton Priory, in twelfth-/thirteenth-century waterlogged remains from Chester, twelfth- and fourteenth-century deposits at Dean Court Farm (Oxon.) and Raunds (Northants.) (L. Moffet pers. comm.; P. Murphy pers. comm.; Greig and Osborne 1984; Greig in preparation a; Moffet in preparation c; J. Ede pers. comm.). So here is an archaeobotanical picture emerging to complement and indeed amplify the historical record of the cultivation of this wheat. Rivet wheat is a tall and productive grain when it grows well, and is practically immune to rust fungi, but it is sensitive to bad weather and poor soil, and grows slowly from autumn sowing. It is not very good for making light loaves. Rivet wheat is perhaps the most 'typical' foodgrain of the medieval and post-medieval periods because it seems hardly to have been grown before. Its history and origins are somewhat obscure, but it might have come to Britain from the mediterranean countries (Percival 1921, 241–3).

Spelt wheat (*Triticum spelta*) has occasionally been found in medieval deposits in the south of England and from the depths of Wales, identified either from the typical grains, or more usually from the spikelet forks (part of the chaff) (Green, 1979a; Hillman 1982). However, in many cases there is some doubt whether these are truly medieval deposits or if there might also be residual Roman material disturbed and redeposited by later activities on the same site, as at Collfryn (Jones and Milles 1984). The role of spelt wheat in medieval Britain is, therefore, open to some question. It does have the advantage of surviving a worse climate than any other wheat, so spelt cultivation in some places would be understandable (Hillman 1982).

Barley (*Hordeum vulgare*) was grown as a spring-sown crop and could be used for food, or drink in the form of ale. Coarse barley bread seems to have been the staple in lowland Scotland, north-west England, and in parts of Wales and Cornwall and five of the food allowances to retired peasants were of barley alone (Wilson, C. A. 1984, 220; Dyer 1983, 202). Malting is the main use for barley now (apart from animal feed) and in the past ale was important as a wholesome and nutritious drink (Corran 1975). Allowances of ale seem generous by present standards, for example a gallon per head per day, although some of this was weak small beer. Barley may have been mainly malted for brewing when there was sufficient bread-corn available, otherwise it would have been used for food (Dyer 1983, 193, 204). Charred remains of barley are ubiquitous in medieval sites, but only here and there is it the main cereal. Examples of finds which are mainly of barley include three sites in Norwich, Whitefriars Street (tenth to twelfth century), Pottergate (thirteenth to sixteenth century) and Alms Lane (thirteenth to fifteenth century), and one fifteenth- to sixteenth-century deposit in Northampton (Ayers and Murphy 1983; Murphy 1985a; b; Straker 1979). The Alms Lane finds also included two-row barley. Brewing was suspected at this site because the barley was sprouted as if for malting, and a millstone, ovens, steeping pits and possible malting floors provided supporting archaeological evidence. Murphy suggests that if the grain was to have been used as bread corn, it would probably have reached the site already milled, thus reducing the chance of finds of grain being made. Barley bread was certainly eaten in East Anglia according to documentary evidence so one ought to suspect that this cereal had been used for brewing only when malted grain is found, as at Alms Lane or at Winchester (C. Dyer pers. comm.; F. Green pers. comm.).

The common oat (*Avena sativa*) and the bristle oat (*A. strigosa*) were widely cultivated as a spring crop either on their own, or together with barley as 'dredge' and they could be used either as food or as fodder. There are various wild species such as *Avena ludoviciana* and *A. fatua* which are still persistent cornfield weeds, so not all oat finds are necessarily cultivated crops. Oat cultivation was most important in the north and west where the climate was less suitable for the success of other cereals and elsewhere where there was a market for fodder, for example around London and Winchester. Oats seem to have been the main food grain in the north-west and uplands but less commonly used as food in the lowlands. According to the maintenance agreements, they do not seem to have been issued alone (Dyer 1983, 201, 205). Archaeobotanical finds of small amounts of oats are ubiquitous in charred material, but these tell us little. Larger concentrations of charred oats could represent food, fodder or straw fuel. None the less oats are the main cereal at sites such as thirteenth-century Cefn Graeanog, Gwynned, at a place where few other cereals could have been cultivated, and at the fifteenth-century Welsh rural site at Collfryn which is in an area of high rainfall, where one might expect oat cultivation to have been important (Hillman 1982; Jones and Milles 1984). In these cases there is no evidence to show whether the oats were eaten by people or animals, or used as fuel in the kiln. Finds that were mostly of oats have also occurred at many different sites, such as Riggs Hall in Shrewsbury, Lydford 'B' in Devon and Upper Bugle St, Southampton and they support the documentary evidence for extensive oat cultivation in lowland areas (Colledge 1983; Green 1982).

Rye (*Secale cerale*) was one of the normal cereal crops of the medieval period, according to the Tudor farmer-writers and surviving account rolls (Campbell in preparation). It was also grown with wheat as a mixed crop of 'maslin' or 'mancorn' although the different ripening times could cause problems at harvest (Grigson 1984, 34). Rye was perhaps the least important cereal, although very widely grown, particularly in the eastern counties on the lighter soils there (Campbell in preparation). In most of the food allowances to retired peasants, rye played only a minor part, although in some areas, for example in parts of Norfolk and Worcestershire, it may have been the principal foodcorn (Dyer 1983, 205; Wilson 1984, 220). Rye bread is dark and heavy, not to everyone's taste, and it may have been regarded mainly as food for the poorer folk and thus considered to be less desirable than whiter wheaten bread (Wilson 1984, 220; see Palliser 1982).

Rye straw is extremely long, sometimes more than 2 m, and this may also have been a further useful product from the crop. Long lengths have been unravelled from daub in half-timbered buildings in Germany (Willerding in preparation). When preservation is adequate, rye can be identified from its tapering grains and also from its chaff and its elongated pollen grains. Finds of rye are frequent, and sometimes it is the most abundant cereal found, as for example at Lydford 'B' in Devon and at Hunter's Walk, Chester (Green 1984; Greig in preparation a). Elsewhere, rye has been found as the second most abundant cereal in remains, as at Stafford (Moffet in preparation b), although in some regions it is usually present only in trace amounts, as in the Winchester area (Green 1979a). Rye seems to have been first cultivated as an important crop in Saxon times. Although it was certainly present before then, it is not always clear whether it was really grown as a crop in its own right in pre-Saxon times or merely grew as a weed among wheat. Rye is productive on soils that are too poor for wheat, and since shortage of dung seems to have been a limiting factor for medieval crop husbandry, perhaps the main value of rye was that it succeeded on such poor land, especially on rather sandy soils.

The growing of a range of cereals would have provided products with rather different uses including grain for food, drink or fodder and straw for fodder, building material and fuel. The variety of cereals grown would have given some insurance against the failure of a particular crop in a given season. The cultivation of both spring-sown grain such as barley and oats, and autumn-sown ones such as wheat and rye would have spread the work of ploughing, dunging and sowing more evenly over the year and facilitated crop rotation.

Other field crops such as peas, beans, lentils and vetches could be used as food or fodder and they were grown alone or as a mixture (for example, peas and beans), sometimes as field crops or in gardens (Campbell 1983a). They were most important in the south, east and midlands, later spreading to most regions except western Britain (Campbell in preparation). Pulses represent about a tenth of the food mentioned in the maintenance agreements, which might be an approximation to their importance in the diet of ordinary people (Dyer 1983, 201). Indeed they were regarded as the basis for the pottage of householders and their labourers (McLean 1981, 201–2). The pea (*Pisum sativum*) evidently existed as white, grey-green and black varieties. The white and green peas were cultivated mainly as a crop to be dried and stored, although fresh green peas were also eaten, as peasecods. Otherwise, the pea crop and vetches were used for fodder, sometimes unthreshed (*in siliquis*) (Campbell 1983a, 32). According to historical evidence, other crops such as lentils (*Lens culinaris*) seem scarcely to have been grown.

Archaeobotanical evidence for legumes is rather infrequent although they are probably under-represented (Green 1979b). They do not often appear charred since their straw is too insubstantial to be of much use as fuel, but there are occasional finds, as at the rural site at Cotton (Northants.), and a scatter of other finds from southern England including some in daub (J. Ede pers. comm.; Green 1979a; F. Green pers. comm.). The eleventh-century find of charred beans and peas from Oxford, together with a bean weevil (*Bruchus*), seems to show that they were grown as a mixed crop (Robinson 1984). Waterlogged remains are also scarce, although the hilum (the 'eye') and fragments of epidermis (the 'skin') can sometimes be found in very well preserved material as at Hunter's Walk, Chester (Greig in preparation a). Pod fragments were found at Gloucester (Green 1979b) and a few pollen grains are usually to be found in sewage (Greig 1982). Peas and beans do not usually feature in pollen diagrams from natural deposits, although the occasional grain is sometimes found as at Cookley, Worcestershire (Greig in preparation e). Lentil has been found in twelfth-century remains at Dean Court Farm, near Oxford, from sixteenth-century pits at Wolvesey Palace and from Hyde Abbey, Winchester (Moffet in preparation c; F. Green pers. comm.; Green 1979a).

Buckwheat (*Fagopyrum esculentum*) is another 'marginal' crop which was relatively little grown, although it may have become more popular at the end of the medieval period (Grigson 1984, 114). Its distinctive pollen has occasionally been found, for instance at Broad Sanctuary, Westminster (Scaife 1982).

Weeds, and the tools to destroy them, are often mentioned (figure 2.4; p. 99; Skeat 1882, 29–30). There are records of poor harvests being blamed on weeds (Mate 1985, 25) and an immense amount of effort must have gone into fallowing, ploughing and weeding the standing crops, in order to try to control the weed growth. Although some of these weeds, such as dock, thistle, dead-nettle and charlock are still common, others such as cornflower (*Centaurea cauanus*) and corn cockle (*Agrostemma githago*) have become rare. As one would expect, corn marigold or 'boddle' (*Chrysanthemum segetum*) is mentioned as a weed especially of spring-sown crops such as pulses and barley, and cornflower or 'hawdods' as a weed of rye (Skeat 1882, 30). Corn cockle has large, somewhat poisonous, seeds yet Fitzherbert commends it as being useful for its flour content (Hall, A. R. 1981; Skeat 1882, 30). Plant remains from medieval sites have a distinctively rich weed flora, so the battle against the weeds was apparently not won.

Gardens were mainly used for the cultivation of vegetables and other plants such as herbs. There were manorial gardens, but they evidently fell outside the scope of the crop husbandry described in *Walter of Henley* (McLean 1981, 203; Oschinsky 1971). Peasants often seem to have had gardens in addition to their holdings in the open fields (p. 50). By Fitzherbert's time the garden was the domain of the housewife, and seems to have been used for flax, hemp and herbs – vegetables are hardly mentioned (Skeat 1882, 96). 'Ion the Gardener' names a great variety of herbs and vegetables in his fifteenth-century poem on gardening (Amherst 1894, 163–6), but one might wonder how many of these were commonly grown either in urban 'garthyngs' (enclosed ground) or in the countryside. Orchards are mainly known for their fruit trees, although nuts and other crops such as flax were also grown there.

The vegetables that were most important in the gardens seem to have been members of the cabbage and onion families. Cabbages, 'cole', seem to have been mainly consumed by poor people, and vegetables were regarded as food for the lowly (Dyer 1983, 208). However, the demand was enough for the production of cole seed, recorded in Norfolk, to have been worthwhile (Campbell 1983a). Archaeological remains of the cabbage family, which also includes mustard, are hard to detect because the plants themselves are soft, and their seeds are difficult to identify. There are however, many records of *Brassica* or *sinapis* seeds which might represent this group. We do know that onions, leeks and garlic were popular, and indeed were frequently recorded as being imported, as was onion seed (Gras 1918, 453). Although the pollen and seeds of this plant group are not distinctive or tough enough to provide much archaeobotanical evidence, recently it has been possible to detect traces of the onion family from remains of the skin, which has a distinctive cell pattern. The leaf edge and a seed have provided evidence for leeks in York and Chester (Tomlinson in preparation; Greig in preparation f). Whole pieces of garlic have sometimes been found charred, but the only medieval example is the possible garlic find from a sixteenth-century context in Norwich (Murphy 1985b). Other vegetables are less frequently recorded in documents and may have been less important, but seeds of beet (*Beta* sp.) have been found in Saxon deposits in Winchester, and sixteenth-century deposits at Hill Hall, Essex (F. Green pers. comm.; Murphy unpublished).

Hops (*Humulus lupulus*) have been included as a garden crop, although they were also grown as a specialist field crop in certain areas such as in Kent and Worcestershire. The works on crop husbandry do not mention hops, and indeed the practice of brewing beer with hops seems to have started in Britain only in the later middle ages (Corran 1975). There is also late evidence of imports of 'pokys of hoppes', such as the customs records for Lynn in 1503–4 (Gras 1918, 652). Archaeological finds of hops seeds occur, but are rather infrequent; while they do not necessarily represent cultivated hops, it is hard to imagine how such wild plants would be brought to a habitation site, except for a particular use. Hops were found in the early medieval remains at Whitefriars Street, Norwich, but they were not necessarily cultivated or used here (Ayers and Murphy 1983). A fifteenth-century find of charred hops in cesspit deposits in Norwich more strongly suggested human use (Murphy 1985a). However, since brewing waste was probably used as animal feed, the small number of preserved remains is perhaps not suprising.

Feeding People: Non-staple Foods

Herbs and spices were very important in providing some flavour to the staple food mainly prepared from grain or dried legumes. The records, mainly from urban deposits, show some of the herbs used – seeds of parsley (*Petroselinum crispum*), summer savory (*Satureja hortensis*), catmint (*Nepeta cataria*) and mint (*Mentha* spp.) have been found, although it is the leaves that are usually used for flavouring. Since both the leaves and the seeds of celery (*Apium graveolens*) and camomile (*Chamaemilum nobile*) can be used, it is easier to understand the finds of these seeds (Greig 1983; Hall, A. R. 1986; Greig in preparation a). Fennel is one of the more commonly found herb plants. It was found at Worcester and at the rural moat at Cowick, Humberside and with coriander at Wolvesey Palace, Winchester (Greig 1981; 1986; Green 1979a). Pot marigold (*Calendula officinalis*), possible dill (*Anethum graveolens*) and celery seed have been found at early medieval Norwich (Ayers and Murphy 1983). Mustard (*Brassica nigra*) and opium poppy (*Papaver somniferum*) seem to have been widely used since their seeds are frequently found in sewage. Pepper (*Piper nigrum*) is well known from documents, perhaps because it was exotic and therefore expensive, but the earliest archaeological find is from the battleship *Mary Rose* (F. Green pers. comm.).

Fruit growing (figure 6.2) is supported by fairly plentiful historical evidence in the medieval period and is summarised by McLean (1981), but most refers to urban and suburban gardens and orchards rather than to the countryside itself. Fruit growing by peasants was probably rather unusual, as it is seldom mentioned in documents. On the other hand, wild and semi-wild fruit was probably gathered from the hedgerows and scrub. Much of this fruit may have been consumed cooked, perhaps with cereals in a murrey, for fresh fruit was

6.2 *Fruit picking, from a Flemish calendar (Bod. Lib. Add. MS A. 46. f. 3v).*

considered unhealthy (Wilson 1984, 299, 311). Fruit was also imported in bulk. For instance, customs dues '*pro fructibus appreciatis* £28' were levied on Pedro of Spain's cargo in Chichester in 1323–4 (Gras 1918, 393). We do not know what the fruit was, nor whether it was fresh or dried, although the sheer quantity hints at the latter. In the later medieval period private gardens and orchards had developed, for Fitzherbert mentions apples, pears, wardens (cooking pears), plums and cherries (Skeat 1882, 90).

The archaeobotanical evidence for fruit is plentiful, especially from later medieval cesspits and latrines. Here fruitstones are readily preserved by waterlogged conditions and by mineralization (figure 6.1), and some whole fruit have even been preserved by charring. Latrines are often identified by the fruitstones that are visible even during excavation, and the archaeobotanical results show a 'medieval fruit salad'. Most of this evidence is from towns, and probably represents the harvest from urban or suburban orchards and imports rather than produce from the surrounding countryside (Greig 1982). The evidence from cesspits may therefore give a somewhat exaggerated picture of the importance of fruit in diet. By contrast, finds such as those from the early thirteenth-century rubbish deposits at Taunton Priory and the moat at Cowick are much rarer (Greig and Osborne 1984; Greig 1986). Where the fruit such as sloes and damsons is wild or at least widely naturalised, there is rarely any proof that the remains were actually eaten rather than being naturally dispersed.

Apples seem to have been among the most widely cultivated of fruit and there is plenty of historical and archaeobotanical evidence for apple growing, the latter from apple pips and sometimes also fragments of endocarp from the apple core. Pears were also grown but probably less widely than apples, for they are less frequently mentioned in documents, and far fewer pear than apple pips have been found.

Damsons and cherries were often grown, although archaeobotanical evidence shows that the varieties were primitive. Damsons and sloes are sour and were often left on the tree until well frosted, or stored in straw, in order to modify the acidity. Some were pressed for verjuice, a kind of vinegar, although many were eaten, often cooked with flour into a murrey, or used as cattle medicine (McLean 1981, 237; Wilson 1984, 299; Grigson 1984, 46). Dried prunes do not seem to have been much imported, although there is the occasional reference such as the '1 box prunys' with a varied assortment of other foodstuffs (Gras 1918, 514). Strawberries were grown or gathered from the wild, and brambles, elderberries, blaeberries, haws, rosehips and wild raspberries were probably also consumed, as their remains have been preserved (Greig 1983; Hillman in press).

The fig (*Ficus carica*) does not seem to have been grown in medieval England according to documentary evidence. However, figs were certainly imported according to the customs records (Gras 1918, 318–21). In cesspits, fig pips are ubiquitous and, since each fig contains nearly a thousand of them, often abundant too. Grapes may have been grown only in certain parts of the country and, although English wine was produced in some of these areas, the grapes were often used for verjuice. Grape products such as raisins, '*racemi*' and currants, '*corones*' were imported (Gras 1918, 393). Grape pips (*Vitis vinifera*) have been found from tenth- to early eleventh-century deposits in Norwich (Ayers and Murphy 1983). There were also grape pips found at Winchester in Saxon deposits at Cathedral Green and in deposits dated to the first half of the eleventh century and the late twelfth to mid-thirteenth century at Brook Street, showing at least something approaching continuity of presence here. However, we do not know whether they were locally grown or imported via Southampton (Green

1979a). Grape remains become more common and abundant in the later medieval urban sites, either because they really were so, or because there are more cesspits from that period (Greig 1983). Amongst the rural sites, the medieval moat at Cowick produced a few food remains, including grape – perhaps a sign of urban sophistication at this royal hunting lodge (Greig 1986). An unusual find of charred grape pips dating from the fourteenth century was made at Dean Court Farm near Oxford and there is also evidence of viticulture from nearby Abingdon Abbey (Moffet in preparation c; see pp. 33, 233).

Nuts are mentioned as being used as payments – *Walter of Henley* mentions '. . . rents from nuts, furze, broom, fern (bracken), reedgrass, peat and stubble . . .' and '. . . the rents in nuts given for the right to go into the woods and gather dry brushwood and such small things as can be found in the woods.' (Oschinsky 1971, 435). The commonest nuts are those of the hazel (*Corylus avellana*) and hazel nutshell is almost ubiquitous among archaeological plant remains. Hazel nuts may have been imported as well (Gras 1918). Walnuts ('great nuts') were also grown; pollen remains have been found in the ditch deposits at Cowick (post-1329), at Nantwich (late fourteenth/early fifteenth century) and at Broad Sanctuary in London, suggesting the presence of walnut trees at these sites (Greig 1986; Colledge 1981; Scaife 1982). Walnut shell, which could have been either home-grown or imported, has been found at a variety of sites dating from the early to the late medieval period (Green 1979a; Ayers and Murphy 1983; Franks 1977; Greig in preparation d). Sweet chestnuts (*Castanea sativa*) were apparently grown in the medieval period, mainly for their wood, and there is a pollen record, from Hampstead Heath (Greig in press b).

Honey, being derived from flowers, can be included as a plant material. It seems to have been produced throughout the medieval period, although it was also imported (Oschinsky 1971, 422–3; Gras 1918). As the only sweetener available until the start of sugar cane imports in the late medieval period, one would expect honey to have been important, especially in view of the large amounts of sour fruit consumed. So far, there is only indirect evidence of honey from pollen records of insect-pollinated plants in sewage (Greig in preparation b; c).

Feeding Animals

Apart from the grain being the main source of food for people, both the grain and the straw of cereals were an important source of fodder for animals, and would have been most important in the winter when grazing was scarce. The different kinds of winter fodder had various values and also palatabilities, so Tusser suggests that the animals be given first rye straw, then wheat straw, followed by peas, oat straw, barley and finally hay (Grigson 1984, 56). The fodder rations also depended upon the animals in question. Working animals such as horses and oxen were better fed: 'and if a horse bee kept in plighte to doo his dayes woorke, he ought to have at the least every nyght the sixthe parte of a bushel of oates, of the price of a half peny and of the least xii den. in grasse in summer . . . and if the oxe bee kept in point to doe his woorke, then it behoveth that he have at the least weekely three sheves and a halfe of oates [for the cost of 1d.] and in the summer season xii d. of grasse . . .' (Oschinsky 1971, 319). Fitzherbert says that horses must have both hay and corn (Skeat 1882, 84). As well as oats, horses were fed peas, especially the grey variety, or horse beans. Sheep were fed coarse hay or oat straw, otherwise pea straw and pods according to *Walter of Henley* (Oschinsky 1971, 338–9). Plants such as common vetch (*Vicia sativa*) were used, and were cultivated for this purpose from the mid-fourteenth century onwards (Campbell 1983a, 32). Even the weed vetches (tares) that had smothered the grain crops could be mown for fodder (Skeat 1882, 30).

Archaeobotanical remains of such animal fodder can be hard to recognise. Cattle dung and sheep droppings are very finely divided after the chewing of the cud and therefore poor in identifiable remains. Horses tend to pass more of their fodder whole (Wilson 1979). Stalled animals spill some of their fodder which can be preserved when mixed with dung and thrown into a pit. Cereal remains and cornfield weeds are often found preserved in medieval mixed rubbish pits, but it is sometimes hard to tell whether they represent the remains of animal fodder, bedding or some other material mixed with dung. When such remains occur together with stable flies, bracken, and horseshoe nails, one can suggest that the cereals may have been used as fodder, as at Hen Domen (Greig et al. 1982). Remains of cereals, such as oats, that were used for fodder are often found in archaeological contexts, but they rarely seem to be from animal dung. In 144 Saxon and medieval contexts from the south of England only three (from two contexts in Winchester and one in Southampton) were mainly of oats, and they may have come from animal dung used as a binding agent (Green 1979a). Vetch seeds have been found, for example, in fourteenth-century deposits at Dean Court Farm (Moffet in preparation c).

Hay was also much used for fodder (figure 6.3). Areas for permanent hay meadow were traditionally set aside for this (Greig in press a) as well as odd pieces of grassland (Grigson 1984, 115). There is less documentary evidence for hay meadow management than for arable farming, perhaps because the hay harvest was likely to have been somewhat more reliable than that of corn, and it was only one of many sources of fodder. The changing price of food-corn on the other hand, was of vital importance. However, during scarce times such as during the early part of the fourteenth century, numerous stock as well as people died, showing that perhaps the animals were also weakened by undernourishment (p. 154).

Domesday records the hay meadows, '*prata*', for most of England, showing them to be mainly in the river valleys and usually under 5 ha, but sometimes over 20 ha (Darby 1936). Other written sources give rather few clues about grasslands, as if they were taken for granted and part of the normal landscape. One or two of these valley meadows, such as North Meadow at Cricklade, have survived apparently more or less unchanged since Domesday. This particular area, now a nature reserve, is on land which floods easily in winter, and which might not therefore be suitable for arable crops. Other meadowland was

6.3 *Mowing the hay meadow, from a mid-fifteenth-century calendar, illuminated in France
for the English market*
(Bod. Lib. MS Auct. D. inf. 2.11, fol. 6r).

ploughed up from time to time, or even alternated between pasture and ploughed land in response to changing needs (Mate 1985, 29–30). Some ancient meadow lies over ridge and furrow from former cultivation, such as Eades Meadow (C. Dyer pers. comm.), but other meadowland is on valley bottoms which tend to be flooded in winter. A logical use for much low-lying land in river valleys was as hay meadow, particularly as it was realised as early as Fitzherbert's day that grazing on such land could cause problems such as fluke infestations (Skeat 1882, 51, 2). On the permanent meadow, grazing ceased in late winter, the molehills were dispersed (Grigson 1984, 85) and the herbage was then allowed to grow until June or July when mowing would take place. Haymaking would be finished before the grain harvest so that the grass would not have become too tough (Skeat 1882, 32–4). The valley meadows were traditionally mown somewhat later in the year.

The summer grazing land was also a vital resource, because its quality was directly related to the amount of animal growth and productivity that would result. The pasture could be permanent and on land not cultivated because it was too steep, rocky or otherwise unsuitable, or on pastures fenced from the other fields or on fallow land. Heathland and wood pasture were also used (p. 133; VCH 1979, 7). Management seems to have consisted of removing bushes, sticks and stones, filling in holes and fencing. Good management consisted of allowing grazing on some pastures, and saving others until needed (Grigson 1984, 75–6, 85). Further pasture was made available in autumn on the stubble after the harvest of corn or legume crops, and on the meadow after the hay harvest, although Fitzherbert warns of the danger of overfeeding on the latter (Skeat 1882, 63).

If the hay ran short, leaf fodder of tree branches could be used instead, and there are a number of records from the early fifteenth century which mention hundreds of cartloads of branches being sold for this purpose (VCH 1979, 47). Mistletoe (*Yiscum album*) and ivy (*Hedera helix*) could be used to provide winter fodder (Grigson 1984, 74), a practice that goes back to prehistoric times.

Evidence for grassy fodder is sometimes to be found in urban rubbish deposits where seeds and pollen of grassland plants may indicate dung, although usually the grassland plants are far less abundant than the cornfield weeds. Occasionally a good find of grassland material in an unmixed state is found; the rural medieval well fill from Claydon Pike, Oxfordshire had 24 grassland taxa, some of them very characteristic of traditional hay meadow (M. Robinson pers. comm.). Grassland plants and dung beetles occur on other sites, usually in mixtures of organic rubbish: at Hen Domen, there were grassland plants such as knapweed (*Centaurea nigra*) and marshland ones too, probably from hay. There were also some grassland remains at Taunton and at Cowick (Greig et al. 1982; 1986; Greig and Osborne 1984). A recent approach to the history of grasslands is through the study of snail shells, since it is possible to distinguish pasture from meadow mollusc assemblages in the base-rich soils of the Thames valley. The ancient origin of some of the 'old meadows' such as Pixey Mead, near Oxford has been demonstrated by this method (M. Robinson in preparation).

It is often hard to find archaeobotanical evidence for the use of other land for grazing, since clover flowers, for example, could have come from hay, grazing or heath and furze remains could have been derived from bedding or fuel.

Using Plants

According to Fitzherbert, who included their cultivation as part of the wife's duties about the household, the two main garden crops were flax (*Linum usitatissimum*) and hemp (*Cannabis sativa*) (Skeat 1882, 96–7). Flax was mentioned only as a fibre plant by Fitzherbert; when used for this purpose it would be sown in spring, pulled up when ripe, retted (soaked) in a pool of water, then processed to separate the linen fibres, spun and finally woven. Not all flax was home grown, for there are frequent records of the import of bales of flax and of finished linen from the continent (Gras 1918, 274). Linseed, the seed of the flax plant, can be eaten in bread and in stews. There are frequent finds of flax seeds and capsules in waterlogged deposits, and sometimes evidence of flax straw as well. Some of these are retting sites (M. Robinson pers. comm.), and others are organic rubbish deposits. The linseed found in sewage deposits suggests that it was being eaten. Since flax fibre only survives where preservation is exceptional, records of this are rare.

Hemp (*Cannabis sativa*) was also grown for its fibres, and used for canvas and other coarse cloth, and cordage – 'hemp is sown on the manor to make ropes for carts, harnesses and other necessary items' (Oschinsky 1971, 439). Tusser mentions different sorts of hemp, the yellow one used for spinning and the green one for shoe thread, harness and rope (Grigson 1984, 116). Although mostly a minor crop, it was the main one in parts of the fenland (Thirsk 1984, 137). Like flax, hemp was retted to separate the fibres from the other plant parts and Tusser suggests first beating out the seed, then retting where the water thus fouled would not poison the cattle (Grigson 1984, 35). Hemp seeds are occasionally found in archaeological deposits and the pollen is sometimes abundant, although it is very difficult to distinguish it from that of hop. Some bogs, such as Askham Bog near York, have been found to contain extremely large amounts of this pollen, sometimes together with hemp seeds and are evidently places where hemp was retted (Bradshaw et al. 1981). Apart from the cables from the *Mary Rose*, the Tudor warship, hemp fibres do not seem to have been found. Oil from linseed and hempseed (and also walnuts) was extracted and used (Oschinsky 1971, 429).

Plants were certainly prized for their medicinal value (figure 6.4). Sometimes the same herbs were used for both medicinal and culinary purposes. There were

6.4 *A blackberry, illustrated in a twelfth-century herbal (Bod. Lib. MS Bodl. 130f. 21r).*

monastic herb gardens, and individuals grew herbs as well (McLean 1981, 176). The plants which could not be grown were brought in, for example the cumin, liquorice, aniseed and sugar mentioned in the Abingdon accounts (Kirk 1892, xxxvii). It is very difficult to decide if any of the plant remains found could represent medicinal use. The finds are usually as rubbish, thus giving little clue whether the plants were actually used or not, although sewage can show which plants were probably eaten. Seeds of narcotic plants such as henbane (*Hyoscyamus niger*) and deadly nightshade (*Atrope belladonna*) are fairly common in medieval deposits, but they may well have been growing as weeds on dungheaps or other waste places. Better evidence is provided when unusual plants, such as the caper spurge (*Euphorbia lathyrus*) at Coppergate, York, are identified from sewage (A. Hall pers. comm.). This plant is a violent purgative and emetic (Grieve 1984, 765), mentioned by Chaucer in the tale of Chanticleer (Coghill 1960, 264). Future archaeobotanical work will doubtless provide further information on medieval medicines.

Tanning, dyeing and cloth processing used special plant products and the leather and cloth trades were of great importance, especially from the fourteenth century onwards. Cloth working may not have been restricted to towns (Campbell 1983a), and even when it was concentrated there the dyeplants would have been country products. There is historical evidence for the cultivation of the well known dyeplants: the Saxon Sagacious Reeve mentions the dyeplants madder (*Rubia tinctorum*) and woad (*Isatis tinctoria*) (Addyman 1976, 319). Madder is mentioned in the accounts of East Anglian manors and those from the manors of Glastonbury Abbey for the years 1333–4 (C. Dyer pers. comm.; McLean 1981, 204). Some of the dyestuffs, such as the Picardy woad recorded in the 1509 customs records from London, and tanning and cloth processing products such as galls and 'tazilles' [teasels] were imported (Gras 1918, 560).

Dyeing is one of the industries that might be expected to leave a good archaeobotanical record, but only recently have the remains of dyeplants been recognised (Tomlinson 1985). Remains of dyers' greenweed (*Genista tinctoria*) which gives a green were found at King's Lynn and at York, where there were also remains of woad, used for a blue, weld (*Reseda lutea*) used for a yellow and madder, used for a red (Franks 1977; Tomlinson 1985). This last plant has now also been found at Bristol (Jones and Watson in press). The remains identified were pod fragments of woad and dyers' greenweed, the roots of madder, and seeds of weld. In addition, the non-British clubmoss (*Diphasium complanatum*) was found at York, where it had perhaps been used as a mordant (Tomlinson 1985). Beverley, famous for its clothworking, also provided leaves of sweet gale (*Myrica gale*) and weld which both gives a yellow colour (Hall and Tomlinson 1984).

Other useful plant products such as peat were obtained from bogs and fens for fuel (turbary). Medieval peat-cutting was sometimes very extensive, and is thought to have been responsible for the creation of the Norfolk Broads, for example. Even quite small bogs, such as Askham Bog, just outside York, were cut for peat – here peat-cutting was regulated by law in order to conserve this fuel supply (and see p. 26). The old peat cuttings were used for retting hemp and flax (Fitter and Smith 1979, 14). Marshland could be used for its hay crop, and it was a source of reed for thatching. Possible reedgrass (*Phragmites*) culm nodes (the thickenings of the stem) were found in destruction layers from a house fire in Norwich (Murphy 1985a), but in general there is surprisingly little sign of the thatching material which must frequently have been used, even in places with good preservation such as York (A. Hall pers. comm.).

Mosses were gathered from such places as woodland where they grew thickly, and were used for packing the gaps in wooden walls and stone slate roofs, and in towns for wiping material equivalent to today's toilet paper – large deposits are sometimes found in cesspits as, for example, at Dublin and Oslo (Hall et al. 1983). Bracket fungi were used for tinder, and some were even imported from Germany for this purpose; whole fungi have also been found at York and on the *Mary Rose* (A. Hall pers. comm.; F. Green pers. comm.).

Heathland products include heathers, which appear on some archaeological sites in quantity and may have been brought in as animal fodder, bedding, for brooms or as building material. Gorse, or furze, whose spiny leaves are found from time to time, seems to have been used as fuel for bread ovens.

Discussion

The choice of crops in different parts of the country depended upon many local and changeable factors such as how well they would grow, the availability of land and labour, grain prices, access to markets and the balance between food and fodder requirements. The analysis of all surviving account rolls suggests that there was indeed a complex regional variation in plant husbandry, as well as in other aspects of agriculture, which had already emerged by the late thirteenth century (Campbell in preparation). Archaeobotanical results are still too few to provide much comment or comparison.

Changes with time have been demonstrated by the documentary record; of the autumn-sown corn, wheat was always the preferred crop, but less rye was grown in the later medieval period. The spring-sown corn was initially mainly oats, but barley increased in relative importance after about 1325 so that a century later it almost equalled oats (Campbell 1983a; in preparation). Archaeobotanical evidence for cereals, however, seems to show little or no change with time. For example, at Alms Lane in Norwich, barley is always the dominant cereal, followed by traces of wheat, oats and rye (Murphy 1985b). Of course, the ratio of plant remains found need not necessary reflect the ratio of crops grown.

Documentary sources show that there was a dramatic increase in the cultivation of legumes (peas, beans and vetches) in the fourteenth century, when the area cultivated doubled (Campbell, in preparation). The detailed plant records from southern Britain (Green 1979a) do not reflect this, but since most of the legumes are likely to have been used as fodder and thus had little chance of being preserved, this is perhaps not surprising.

Archaeobotanical evidence, mainly from urban contexts, suggests that the range of fruit and herbs increased steadily through the medieval period showing a growth in sophistication as new arrivals were first expensive and rare, and then later diffused down through the layers of society (Greig 1983). A good chance to examine change with time was provided by the 35 samples analysed from Brook Street, Winchester, ranging from the early tenth through to the late fifteenth century (Green 1979a). A range of fruit including bramble, plum, bullace, sloe, apple and cherry is present throughout the period covered. The grape first appears in early eleventh century, and was much rarer than the other fruit, being represented by only five samples. Fig appears in the thirteenth century and is represented by only a single sample, and there were also single finds of strawberry and peach. Many of the Brook Street samples contain only weeds and cereal remains, and seem to be normal domestic rubbish, but 22 also contain fruit. The pattern suggests that wild fruit was available throughout the period, but cultivated or imported fruit was much rarer until the late medieval period. Grapes and figs are sometimes common in late medieval cesspits, perhaps because they were cheap to import by then. Finds of morello cherries also became more frequent, providing evidence that cultivated varieties had become established, since these are not native fruits.

The first appearance of new foodplants is usually first shown by the documentary record. Pepper is first documented in the eleventh-century Billingsgate tolls, and thereafter more frequently (Gras 1918, 153). The earliest British peppercorn finds so far seem to be those from the *Mary Rose*, where they were in storage (F. Green pers. comm.). Initially the pepper would have been relatively rare and expensive, and it would have doubtless have been used carefully. If peppercorns were ground up, traces in sewage could easily escape detection by archaeobotanists. Later as pepper became cheaper it become more widespread, thus increasing the chance that its remains would be found. For many other foodstuffs the archaeobotanical records usually occur considerably later than the first documentary references.

Possible climatic change has often been discussed as a factor determining events in the medieval period (p. 232; Lamb 1985). There are some events which might appear to hint at a deteriorating climate, such as the decreasing production of the vineyard at Abingdon in the years 1369, 1388, 1412 and 1450 (McLean 1981, 266), but this cannot be demonstrated in the archaeobotanical record as we cannot distinguish locally grown from imported vine fruits.

One would expect there to be some seasonality in the diet because some fruit and vegetables are only available fresh for a limited season, and there were few ways known of preserving food in the medieval period. The staple foods, such as cereals, peas and beans, could be dried and were available throughout the year. Figs and raisins were also available dried, although they were mainly eaten during the winter, especially at Christmas and during Lent (Wilson 1984, 298). Sloes, apples and pears were stored to extend the period of their availability (Grigson 1984, 46; Wilson 1972, 296). One would expect evidence for seasonality of diet to be found in latrine deposits, as Tusser suggests that a clearing-out of the latrine every November was the order of the day, and one might thus expect a year's deposits to have accumulated, at least in some cases (Grigson 1984, 51). However, latrines such as the Worcester barrel-latrine appear remarkably uniform in content from the top to the bottom, with large amounts of fruit remains throughout (Greig 1981).

Status can be indicated by the presence of food known to be expensive. These foods include peppercorns and a variety of fruit, such as quinces, medlars, peaches, mulberries and figs; the latter cost a penny-ha'penny a pound in the later medieval period, the equivalent of the daily wage of a labourer (C. Dyer pers. comm.). Records indicate that quinces (*Cydonia oblonga*), for example, were grown in gardens of the wealthy, and that the trees were very expensive. The purchase of trees for the Tower of London gardens in 1275 included 100 cherries at 1s 6d and 4 quinces at 2s (McLean 1981, 235), so these may never have been more than an exotic rarity in the gardens of the rich.

There is little archaeobotanical evidence for luxury living; the evidence from latrines usually seems to reflect townsfolk of moderate status, although Brook Street, Winchester was evidently a slum (F. Green pers. comm.). Some exotic fruits appear in the archaeobotanical record. The medlar, whose stony pips are both durable and easily recognised, has been found at Bristol (Jones and Watson in press). Peach stones have been found at twelfth-century York, in a fifteenth-century grave at Winchester and in Bristol (Green 1979a; Hall 1986; Jones and Watson in press). The mulberry (*Morus nigra*) whose red juice was used with cereals to make a murrey has appeared in later medieval deposits in York (Wilson 1984, 299; Hall 1986). Perhaps by the late medieval period some of these fruits were no longer such luxury items as they had been earlier. Food remains from a clearly high status context at Barnard Castle, County Durham included only four different plants, in contrast to a great range of animals, birds and fish (Donaldson et al. 1980) but the royal hunting lodge at Cowick, Humberside, did provide both fig and grape from the moat, signs of at least moderate sophistication in the depths of the countryside (Greig 1986).

7

Woods and Parks

Paul Stamper

The amount, type, and distribution of woodland in England have always been subject to change, perhaps never more so than in the middle ages. In recent years great strides have been made in the study of woodland, charting and explaining these changes, and demonstrating the vital and intimate role that it had in men's lives.

Studies have built up a fairly full picture of the distribution of woodland and how it was exploited in the relatively well-documented centuries after the Norman Conquest. In contrast, from the preceding Saxon period little evidence survives, and consequently even rudimentary and crucial questions remain debated and unresolved. W. G. Hoskins (1955, 56) expressed the long-held view that the end of Roman administration was followed by a collapse of the economy and of the population. The Anglo-Saxon settlers, he argued, faced a virgin country of damp oak–ash forest, much of it covering previously cultivated land, the England of 1086 being a colonial place of pioneers, frontiers and forests. The general premise of the above argument later came under attack as researchers proposed instead that there was an essential thread of continuity between Roman Britain and Saxon England with relatively little dislocation in the countryside.

Now, however, it begins to look as if Hoskins was more right than wrong, as evidence accumulates of the large-scale abandonment of cultivated land at the end of the Roman period and its gradual return to woodland in the fifth and sixth centuries. In midland England this has been shown, for instance, in several areas of Oxfordshire (Bond 1981, 201; Schumer 1984, 11–16; Steane 1985, 41) and in that part of Northamptonshire later to become Rockingham Forest (Petit 1968, 15; Taylor 1983, 121). Just how quickly regrowth could occur is revealed by a Domesday entry concerning eleven waste manors in north-west Herefordshire and the adjacent parts of Radnorshire. Here 'on these waste lands there have grown up woods in which Osbern [Fitz Richard] hunts' (Atkin 1971, 84–5). This waste probably resulted from Welsh raiding just 31 years before. Overall it seems about one-third of England was wooded in AD 586 (Rackham, O. 1980, 133).

In the sixth to eighth centuries massive clearances began in various parts of the country. 'Wold' and 'weald' both mean woodland, and at least some of those parts of the country that today have those names were wooded until they were cleared in Saxon times. It is true, for instance, of both the north and south Cotswolds, the Leicestershire Wolds, and the east Kent Weald (Everitt 1977, 10–17; 1979, 67–78; Hooke 1978, 333–41; Slater 1979, 213–18). There was also much piecemeal clearance, evidenced in part by '-leah' placenames, and by 1086 only 15 per cent or so of the country was wooded (Rackham, O. 1980, 126).

England was then a prosperous country whose population was growing, as it would continue to do for at least the next two centuries. In many parts of the country there was a real and urgent need for more agricultural land on which to grow food, and whatever other kinds of land, such as fen and waste, were brought into cultivation, considerable amounts of woodland were felled to that end. Particularly extensive clearances were made in the Chilterns and in the Sussex Weald, where *c.*180,000 ha of woodland were cleared in at most 260 years. There was also considerable assarting (that is, the clearing of land for cultivation) in the Arden region of Warwickshire and in north Worcestershire, in Lyme (Cheshire), in Surrey, Berkshire and north Hampshire, in the wooded areas of Derbyshire, Staffordshire and Yorkshire, in Neroche in Somerset, in Dorset, and in north-east Suffolk (Rackham, O. 1980, 134; Stamper 1983, 47–52). By 1350 the area of England that remained wooded was at most 10 per cent (Rackham, O. 1980, 134).

Woodland was a vital, much-used, and financially valuable resource in the middle ages; its products housed and heated all sections of society, and supplied the raw materials for a wide range of manufactured goods. Moreover, woodland often served as grazing land, usually much needed and sometimes the only common land on which animals could be put. Little wonder, then, that woodland became increasingly carefully managed and conserved as the amount available was whittled away.

Domesday and Woodland Systems

In 1086 woodland was noted in six different ways, reflecting the recording methods adopted by the different groups of commissioners rather than inherent regional differences in woodland management practices:

1 acres, especially in Lincolnshire;
2 length of the wood, as in Shropshire;
3 length and breadth in furlongs or leagues, a very widespread quantification;

4 'wood for *x* swine', an assessment nominally related to pannaging (the autumn fattening of pigs in woodland), the usual record north and west of London;

5 swine rents, the number of pigs paid each year by tenants for pannaging or grazing rights, predominant in the south-east;

6 miscellaneous other entries, such as 'a grove for fences'.

Woodland entries are as teasing as any in Domesday, and it is usually difficult even to be sure of the location of specific woods. As later, many vills, settlements and their lands, had little or no woodland within their bounds, but instead had the right to take timber and wood, and to graze animals, in woods some distance away. In Shropshire, for instance, much of the area around the Ironbridge Gorge was then wooded, and it was here that many of the agricultural communities to the north had their woodland rights. For instance, in 1086 the Saxon royal manor and hundredal centre of Wrockwardine had a wood one league long and half a league broad. This can be identified as Wrockwardine Wood, which lay seven kilometres to the east of Wrockwardine and which remained a detached part of that parish until the nineteenth century. Contiguous to Wrockwardine Wood in the middle ages were the townships, subdivisions of the parish, comprising a settlement and its land, of Donnington Wood and Hortonwood, which belonged respectively to Lilleshall parish and Horton, a township in Wellington parish. Both these woods, if the identification is correct, were recorded in Domesday under those parishes as being a half league in length. Here then is a case where, by the late eleventh century, a single large wood was shared among communities, some several kilometres away, and was possibly physically divided by 'trenches', that is cleared strips along the boundaries. Almost certainly there were other communities which had rights in that woodland in 1086, although no mention of this is made in Domesday Book. Eyton upon the Weald Moors and Preston upon the Weald Moors, for instance, both had rights in Hortonwood in the early middle ages and intercommoned there. Both communities' animals fed there until 1238 when the wood's northern part was physically divided between them (VCH 1985a, passim). Many similar instances of detached woodland rights have now been identified. Most estates on the coastal plain of Sussex and Kent had woods or woodland rights on the Weald to the north (for example, VCH in preparation a, 130–1), while in Oxfordshire, vills sixteen km from Wychwood had rights there (Schumer 1984, 20–1).

Almost all medieval woodmanship was based around the principle of cutting wood in such a way that natural regrowth was ensured and encouraged. Most native species – alder, ash, crab apple, elm, hawthorn, hazel, and oak, for instance – will send up new growth, either from a stool or by means of suckers, when cut down to ground level (figure 7.1). A large number of straight, quick

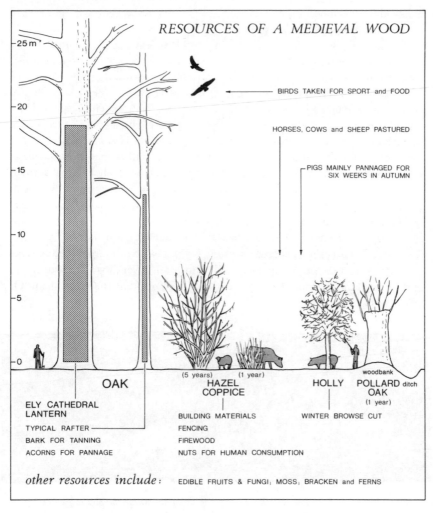

RESOURCES OF A MEDIEVAL WOOD

BIRDS TAKEN FOR SPORT and FOOD

HORSES, COWS and SHEEP PASTURED

PIGS MAINLY PANNAGED FOR SIX WEEKS IN AUTUMN

OAK

HAZEL COPPICE (5 years) (1 year)

HOLLY

POLLARD OAK (1 year)

woodbank ditch

ELY CATHEDRAL LANTERN

TYPICAL RAFTER
BARK FOR TANNING
ACORNS FOR PANNAGE

BUILDING MATERIALS
FENCING
FIREWOOD
NUTS FOR HUMAN CONSUMPTION

WINTER BROWSE CUT

other resources include: EDIBLE FRUITS & FUNGI; MOSS; BRACKEN and FERNS

7.1   *The resources of a medieval wood.*

growing poles are produced, which are usually cropped when between four and eight years of age and perhaps 6 m high. This is coppicing; whole woods worked in this way are called 'coppices', Domesday's *silva minuta*. In most medieval woods there was a mixture of coppice wood, here usually known as underwood, and larger, mature trees, known as standards. Normally oaks were allowed to mature, for perhaps 70 years, until they were ready to be cut and then sawn or split into major timbers for use in building works. Grazing animals, such as pigs, sheep, goats, and cattle, were usually excluded from coppice woods by banks, ditches and hedges, at least for the first few years of regrowth, in order to prevent the tender shoots being eaten.

The second system, that of wood pasture, Domesday's *silva pastoralis*, was a less intensive form of land use. Interspersed in what was often a very extensive tract of rough grazing land were mature trees such as oaks and beech, whose nuts when – or more correctly if, for the crop was intermittent – they fell in the two autumn mast months between mid-September and mid-November provided a valuable means of fattening pigs ready for slaughter (figure 7.2). The trees were either left to mature as standards, or else were pollarded. This was another way of producing a regular crop of poles in which the cut, rather than being made at ground level, was made across the trunk of the tree above the height that animals could reach. An important feature in the wood pasture landscape was clumps of thorns, for it was within these, out of the reach of animals and wood thieves, that the future standards were able to gain their vital first few years of growth. Domesday Book clearly indicates that the amount of wood pasture was then declining, in East Anglia at least, presumably in favour of more intensive types of land use as the population increased. However, overall wood pasture was probably still the most usual type of woodland in England in 1086 (Rackham, O. 1976, 60).

7.2   *Pannaging. The swineherd is beating down acorns for the pigs to feed on (Brit. Lib. MS Cotton Tib. B V Pt. 1, fo. 7).*

Domesday Books gives particulars of about 7,800 woods, which means that about half the places recorded had their own woodland. In the home counties most vills had their own woods, while in areas such as the midland vales, the fens, the brecklands and east and north-west Yorkshire there were large tracts of land with little tree cover. The largest single wood covered about 9,600 ha and formed part of the later Cannock Chase (Staffs.). Most woods, of course, were much smaller; many were of two ha or less, and one at Willoughby-with-Walesby (Notts.) was only about 25 m square (Rackham, O. 1980, 112–16).

Common Rights

Three categories of woodland ownership can be broadly defined in the middle ages. Most frequent were woods owned by an individual but within which others had certain common rights (figure 7.3). Some woods were by tradition entirely common, albeit perhaps only to certain parishes or manors, and there were a few woods which were entirely private. It is often difficult to be sure when such differences in status emerged, but in the Chilterns private and common woods were clearly separate by the end of the twelfth century (Roden 1968, 61), as they were in the extensive manor of Wakefield (Yorks.) in the thirteenth century (Faull and Moorhouse 1981, 690). Despite supervision intended to prevent it, common woods often lost much or all of their underwood through over-use, lack of management, or neglectful ignorance, becoming fairly 'open', with occasional mature trees standing in grass or scrub. In the Chilterns common woods were sometimes completely cleared, and evolved into greens. Breachwood, in King's Walden (Herts.), was woodland in 1300, but the felling of the best trees, authorized in 1333, followed by intensive grazing, had produced an open green by the end of the century (Roden 1968, 67–8).

Where they existed, common rights were usually strictly defined by this period in an attempt to prevent over-use. Grazing rights were usually confined to finite numbers of specified types of animals at certain times of the year. In 1227, for intance, each of the tenants of Escrick (Yorks.) could graze 10 cattle, 10 pigs and 20 sheep in the manorial woodland (VCH 1976, 22). By the end of the middle ages grazing rights were normally subdivided into three categories by the officials charged with their regulation. Agistment was the right to pasture cattle, which could often be left out all year because of the protection from the weather afforded by the woodland (Donkin 1960, 125), while pannage was the right to put pigs into a wood to forage, particularly during the autumn. In both cases, unless the wood was entirely common, its owner would usually collect a small annual payment in cash or kind for each beast pastured. Thirdly, there was common of pasture, the right sometimes claimed by the inhabitants of ancient houses in woodland areas, especially in forests, to put their cows, bullocks and horses into the wood. In forests like Rockingham it was argued that this was in recompense for the unhindered access deer were allowed to the villagers' lands under forest law (Petit 1968, 153). As time passed, and often the area and quality of the woodland diminished, certain animals, especially sheep and goats but also asses and geese, came increasingly to be excluded from common woods because of the damage they caused by eating bark and young growth (figure 8.7). Such was undoubtedly the reason for the ban against which the men of Stonesfield, Combe and Hanborough (Oxon.) petitioned the king in 1232. They claimed, perhaps correctly, that in the time of King John they had been allowed to put their sheep

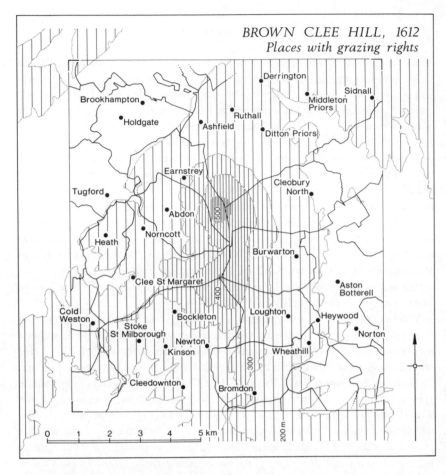

7.3 *Places with grazing rights on Brown Clee Hill in 1612. The Clee forest in Shropshire was a private forest owned by the Cliffords, lords of Corfham. Even long after the forest's demise in the late middle ages the surrounding vills retained grazing rights in the woods and pastures on the Brown Clee hills that had lain at the heart of the forest. Inhabitants of vills adjoining the hills had greater rights than 'strakers' who lived in more outlying ones (source: Shropshire Record Office, 334/2).*

and goats into Wychwood Forest, and that this right was now denied them (Schumer 1984, 44).

Apart from grazing, the other important common right which might be enjoyed was that of taking certain types of wood and timber. Most frequent, and most vital, was 'firebote', the right to take wood, usually deadwood, for the household's fire. This right might well come to be quantified as being limited to so many cartloads a year, to be taken under the supervision of a manorial official, such as a woodward (Roden 1968, 67). The right to take greenwood, and especially timber, was always more limited. Commoners did, though, often enjoy the right to take wood for building ('housebote'), for fencing ('fencebote' or 'hedgebote'), or for making agricultural equipment ('ploughbote') (Rackham, O. 1976, 83–4). As for grazing rights, a small rent was usually paid to the owner of a wood for such privileges. Traditionally, hens or eggs seem often to have been given; in thirteenth-century Spelsbury (Oxon.) every villager gave a hen, known as the 'woodhen', each year for the right to gather deadwood in the manor's woodland in Wychwood (Homans 1941, 258–9).

Common rights of any sort could not be lightly ignored and, if an owner wished to fell, enclose or otherwise alter the status of woodland where such rights existed, he usually had to provide compensation, most often in the form of rights in lieu. In 1296 the villeins of Brightwalton (Berks.) came to the manor court and surrendered their right to common in the abbot of Battle's wood called *Hemele*. In return the abbot conceded common rights in the village's East Field and in the villeins' wood called Trendale (Homans 1941, 330).

The imposition of conditions which limited how woods, or even specific trees, might be treated was usual when lands were leased. Invariably lessors reserved to themselves growing timber and wood, a valuable financial reserve against times of need, and the right to enter their tenant's land and fell trees if they wished. Lessees might be allowed fire-, fence- or housebote, or certain defined grazing rights, but Fountains Abbey was not exceptionally restrictive in only allowing most of its tenants deadwood and winter forage (Michelmore 1981, lxii, 206). And while Haughmond Abbey (Shrops.) generally allowed its tenants house-, fire- and fencebote (specifying the use of blackthorn and alder to enclose gardens in 1334) it was careful to note where mature trees were to be left. A life-lease to Sir Roger Corbet of the demesne at Medlicott *c.*1320–30 specified that at the termination of the lease there were to be, as then, 80 oaks in a certain wood (Rees 1985, 45, 154). It is paradoxical, as West (1964, 214–15) has noted, that lords required tenants to keep up their buildings, yet denied them the easiest way of obtaining materials to do this, and that it could be as much an offence for a tenant to plant trees as to fell them.

The Uses of Wood and Timber

It has been seen that, by and large, continuity of wood and timber supplies was ensured by management methods which encouraged regeneration. Some lords, though, took more active measures to keep up the quality of their woods by collecting and setting acorns in them. Others raised trees in special enclosures for transplantation. The field names 'impyard' and 'impgarth', found from the early twelfth century, have as their prefix an Old English word meaning a graft, scion, young shoot or sapling (Harvey, J. 1974, 22). In 1383 several men were presented at court for having entered the impyard on the Bishop of Lichfield's manor of Longdon (Staffs.) and cutting down ash trees there (Staffs. RO, D. (W.) 1734/2/1/599, m. 4), while in 1413 in the Aire valley (Yorks.) there were impyards containing young oaks (Harvey, J. 1974, 22–3).

More common was the propagation of trees, particularly fruit trees, in gardens and orchards, and J. Harvey has argued that plantsmanship was well developed in England before the end of the eleventh century (1974, 16). The household of Henry III was kept well-supplied with apples, several varieties of pears and nuts from the royal orchards and gardens. It was, though, perhaps as much for their blossom as their fruit that the same king planted a hundred pear trees in 1264 at the idyllic retreat near Woodstock where his grandfather had earlier kept his mistress, the Fair Rosamund. Here Henry may have been imitating Sicilian gardens, or the landscape described in the popular twelfth-century romance *Tristan and Isolde* (Brown et al. 1963, 1015). While this garden may have been unparalleled in its sophistication, pleasure gardens were a normal adjunct of the greater houses in the middle ages, and some of the trees which first appeared in England in the fourteenth century, such as the Norway Spruce, the Scots Pine, the Laurel (or Sweet Bay) and the Oriental Plane, may first have been imported as ornamental trees for the gardens of the nobility (Harvey, J. 1974, 18).

By far the most common tree in the medieval countryside seems to have been the oak. It is a wood that is strong and durable, yet pliable and workable for months or even years after felling. It then hardens, becoming virtually impossible to saw or axe across the grain, although the skilled woodworker can easily split it into structural members, billets (fuel) or roof shingles. The main determinant of the size and shape of an oak is not species but environment, and the woods of the two native species, the pedunculate (*Quercus robur*) and the sessile (*Quercus petraea*) are, at least as far as the carpenter is concerned, virtually indistinguishable and have the same properties. The parkland tree may have a spread of canopy 25 m across, with massive branches sprouting from the trunk a little above head height. The close-growing woodland tree, or flittern, tends to be pole-like, tail and straight, and may be largely branchless for its lower 9 to 12 m. It was 60–100-year-old trees like this which were most in demand for framed buildings, carpenters often constructing building frames within the wood where the timber was cut. Crucks, great paired, curved, timbers which formed the main uprights in one of the most simple, yet long-lived, forms of framing, came from a very different type of tree, one which was naturally bent. Such trees were most often found on steep, exposed sites, which may go some way to explain why cruck buildings are more common in the more rugged landscapes of the west and north (Charles and Charles 1984, 40–2, 47–50).

There was a constant demand for great trees in the middle ages. In the thirteenth century windmills began to be built across the countryside and each had at its heart a massive post which suported it and around which it revolved to catch the wind. This post was perhaps 12 m long and 600 mm thick, and weighed 3–4 tonne (Rackham, O. 1980, 152; Steane 1984, 170–1). The great gothic buildings, such as cathedrals, could demand timbers of an even more prodigious size, which would be today virtually unobtainable and in the middle ages were often only found after an extensive search (figure 7.4). Such was the case in 1328 when oak posts 19 m high and 800 mm in diameter at the top were needed for the lantern of Ely cathedral (see figure 7.1). The 52 huge trees for the double hammer-beam roof at Westminster Hall in 1395 had to be fetched from near Farnham, and each needed two carts and 16 horses to transport it (Charles and Charles 1984, 47).

Among the other trees elm, which grows at twice the rate of oak, was the

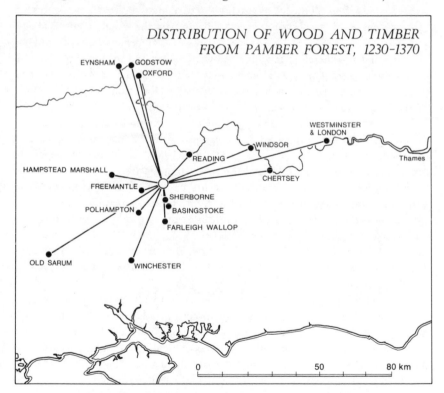

7.4 *The distribution of wood and timber from Pamber Forest, Hampshire 1230–1370.*
Although a small forest, the way in which its products were widely transported to royal houses
and to the recipients of grants, such as monastic houses, was typical
(source: Stamper 1983, 45).

second most widely used building timber in the middle ages, being especially favoured where unusually long or thick timbers were demanded. While it can be 'treacherous', rotting quickly from the centre outwards, it lasts better than other native timbers when permanently wet, and was accordingly used for weather-boarding, conduits, piles, coffins and ships' keelsons (Charles and Charles 1984, 43; Rackham, O. 1980, 267). Ash, often found with oak, was rarely used by choice in buidings as it is too pliant for load bearing and is suceptible to beetle. However, a choice of timber was a luxury perhaps not always available to the poorer sections of society. When Thomas of Merdene died in 1303 his son moved into the parental home in Halton (Bucks.), giving his mother 2½ marks of silver and three ash trees 'of the better sort' with which to build herself a house (Homans 1941, 183–4). However, ash is the best of all woods to cleave, and with its elasticity this made it the preferred wood for tool handles and for the frames and shafts of vehicles (p. 93; Charles and Charles 1984, 43; Rackham, O. 1980, 206). It was also favoured, along with beech, by coopers for making cups and bowls because the sap did not taint the vessel's contents (Faull and Moorhouse 1981, 682–3). Hazel, grown as underwood, twists without breaking and was therefore favoured for wattle work and in thatching. Its nuts were collected, sometimes as a labour service for the lord of the manor, and possibly, as later, nutting was a social occasion (Rackham, O. 1980, 206). Willow, too, was used to make wattles and hurdles, and in basketry. Hornbeam, or 'hardbeam', was usually grown as underwood, or pollarded. It was highly thought of as a fuel and, with beech, was probably the main fuel supplied to medieval and Tudor London (Rackham, O. 1980, 224). Beech, popularly thought of as a chalkland tree, and the most common tree in the woods of the Chilterns (Roden 1968, 60), actually occurs on soils of most types. Thus, in Windsor Forest in the thirteenth and fourteenth centuries, Inwood and Altwood were described as beech woods, boat building being one of the specific purposes for which the timber was used (VCH 1907a, 343–5). Birch, coppiced extensively in the Chilterns in the middle ages, although also grown as a standard or pollarded, was also favoured as a fuel (Rackham, O. 1980, 305, 321; Roden 1968, 62).

The specific properties of other woods were well known and exploited accordingly. Maple, lime and alder, for instance, could be found in the greater houses, used variously in furniture, panelling and musical instruments. Lime was also used to make *sadaltres*, the wooden frames of saddles (Faull and Moorhouse 1981, 689), and its bark to make 'baston', or binding, ropes (VCH 1979, 12). Alder, light and straight, was employed as scaffolding. Holly was widely coppiced and pollarded for use as a winter food for sheep and deer, a vital reserve if the hay crop had been poor or the winter long (Rackham, O. 1980, 207, 242, 305, 345).

An important and profitable use of oak bark, especially near centres of the leather industry, was in the tanning process. Oak bark, particularly that from young trees, contains a relatively high percentage of tannin. Yields are generally in the order of one tonne of bark to every three to five of wood. The bark can be stripped with relative ease only in the spring when the sap is rising and the trees are starting to come into leaf. The favoured method of stripping, at least the end of the middle ages, was to peel standing trees, the workers operating from ladders and clambering around the crown of the tree. Once barked, trees were usually left standing for a year to dry out before being felled, the delay enabling trees in hedges and in fields to be felled after any arable crop had been removed (Linnard 1982, 87–94).

As a fuel, charcoal was superior in almost all respects to wood; coal was not to gain general social acceptance as a domestic fuel until the later sixteenth century (Brimblecombe 1982, 19–20). The expense of charcoal's manufacture and transport limited its availability, however, and it was probably only the wealthy who burned it in their houses. In 1385–6, for instance, charcoal was made in the great park at Framlingham by William Colyere – whose name suggests that this was his full-time occupation – and carried to the castle in old flour sacks (Ridgard 1985, 127). While charcoal making was sometimes permitted in the forests, the charcoal burners from the Oxfordshire villages of Ditchley, Finstock and Ramsden who were imprisoned in 1272 clearly had not had the approval of the forest officers to work in Wychwood (Schumer 1984, 56).

While almost any charcoal can be used to smelt iron, it needs to be strong enough not to crumble. Hence oak, beech and birch charcoals were preferred (Tylecote 1986, 225). A small woodland bloomery like Tudeley (Kent) with an output of four tonnes of iron a season required about 40 ha of well-managed underwood cut on a 12-year cycle to fuel it (Cleere and Crossley 1985, 100). The damage that unsupervised ironworking could do to woodland was clearly appreciated. Flaxley (Glos.), a Cistercian house founded in 1151, worked the iron deposits in the Forest of Dean. Royal grants permitted the monks to take deadwood, underwood, and the like for fuel, yet in 1229 they were ordered to limit their itinerant forge to the thorn thickets on the margins of the forest (Donkin 1960, 48). Wood, or 'white coal', was used for smelting lead near Baxenden in Rossendale (Lancs.), probably first having been dried in a kiln (Tylecote 1986, 223). Raw wood was also used to fire pottery and tile kilns. The quantities that the full-time industries absorbed meant that they were invariably sited in or near woodlands, and the larger concerns presumably ensured future supplies of fuel by encouraging coppicing. Certainly this was done by the Laverstock potters in Wiltshire *c.*1300, who fired their kilns at least in part with brushwood from coppices in Clarendon Park and Forest (Musty et al. 1969, 90). Others, if not so closely supervised, could be less prudent; in the sixteenth century a potter of Lingen (Herefs.) was said to have carried away 500 great oaks and saplings in seven years from Penyard Wood (Rowley 1986, 150).

Wood ash, rich in potash, was used in the middle ages to make soap and in dyeworks. In 1271 three men and a woman, with the connivance of two foresters, worked in Alrewas Hay (Staffs.) burning birch, lime and other trees to make ash for sale to dyers (Linnard 1982, 42; VCH 1979, 12). Fern ash and the ash of beech wood was also used in glass making, for instance by Vale Royal Abbey (Cheshire) in the late thirteenth century (Donkin 1960, 127; Salzman 1923, 190).

Parks and Hunting

A park differed from other demesne woodland mainly in that it contained deer and was accordingly securely fenced. Woodland enclosures or 'deer folds' were found in late-Saxon England, for instance at Ongar (Essex), but parks, like forest law, were essentially a Norman introduction (Cantor and Hatherly 1979, 71). A park provided a lord with a ready supply of fresh venison, a meat that was seen, at least by the aristocracy itself, as reserved for its tables and especially the feast. As important as the meat itself was the way in which it was taken, the park being an enclosed hunting ground, where the pleasures of the chase could be enjoyed by the lord and his chosen companions. Throughout the middle ages deer hunting was the preserve of the king and the aristocracy, and the acquisition of a park was one of the marks, at least in the eyes of its creator, that he was joining their ranks.

Domesday Book records 35 parks, and there were probably a few more, like Bramber (Sussex), that went unnoticed (Cantor 1982, 76). It also records a number of 'hays' (literally meaning hedges) especially in the west midlands. These seem to have been the successors of late-Saxon deer folds, places where deer were temporarily enclosed before the hunt. They were perhaps also breeding enclosures (Darby 1973, 55; Rowley 1986, 149). Over the next century, while the number of parks increased, forest law seems to have limited their proliferation. But from the early thirteenth century their number began to increase rapidly as the area under forest law was reduced. Lords' incomes were rising and with them their desire to invest and enjoy their new found wealth in such things as hunting parks. Many lords found it necessary to purchase a licence from the king permitting them to construct a park. There seems to have been no hard and fast rule about when a licence would be demanded, although the closer the park was to a royal forest the more likely it was.

By the early fourteenth century there were perhaps 3,200 parks in England (Steane 1984, 168), varying in size from just a few hectares to several hundred. The main concentrations were in the west midlands, Staffordshire and Worcestershire, the home counties, Essex, Herefordshire, Buckinghamshire, Surrey and Sussex. Relatively few parks lay in East Anglia, Cambridgeshire and

Lincolnshire and in the more remote parts of Northumberland, Cumberland, Durham, Devon and Cornwall. Within individual counties parks tended to be most common in the areas with most woodland (Cantor 1983, 4–5).

Invariably parks contained a mixture of woodland and grassland. While the former provided cover for the deer and a forest ambience for the hunter, it was the latter that was the more important, as deer are primarily grass feeders. Rackham has argued that medieval parks can be divided into two distinct categories according to the way in which these two resources were mixed. The first he calls the wood pasture park, where trees and grass were intermixed. The second, where the production of wood was maximized, was the compartmental park, and here grassland launds or glades were kept separate from the enclosed and usually coppiced woodland (Rackham, O. 1986, 125–6).

The most distinctive feature of a park was its boundary, generally a pale of tall, cleft oak stakes set in a broad, high, earth bank with an internal ditch. Sometimes between the bank and ditch there was an open strip of ground, known as the freeboard, which allowed access to the pale so that repairs could be made. Sometimes a quickset hedge was used in place of a pale or, in areas where stone was readily available, a stone wall. Woodstock Park (Oxon.) had a stone wall by the early twelfth century (Harvey, J. 1974, 15), and examples can still be seen at Beckley (Oxon.), Moulton (Northants.) and Newton Blossomville (Bucks.). But, whatever the medium, the boundary had to be formidable, for deer can leap up to 3 m vertically or 6 m horizontally, and the upkeep of the pale was a constant and considerable expense for the lord with a park. Sometimes it was made a customary work or labour service, particularly where tenants enjoyed common rights within the park (for instance, VCH 1988, 106). As early as the thirteenth century the repair of the wall of the king's park at Moulton was largely the responsibilty of the surrounding townships, and by the sixteenth century these obligations were recorded by stones bearing the townships' names set into the wall (Steane 1975, 213).

In the early middle ages the king was considered to own all deer in the forest, and therefore the stocking of a park with deer necessitated his aid or compliance. Many grants are recorded from the king of live deer – usually of several times more does than bucks – to stock parks. The long-distance carriage of livestock was clearly routine, and in the fourteenth century Windsor Great Park, for instance, was stocked from Chute Forest in Wiltshire (Cantor and Hatherley 1979, 73). In other cases the king might authorize the construction of a deer leap, which allowed deer to enter but not leave the park, consisting of an external ramp and an internal pit in a gap in the pale. Clearly such devices could steadily reduce the number of royal deer running freely in the forest; their construction was strictly controlled, and some licences to impark specifically prohibited them.

A parker was usually employed to care for and oversee the park. A house or lodge was often provided for him within the pale where, like any good herdsman, he would be in constant contact with his charges (figure 7.5). Presumably it was also hoped that his presence would deter poachers. Like so many contemporary isolated woodland dwellings, lodges were often surrounded by a shallow moat. No one knows why this should have been, but perhaps a moated residence was felt to add to the atmosphere and illusion of the park as a milieu that was wooded and mysterious, yet above all distinctly aristocratic. To what extent there was a sensibility towards a beautiful natural landscape in the

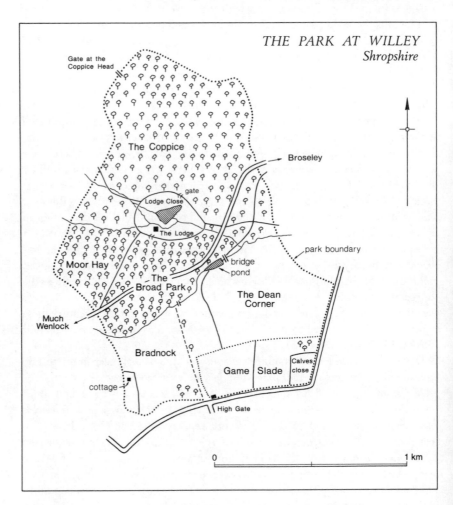

7.5 The park at Willey, Shropshire, is first documented in the thirteenth century, and was mapped in 1618. The wood and field names indicate the economic functions of the park. The park was crossed by a road, an unusual but not unique feature
(source: Shropshire Record Office, 1224/1/9).

middle ages is difficult to grasp; that it could exist is demonstrated by the construction in 1354 of a balcony at Woodstock Palace to give Princess Isabella a view of the park (p. 7; Brown et al. 1963, 1016–17).

As the size of parks varied so did the size of the herds they contained, although almost invariably it was fallow deer that were kept (p. 165; Rackham, O. 1986, 125). In Cornwall the Duchy had seven parks in the middle ages; in 1337 the two smallest, attached to Launceston and Taunton Castles, had just 15 and 42 deer respectively, while the largest, Restormel, had 300 (Hatcher 1970, 179). The largest parks were capable of supplying great quantities of venison. In Woodstock Park 200 does were killed in 1250 and then salted down and sent, presumably packed in barrels, to Winchester for Christmas and to Westminster for the feast of St Edward (5 January). These would have been culled by the king's huntsmen, who were usually also responsible for taking any deer that the king might grant to others. Occasionally others might be permitted to hunt in the king's parks; in 1444, for instance, Henry VI granted Abingdon Abbey the right to take four bucks and two does a year from Woodstock, in lieu of the abbey's loss of hunting rights in Windsor Forest (Cal. Pat. Rolls 1441–6, 277).

Of course, those who hunted were those who were legally empowered to do so and, while Robin Hood may have been a fictional character, his type was familiar, and the judicial records provide many examples of the criminal band. Like Hood's 'merry men', many band members were outlaws – fugitives from justice – and lived in forest areas. In Feckenham Forest in the 1280s Geoffrey du Park – whose name suggests a long familiarity with woods and deer – and a band that at times numbered a hundred men established themselves in a stronghold at Gannow (Worcs.). Typical was the presence in the band of a renegade priest and the way in which it was joined for certain expeditions by members of the gentry, 'vigrouse gentz' from Sherwood. The crimes committed by the band were wide-ranging and violent. They murdered, burned and looted in villages and on the highway, and as much from the very poor as from the rich (West 1964, 42). While other aspects of the story of Robin Hood may have been familiar to the balladeer's audience, his social discrimination would have rung false. Venison clearly made up a good part of the diet of du Park and his men, and many deer from Feckenham fell prey to them. Less spectacular, but far more frequent and widespread, was the taking of single deer by individuals or small groups of family or friends. Detection by the forest or manorial officials of such offences was difficult, and the proportion of offenders caught and presented at court was presumably low. Even so, 200 named poachers were presented in Cannock Forest and 250 in Kinver at the three Staffordshire eyres in the late thirteenth century, and in Dean over 300 at the eyres of 1270 and 1282, and in Rockingham over 230 in 1272 and 1286. Overall, it seems likely that as many deer were taken from the forest illegally at this time as legally (p. 165; Birrell 1982, 10).

While the hunting of the so-called lesser beasts of the chase – wolves, wildcats, badgers, foxes, hares, rabbits, pigeons, pheasants and partridges – is less frequently recorded, it was certainly popular. In areas under forest law manorial lords increasingly purchased the right of free warren, that is the right to hunt these animals across their own lands, and by the early fourteenth century there were probably as many manors with as without this privilege (figure 7.6). For some, the acquisition of this right simply meant that they could now legally control vermin and supplement the household diet with game. Others, though, clearly enjoyed the chase, albeit of the fox rather than deer, as much as the king. Chaucer's monk, for instance (Coghill 1960, 23–4),

> . . . rode the country; hunting was his sport . . .
> Greyhounds he had, as swift as birds, to course.
> Hunting a hare or riding at a fence
> Was all his fun, for he spared no expense.

Neither was hunting entirely a male preserve; one of the earliest recorded sporting prelates was the Abbess of Barking (Essex), who in 1221 was permitted to hunt foxes and hares in Havering Park (Essex) (VCH 1907b, 118).

The breeding of rabbits in specially constructed warrens – long, low,

7.6 *An elaborate charter of free warren granted in 1291 to Roger de Pilkington. Around the edge are shown the animals that the recipient was thereby permitted to hunt on his own land (Fitzwilliam Museum MS. 46–1980).*

earthworks sometimes called pillow mounds – rapidly gained popularity between 1230 and 1250. Warrens were often sited in parks, and in 1413 the scholars of Oxford were banned from entering Woodstock Park because of the nuisance they had made of themselves there by poaching deer, rabbits and hares (Bond n.d.). By the early 1300s rabbits were numerous, warrens were valuable, and there was an export trade in skins (Veale 1957). Rabbits were not the only beasts kept in warrens; in 1372 the Duke of Lancaster's warren at Higham Ferrers (Northants.) also contained hares, pheasants and partridges. It was surrounded by a wall, presumably as much to keep poachers out as the stock in. Certainly in the former capacity it proved unsuccessful (Steane 1974, 179).

Other specialist demesne livestock farming sometimes took place within the relatively secure confines of the park. Parks had to have a water supply for the animals, and streams were frequently enlarged and dammed to form fishponds. The studs where war and other high quality specialist horses were bred were often in parks; in the fourteenth century the Earl of Arundel had important studs in parks near Oswestry and Clun in the Welsh Marches (VCH forthcoming) and the king had a stud in Woodstock Park. Woodstock also had an eyrie of falcons, and it had earlier housed Henry I's extraordinary royal menagerie which apparently included lions, lynxes, camels and a porcupine (Bond n.d.). Another royal park, Windsor, contained a herd of wild cattle (*silvestres*) (VCH 1907a, 344). When lords created parks they sought, whenever possible, to extinguish any common rights that might exist there, sometimes by granting rights in lieu elsewhere. However, in 1255 Lord Braose took a different course, allowing tenants to forgo attendance at his hundred courts in return for their giving up the right to hunt with dogs in some of his lands including Hookland Park (VCH 1988, 107). But in many parks rights persisted, and at times the parks were thrown open for grazing large numbers of cattle, sheep and pigs. In Beverley Park (Yorks.) 400 of the townsmen's animals were pastured in the summer of 1388 and 200 in the autumn, but they were excluded between 30 September and 1 May (VCH 1976, 6).

Parks in the Later Middle Ages

In the early fourteenth century the era of high farming and agrarian expansion began to draw to a close. Subtle long-term changes in the economic cycle were accelerated and overwhelmed by a series of catastrophic agricultural crises in the second decade of the century and by the Black Death of 1348–9 in which at least one-third of the population died (p. 208). The second half of that century was no less fearful for contemporaries than the first, with major outbreaks of plague in 1362–3, 1369 and 1375, which prevented the recovery of population levels and reinforced the trends of social and economic change that had begun in the time of men's grandfathers (Hatcher 1977). England became greener as arable land was put down to pasture, and fields on unprofitable and poor soils were abandoned to return to scrub and in due course to some form of woodland. Lords, as much as peasants, had to adapt to the altered circumstances. As wages and other costs rose many lords were unwilling or unable to afford the luxury of a park keeper to manage what was anyway an unprofitable use of land. An accurate calculation of a manor's profitability was perhaps achieved only on the larger and administratively more advanced estates in the middle ages (Harvey, P. D. A. 1984, 28–9). Even so, lords must have generally been aware that a park tended to be a constant drain on their purse rather than a regular source of income. The Duke of Cornwall, for instance, derived little income from his seven parks, and in the fourteenth and fifteenth centuries they ran at a continual net loss (Hatcher 1970, 180). Over the country as a whole some parks were dismantled, while others became less specialised and ceased to be solely deer farms and hunting grounds. Yet, conversely, at the same time other parks were greatly enlarged as they absorbed poor land that the lord now found unleaseable or not worth farming more intensively (Cantor 1982, 77).

Increasingly parks came to be used for stock fattening, either by lords or lessees. In 1385–6 the lord of Walsall manor drew no income from the herbage in his park as it was enclosed to protect its wood and for fattening 20 heifers and poultry or game birds (Cantor 1965, 5). In Bowland Forest, on the border of Lancashire and Yorkshire, the forest's two parks at Leagram and Radholme had ceased to be effective refuges for deer by the sixteenth century and their pales were in disrepair. It had by then long been the custom for the parkers to take leases of pasture in their parks, either for their own stock or to sub-let to others (Porter 1975, 48).

It is also noticeable that by the mid-fourteenth century parks not uncommonly contained some arable land, and thenceforward lords seem to have been increasingly willing to put at least a part of their parks down to the plough. The reasons are complex and varied, but underlying all was the attempt to keep up income. In Finchingfield Park (Essex) 8 ha of rough, gorse-covered land were assarted in 1340–1 and put down to cereals, mainly oats (Britnell 1977). In 1347–8, on the very eve of the Black Death, 21 days were expended in Petworth Park (Sussex) removing rabbit burrows so that peas could be sown, while in the Great Park there, oats were sown at the same time on newly assarted land (Salzman 1955, 6, 13, 35). By the end of the fourteenth century Kilton Park (Somerset) was divided into enclosures, some ploughed (VCH 1985b, 93).

Towards the end of the fifteenth century there was a fresh phase of park creation or enlargement as a fashion for large amenity parks grew among the greater gentry. These parks were usually larger than their predecessors, encompassing at least several hundred acres. Neither were these, as previously, isolated from the lords's house, but instead were an adjunct of it. Typical were

Bagworth and Kirby Muxloe parks in Leicestershire, both imparked by Lord Hastings in 1475 and both of about 800 ha (Cantor 1971, 12). Part of the impetus behind such emparkments was the return of agricultural prosperity, which encouraged landlords to increase greatly the size of their herds of cattle and sheep, which could be kept within a park. Deer hunting, though, remained as popular at the end of the middle ages as it had been under the Norman kings, and while they might contain hundreds of sheep and cattle, parks remained primarily hunting grounds. In 1549 a Frenchman surmised that there was as many deer in England as people in France, while the widely travelled Andrew Boorde thought that England had as many parks as the rest of Europe put together. William Harrison thought that Elizabeth I alone had 200 (Hoskins 1976, 11, 230).

Some Tudor landlords depopulated villages in order that the landscape might be transformed into one great park. At Wilstrop (Yorks.) the village of that name was depopulated in 1498 by its emparking landlord. The evicted tenants joined forces with some of the local gentry with whom the imparker had a long running feud and on several occasions attacked the park, uprooting the pale and its accompanying quickset hedge. One raid was by a 200-strong crowd who 'hewid and kit doonn 100 walnottreis, and appeltries grafted ii or iii yere before', suggesting that the lord's intention was not only to make a secure enclosure for sheep and deer but also a pleasing environment (Beresford, G. 1957, 205–7).

Predictably, poaching continued to trouble park owners from the king downwards. An act of 1485–6 (Statutes of the Realm 2, 505–6) noted 'tumultuous' hunting in forests, parks and warrens, and made hunting at night or in disguise – with a 'blacked-up' face – illegal. A later act of Henry VII's reign further made it an offence to keep nets, known as deer-hays or buck-stalls, or to stalk deer without licence (Statutes of the Realm 2, 655). Such legislation marks the beginning of the evolution of the later game laws, laws that were to prove no more effective, and equally as unpopular, as the forest law they evolved from and replaced (Petit 1968, 43).

Conclusions

Woodland, as much as arable and grassland, was an essential element in the medieval economy. Timber for building and wood for fuel had to be obtained, the latter on a day-to-day basis, whether locally or from further afield and whether through the enjoyment of common rights or by purchase. As the population level rose and woods were cleared to provide more arable land, the pressure on the remaining woodlands increased. Greater restrictions were introduced on who might take wood, and how much, through by-laws, customs and by the physical division of woods between communities. The production of wood may have been increased by the greater use of coppicing, but this is difficult to assess on a countrywide basis. Concomitant with the physical reduction of woodland was a decline in the amount of grazing land available to communities. This loss was especially serious to smallholders and cottagers whose economic existence was at best precarious, and to whom a couple of pigs pannaged in the village's wood meant a little ready cash in the autumn when one was sold and at least some meat to eat during the winter. Only in the mid-fourteenth century, owing to the successive visitations of the plague which probably halved the population level, did the acute pressure on resources begin to decline. There was little regrowth of woodland over areas that had been cleared in the preceding centuries, but at least there was a little more to go round among those that had survived.

8

Animal Resources

Annie Grant

The primary source of information for this consideration of the exploitation of animals in the medieval period is the archaeological evidence – the bones and bone fragments that are frequently among the most numerous of all finds made during excavation. During the last twenty years or so, a new sub-discipline of archaeology, archaeozoology (or zooarchaeology), has grown up in response to the realization of the potential importance of this bone material for understanding animals and man–animal inter-relationships in the past. As with many new disciplines, the methodologies of investigation are being developed at the same time as the first analyses are being made. Thus while there now exists a body of data in the form of reports made on the animal remains found at a wide range of archaeological sites, there is as yet no universally accepted standardization of methods or approaches (see p. 4).

There are particular problems inherent in any attempt to reconstruct livestock husbandry from the bones of dead animals. The more urbanized a society is and the more complex the relationships of interdependence between different communities and groups, the more difficult it will be to assess the nature of the animal husbandry from food refuse. For example, Kershaw's (1973a) analysis of the Bolton Priory account book shows that between 1304 and 1318, sheep were by far the most numerous of all the livestock kept on the priory estates. However, the larder accounts for the same period show that only 40 per cent of the animals killed for use in the priory's kitchen were sheep. Even more striking is the fact that while only 3 per cent of the priory's livestock were pigs, nearly 30 per cent of the carcasses in the larders were pork (figure 8.1). Any animal bones recovered during excavation of priory buildings would be likely to reflect the proportions of carcasses in the larder and might give a misleading impression of the animals kept on the priory estates.

Some of the extensive documentary evidence for this period makes specific reference to animal husbandry and the anonymous *Seneschaucy* and Walter of Henley's *Treatise* are essentially manuals of estate management (Oschinsky

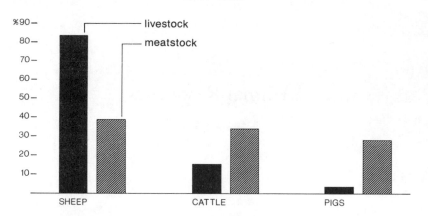

8.1 *Livestock and meatstock at Bolton Priory, 1304–18. The livestock percentages are caclulated from the priory's livestock inventories and the meatstock percentages from the larder accounts*
(source: Kershaw 1973a).

1971). However, high quality documentary evidence for peasant animal husbandry is scarce, although some information on peasant livestock holdings can occasionally be found in inventories associated with confiscations of property and land, lay subsidy assessments and heriots (death duties) in manorial accounts and court rolls (for example, Langdon 1982).

Sometimes, there is documentary evidence directly relevant to the economy of excavated sites, and the two forms of evidence can be used together as, for example, for the castle at Middleton Stoney (Bond 1984; Levitan 1984b). However, in many cases the direct link between archaeological and historical evidence is not possible and the two may be seen as showing rather different and rarely matching fragments of a now very faded picture.

Animal Husbandry and the Rural Economy

The medieval farmers of England inherited a long tradition of animal husbandry that stretched back for over five thousand years. As early as the end of the last millennium BC the majority of the population were involved in the tending of almost exactly the same range of domestic animals as was to be found in the medieval and indeed the modern periods.

The extensive specialization on single animal species for single products – for example, dairy farming and intensive pig production – is only a recent development. Animal husbandry in the past seems always to have been a mixed husbandry for a range of primary and secondary products. However, there have been changes in the relative proportions of the three most common domestic animals, sheep, cattle and pigs.

The medieval period is traditionally viewed as an age when sheep were of particular importance. Both secular and monastic estate accounts record vast flocks of up to ten thousand sheep with very much smaller numbers of cattle and pigs (Carus-Wilson 1962–3, 185). However, although they were kept on a much smaller scale by the rest of the rural population and many peasants had no sheep at all, the documentary evidence suggests that overall, more sheep were raised by peasants than were kept on the estates (Power 1941, 29). English wool was considered to be of especially high quality even on the continent and from the twelfth century was in particular demand: it was thus a vital commodity in the medieval economy. During the decade from 1280 to 1290 the wool of three million sheep was shipped from Boston in Lincolnshire and that of another two million sheep from London (Carus-Wilson 1962–3, 189). Wool sales provided over a third of the income of Bolton Priory between 1287 and 1305 (Kershaw 1973a, 164), and the accounts from other estates reinforce the generally high value of wool. However, there were inevitably regional differences in the scale of sheep farming practised, and thus the place of wool in the economy (Lloyd 1977, 310).

Wool was a major product of sheep farming even in the Iron Age (Grant 1984b, 508), but archaeological evidence from sites with a long occupation suggests that it became increasingly important from at least the eighth century AD (Grant 1982, 106).

The historical evidence tends to put rather more emphasis on sheep and wool production than the archaeological evidence. In fact, taken at face value, some of the historical and archaeological evidence seems contradictory.

At several of the excavated rural sites, sheep remains were either outnumbered by those of cattle (for example, Grant 1975, 152; Harcourt 1969) or accounted for little more than half of the total complement of domestic animal bones (for example, Grant 1975, 153; Noddle 1976; 1980; Pernetta 1973; Ryder 1974). However, at Upton (Glos.), a deserted medieval village of the twelfth and thirteenth centuries, over 70 per cent of the identified bones and teeth were those of sheep, and they were mainly from mature animals, implying a husbandry in which wool production was important (Yelland and Higgs 1966).

Castles and religious establishments, generally situated in the country, may also be expected to have yielded bone assemblages that reflect the economy of their estates, but this is not necessarily the case. The animal bones often seem to show the particular dietary preferences of the aristocracy as much as the local rural economy (p. 180 and see p. 141). Percentages of sheep bones at these high status sites are on average lower than those from both ordinary rural sites and from towns (figure 8.2). However, although in many instances the faunal analyses do

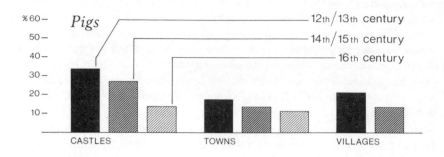

8.2 *Average percentages of pigs, cattle and sheep bones from excavated contexts of the twelfth to the sixteenth century. These figures are given as a very general guide to the relative importance of the three most important domestic animals in castles, towns and villages over this period. The twelfth- to thirteenth-century figures have been calculated from 16 castle contexts, 33 urban contexts and 7 village contexts; the fourteenth- to fifteenth-century figures from 13 castle contexts, 22 urban contexts and 5 village contexts; the sixteenth-century figures from 10 castle and 10 urban contexts − there was insufficient information available to be able to include sixteenth-century villages.*

not make it clear whether the sheep eaten at these sites were predominantly young or older animals, at some castles the majority of sheep do seem to have been sufficiently mature to have yielded several wool clips before being eaten (Jones et al. forthcoming; Levitan 1984b).

The best available archaeological evidence for the way in which sheep flocks were managed in the countryside may come from the towns. In the majority of twelfth- and thirteenth-century urban contexts, sheep bones outnumbered or at least more or less equalled those of cattle (figure 8.2). Furthermore, these sheep bones are predominantly of juvenile animals, killed at an age when they could have provided only one, or at the most two fleeces (see Maltby 1979; Grant 1979a; Cartledge 1983; O'Connor 1982; 1984). Large numbers of juvenile animals in towns imply the presence of very much larger numbers of older sheep in the countryside, especially of breeding ewes, and suggest a husbandry in which surplus animals or weaklings were regularly removed, leaving the better animals for wool production. The culled juvenile animals, together with a smaller proportion of older animals, seem to have been fattened up for sale and would have fetched good prices on the urban market. A large proportion of the many wool-producing sheep of the medieval period may have been eaten by peasants, who may then have added their bones to the manure heaps and later scattered them over the fields where they would be lost to archaeologists (p. 2). The Bolton Priory accounts certainly indicate that only a small proportion of the sheep owned by the estate were actually eaten by the monks (see figure 8.1).

Selling meat animals for cash can be an important element in a rural economy, although the temptation to make quick profits can lead to serious long-term problems. In the sixteenth century, the killing of young cattle for meat led to a real threat of future meat shortage and in 1532 an Act of Parliament forbad the slaughter of cattle under two years old (Jones, P. 1976, 141). The peasants and the owners of the large estates must both sometimes have been faced with difficult choices, particularly when their flocks were cut back by natural hazards such as disease and food shortage. A policy that attempts to provide both meat animals for the urban market at minimum cost and the best quality fleeces is not without some inherent incompatibilities. The best fleeces come from wethers, castrated males, and yet it is generally only the male animals that can be sold off when young for meat, since the majority of fertile females must be kept to maturity to ensure the maintenance of the flock. However, with a healthy flock, plentiful grass, and food for any necessary supplementary feeding, the sheep husbandry system was undoubtedly successful and flocks both increased in size and provided good profits for their owners (for example, Kershaw 1973a, 163).

The archaeological evidence suggests a widespread change in animal husbandry in the fourteenth and fifteenth centuries. Again the urban contexts provide much of the information. The percentage of sheep bones in several towns fell in the fourteenth century but increased in the fifteenth century (for example,

Jones, G. 1983; Maltby 1979; Noddle 1975; Wilson, B. 1983). A similar increase is also seen in castles and village sites, although the average percentage for sheep in castles is still lower than in either towns or villages (figure 8.2).

A change in sheep management is also apparent. At several towns there was a higher proportion of sheep bones from older animals in fourteenth- and fifteenth-century contexts than had been found from earlier centuries (for example, Armitage 1977; Maltby 1979; O'Connor 1982).

Major epidemics of disease caused serious losses to the sheep population in England in the late thirteenth and early fourteenth centuries. Some flocks were reduced by as much as two-thirds (Lloyd 1978, 11; Kershaw 1973a, 80). Archaeozoologists are now beginning to take more account of traces of disease on animal bones, but it is unlikely that such evidence will be able to shed much light on these epidemics since the most likely causes, common sheep scab, sheep pox, infestations of liver fluke and foot and mouth disease, leave no readily visible traces on the skeleton (Lloyd 1977, 12; Hartley 1979, 83). However, studies of the incidence of periodontal disease may make possible some assessment of the extent to which animals were overgrazed, particularly in periods such as the thirteenth century when population pressure led to the use of increasingly marginal land for sheep pasture. Overgrazing encourages gum diseases that can lead to feeding difficulties and malnutrition but it can also increase the incidence of parasitic infestations making the animals much more vulnerable to infection (Grant 1984b, 586). This may have been an important factor in increasing the susceptibility to disease of the sheep population in the fourteenth century. One of the few studies carried out to date is by Sadler (in press) who has shown a marked increase in the incidence of oral pathology at Faccombe Manor (Hants.) in thirteenth- to fourteenth-century contexts.

The reduction in sheep numbers in the early fourteenth century led initially to higher prices for wool which may have encouraged farmers to keep their animals until they had yielded several clips rather than sell them off for meat when very young. In the longer term, wool prices fell, and although by the fifteenth century beef production was becoming increasingly important, (p. 156), the slight increase in the percentages of sheep bones in many contexts demonstrates that sheep were still of considerable economic importance in the later medieval period, both for wool and for meat.

These were of course not the only sheep products utilized. Manorial accounts and other historical evidence show that sheep were also milked. However, the production of milk and cheese, although important, cannot have been more than a relatively minor byproduct of sheep rearing since lactation began with lambing in March or April and generally continued only until mid-August or September. Medieval writers warned against milking ewes for too long as they believed that it weakened them and made them unreceptive to the ram (Oschinsky 1971, 287). Holden (1985, 230) discusses records describing the feeding of lambs with warmed cows' milk so that the richer ewes' milk could be used for human food. This is not a practice that would have encouraged the production of good quality lambs. However, it is difficult to know if it was a widespread custom or reflected particularly hard times with shortages of human foodstuffs, or a high market value for sheep cheese.

In many farming systems, the rearing of animals is intimately related to the growing of crops. Not only are the cereal and vegetable waste products used to feed the livestock, but animal manure is highly valued as a fertilizer. Manure was an important byproduct of sheep farming, particularly on the lighter soils of eastern and southern Britain where a 'sheep and corn' economy was practised in the later middle ages (Allison 1957). Sheep were folded on the stubble, and the manure from stalled animals was spread on the fields around rural settlements (p. 26).

The similarity between the bones of sheep and those of goats makes it difficult to assess accurately the importance of goats in the rural economy. Many archaeozoologists do not attempt to make the distinction and figures given for sheep should strictly be regarded as figures for sheep and/or goats. However, where the distinction has been made, goats seem to have been very much a minority species. At the village of Walton (Bucks.), only 1 per cent of the early medieval domestic animal bones were from goats and a similar percentage was reported from North Elmham Park (Norfolk) (Noddle 1976; 1980). Exceptionally, in some urban deposits at Southampton and Bedford, remains of goats were more numerous (Noddle 1975; Grant 1983), but may here reflect the use of goat horn as a raw material. Documentary sources suggest the possibility of a decline in goat keeping during the medieval period. Goats figure prominently in some of the Domesday records, but are seldom mentioned in later manorial accounts (J. Langdon pers. comm.). With English climate, terrain and vegetation, sheep are much easier animals to manage than goats and the coat of the latter was not nearly as highly valued as sheep's wool. Goats are good milk producers, however, and will eat a wide range of food stuffs (figure 8.7). While there is both archaeological and documentary evidence that, once dead, their carcasses, or at least parts of their carcasses, may have had a certain commercial value (see p. 182), we must assume that they played only a relatively minor role in the rural economy.

Cattle bones form a large component in the faunal assemblages of both urban and rural settlements. Average proportions of cattle bones are similar in towns and at the higher status rural sites in the twelfth and thirteenth centuries, but their proportions in ordinary rural settlements are generally rather lower (figure 8.2). Frequently, the majority of the cattle bones found at all types of site were from mature animals and this reflects the significance of cattle in the agrarian economy

(Maltby 1979; 1982; Noddle 1980: Wilson, B. 1980). Their crucial role seems to have been as providers of traction, and this would have encouraged the keeping of as many cattle as possible as plough animals, with the only young animals sold for meat being the weak and those that were surplus to agricultural requirements. Most of the large estates seem to have maintained cattle herds which were often predominantly of oxen (castrated males) (see, for example, Hockey 1975, 30). Peasants who held land and had sufficient resources kept one or more oxen specifically for ploughing and farm haulage. However, many of the peasants with only one or two cattle may have tried to utilize all the possible resources of their animals. Cows, including those in the early stages of pregnancy, seem to have been used in plough teams (Trow-Smith 1957).

Many of the cattle eaten in towns, castles and villages may have served several years as plough beasts before being fattened up for the table. A study of the cattle bones from food refuse found at Winchester noted a high incidence of injuries to the hip joint, likely to have been induced by the use of the animals to pull heavy loads (Baker, quoted in Brothwell 1981, 239).

During the early part of the medieval period the intensification of arable production led to the ploughing up of land that had previously been cattle pasture, and more marginal areas had to be used for animal grazing (p. 82). This made the keeping of sheep particularly appropriate as they have very much lower nutritional requirements than cattle and can be successfully raised on poorer land. However, the increased acreage of arable required larger numbers of plough beasts for its cultivation — a potential incompatibility within the medieval farming system. During the fourteenth century this problem was relieved when better grazing land became available with the abandonment of previously cultivated land.

The archaeological evidence cannot tell us about actual numbers of animals kept, only their relative proportions. In general, proportions of cattle bones are rather stable throughout the period (figure 8.2), but changes in cattle husbandry are suggested by an increase in the percentage of young or at least juvenile animals in later deposits at some sites. At Exeter, for example, there was a very marked increase in younger animals in the deposits of the fourteenth and fifteenth centuries (Maltby 1979). Despite the deficiencies of the present archaeological record, there is a strong suggestion that while cattle were required primarily as working beasts and breeding animals in the early part of our period, their importance as suppliers of meat increased in the later centuries. The appearance in the later middle ages of the butcher—grazier, based in the towns but leasing land in the countryside for fattening meatstock (Dyer 1981, 17), provides corroboration for this view of changing cattle exploitation.

Milk was an important, although probably relatively minor, byproduct of cattle raising (figure 8.3). The nature of the husbandry, particulary in the twelfth and

8.3　*A woman milking a cow, from a thirteenth-century bestiary (Bod. Lib. MS Bodl. 764 f. 41).*

thirteenth centuries, makes it unlikely that milk could have been very intensively exploited. Yields were low by modern standards, especially where there was a shortage of good grazing for cattle and the milk was only available for part of the year – cows that give milk throughout the year are a product of modern animal breeding (Oschinsky 1971, 333). Dyer (1983, 211) shows that dairy produce was a more important component in the lower-class than in the upper-class diet and a large proportion may have been consumed at home, rather than traded.

Pig bones are found in assemblages from every type of context although they are in most instances rather less numerous than those of cattle and sheep (figure 8.2). There can be little ambiguity about why these animals were kept – pigs are extremely efficient converters of a wide range of organic matter to meat. One particular advantage that a pig has over the other common domestic animals is that it can eat foodstuffs that are inedible or even poisonous to the other species – acorns and beech mast for example. The pig herd driven into the woods in the autumn to forage for 'free' food is a common image in the documentary and pictorial record (figure 7.2) and in the Domesday survey woods are often recorded as 'wood for so many swine' or 'wood rendering so many swine for pannage' (see p. 130). However, even by the twelfth century, substantial areas of woodland in England were rare (Rackham, O. 1986, 75). Woodland was an important but essentially seasonal resource for pigs, particularly valuable for fattening prior to slaughter (figure 10.2). The stubble field and cereal waste also provided food for pigs. However, if too many pigs were kept, for much of the year they may have been in competition with the other domestic animals and even the human population for their food.

Meat production was clearly not the main aim of either the sheep or cattle husbandry and the differences in the way that pigs, and cattle and sheep were managed is clearly demonstrated in the age at which the animals were killed. While many of the cattle and sheep bones are from mature animals, the vast majority of the pig bones in archaeological contexts are those of juvenile animals, killed when the balance between food consumed and body weight achieved was at the most favourable point.

The documentary record shows that the scale of rural pig keeping varied from the intensive pig husbandry of the Peterborough Abbey estates with herds of over one hundred swine kept on several manors (Biddick 1984) to the peasant's single weaner fattened up on scraps and waste. But it also suggests that pig keeping was often for home consumption rather than for income. The Peterborough Abbey records show that the Abbey was essentially a producer rather than a marketer of pigs (Biddick 1984, 176) and the same impression is given by the Bolton accounts (p. 149 and figure 8.1; Kershaw 1973a, 152). A survey of the proportion of pig bones from a wide variety of locations has shown some quite clear patterns. Pig bones are in general more common in rural than in urban locations and they are particularly important at castles and monastic sites. The lower incidence of pigs' bones in the towns may be further evidence that rural pig keeping was more often for home consumption rather than for sale. Pigs were driven, both to market and to woodland areas in the autumn, but they are much less easy to move about than either cattle or sheep and cannot manage the long distances of which these latter animals were capable.

Pig keeping can of course be successfully carried out in the confines of a small back yard and it is not clear to what extent the pig bones found in town deposits do in fact reflect the rural husbandry. Raising pigs makes most sense when there is spare or waste food to feed them on. At Beaulieu Abbey, for example, the pigs were fed with malt dregs, swill from the kitchen and rejects from the granary (Hockey 1975, 28, 39). For pigs to have been raised in urban areas, food had to be available from the surrounding countryside, from the gardens that existed within the walls of many towns in the twelfth and thirteenth centuries, or from the waste products of industrial activities such as brewing.

The presence of the bones of extremely young pigs *may* be seen as possible evidence for pig raising within the town boundaries. At Exeter, while up to 5 per cent of the pigs of Roman date were from animals of under six months, in the contexts dated from 1200 to 1600 there were no traces of such very young animals (Maltby 1979). Very young pigs were also extremely rare at Flaxengate in Lincoln (O'Connor 1982). The pigs eaten in these larger conurbations seem more likely to have been bought at market than raised in the towns. At the much smaller town of Aylesbury, the remains of several very young piglets were found, which could suggest some local pig keeping (Jones, G. 1983).

At some sites, and these are usually of a high status, percentages of pig bones are much higher (figure 8.2). They were particularly common at Barnard Castle (Co. Durham), at Okehampton Castle (Devon), at Middleton Stoney Castle (Oxon.) and at Faccombe Manor (Hants.) (Jones et al. in press; Maltby 1982; Levitan 1984b; Sadler in press). To some extent the better representation of pigs in these sites must be a reflection of their rural locations and perhaps of the amount of woodland, but percentages of pig bones tend to be relatively high even at castles in urban settings such as Baile Hill in York and in Baynard's Castle, the late medieval castle in London (Rackham, J. 1978; Armitage 1977; see p. 181).

There is a decline in the importance of the pig in the archaeological record of the fourteenth and fifteenth centuries which can be seen in all types of context (figure 8.2) and at the vast majority of both urban and rural sites with a long period of occupation. This could be simply explained as resulting from the reduction in the amount of woodland that could be used for pannage, but such facts as are available do not support such a view. If one examines the importance of pig over a rather longer time span, one can see that, relative to the other two main domestic species, pigs were more important in the twelfth and thirteenth centuries than at any time since the Bronze Age. Average percentages of pigs rose from the Iron Age, through the Roman and Saxon period and reached a peak in the early medieval period, after which there was a steady decline. The increase in the proportion of pigs occurred when there must have been a considerable overall reduction in the amount of woodland in England (p. 129).

The peak in the importance of this animal seems in fact to have coincided with a period when the production of grain had intensified, and the amount of good quality grazing land for sheep, and particularly for cattle had declined. When good quality land was at a premium for cereal growing, keeping pigs may have been seen to have been the best way of maximizing the use of those resources that were available. Pigs can be kept in the spring and summer on waste land that is not suitable for cultivation or grazing, and fattened up at the end of the summer on cereal waste and in the autumn in woodland areas. The decline in the relative proportion of pig in the latter part of the medieval period may be another reflection of the return of much previously cultivated land to pasture, making pig keeping less profitable and sheep and particularly cattle raising for meat more attractive.

Woodland was a very important resource, managed for a range of products of which pig food may only have been incidental (chapter 7). Pig herding in woodland can be positively detrimental to the growth of young timber. The traditional equation of woodland and pigs seems to be a gross simplification of the way in which a range of resources was utilized to raise pigs for meat.

Horses had an important role to play in agriculture as providers of traction. In some regions, horses began to be used both instead of and as well as oxen in plough teams from the beginning of our period (see Langdon 1986a, 288; p. 91; figure 5.4). Walter of Henley was against this use of horses except on light soils (Oschinsky 1971, 319), and indeed, several of the excavated villages with particularly high percentages of horse bones are situated in such areas (see, for example, Le Patourel 1974; Noddle 1980; Yealland and Higgs 1966) and some with very low percentage were on heavier soils (see, for example, Noddle 1976; Pernetta 1973). However, the correlation between soil type and the incidence of horse bones is not perfect, as they are also common on clayland sites (Ambros 1980; Grant 1975). From the twelfth century onwards, horses increasingly took the place of oxen for haulage (Langdon 1984) and their breeding and training must have been an important rural occupation in some areas (p. 23).

Horses were also well represented in bone assemblages at some high status sites but here they need not have been from working animals but may have been from those kept for riding, hunting or even for war (figure 8.7; Grant 1985; Jones et al. in press; Griffith et al. 1983).

In the past, and even in some contemporary cultures, horses have been eaten but by the medieval period they were not considered as suitable human food and the eating of horse meat was proscribed (p. 174). Horse bones are only exceptionally found with cut marks that suggest that the prohibition had been ignored.

Assessing the role of both horses and dogs from archaeological evidence is complicated by the fact that these animals were rarely, if ever, kept for food, but animal bones recovered during excavation are often food waste. However, the carcasses of these animals had to be disposed of, and thus their bones do occur in the archaeological record (figure 8.4; and see p. 178).

Finds of dog bones suggest that these animals had a place in rural life. Their remains usually form a small percentage of most village faunal assemblages and they have been found in rather larger proportions at some high status sites (for example, Yealland and Higgs 1966; Grant 1985; Jones et al. in press). Iconographic evidence (for example, Bise 1984, 38) suggests that there were many different types of dogs and indeed the measurement of bones from archaeological contexts shows a wide variation in size. The majority of dogs seem to have had shoulder heights of approximately half a metre, but bones from dogs as large as modern alsatians and as small as toy poodles have been found. Dog bones from rural contexts are likely to have been from animals used for herding and as guard dogs, but they were also frequently used for hunting (p. 178) and some of the very small animals may have been kept as pets (p. 180).

8.4   *The partly articulated skeleton of a dog found at Cauldwell Street, Bedford. The scale has half metre divisions*
(source: Grant 1979c; photo: D. Baker).

Cattle and sheep were undoubtedly the most important animals in the medieval rural economy and the most intensively exploited. The management of both of these animals was intimately related to the agrarian economy. Cattle, and sometimes horses, were the essential working animals on the farm and cattle, pigs and especially sheep provided manure to fertilize the arable land. While pigs give a much smaller range of utilizable resources than either sheep or cattle, they none the less had a role as converters to first class protein of many of the waste products of agriculture that might otherwise be lost to the system.

Animals as Food

Of the three most important domestic animals, only pigs were usually reared specifically for food, but cattle and sheep, important in many ways when alive, were also eaten when they reached the end of their useful lives. Animal bones at rural sites are frequently those of elderly animals, although there are exceptions; at Wharram Percy, many of the sheep bones were from quite young animals, killed before they had made any important contribution to the economy as providers of wool (Ryder 1974).

Old animals were not just eaten by the farmers who raised them, but were fattened up and then sold. The *Seneschaucy* advised that old, barren and broken-toothed cows and 'worthless heifers' should be fattened up on good pasture before being sent to market (Oschinsky 1971, 285). This was one way of taking advantage of seasonal gluts of cereal or vegetable products and of the rich pastures that existed for only part of the year.

The large differences in the body size of cattle, sheep and pigs must be taken into account not only when assessing the amount of beef, mutton and pork in the diet but also when considering the economics of meat production. The proportion of beef in the diet will have been much greater than the proportion of cattle among the livestock or cattle bones in archaeological assemblages. However, although the sale price of cattle may have been higher than that of sheep or pigs, feeding cattle may also be much more expensive. The cost of raising a domestic animal was not only dependent on the availability of fodder, but also on the other contributions that had been made by the animals. A fertile ewe, giving several clips of even medium quality wool, may be seen to have more than paid for her food even before she was sent to market. The same might be said of a good plough ox or a breeding cow, but the cost of feeding a pig, a young sheep, cow or bull could only be repaid by the food it itself provided or the price offered at market.

Information on animal carcass use can be gained from a study of butchery. Analyses of cut marks on animal bones has been used to reconstruct butchery practices, to demonstrate technical developments and also changes in the intensity of carcass utilization (Grant 1987). A feature of medieval food debris is the marked fragmentation of the majority of the bone material: that from the Roman and especially the Iron Age periods in England is typically much less fragmented. The bones of the lower parts of the limbs, which bear very little meat, are often complete and unbutchered in the earlier periods, but are much more frequently broken or butchered in medieval deposits. The implication is that the meat and marrow content of even these bones has been used, suggesting that none of the food resources of the animal carcass could afford to be wasted.

Although it is difficult to find archaeological evidence to confirm it, written records show that meat from the larger domestic animals was not only eaten fresh. Preservation of meat allowed consumption at times of the year when fresh meat was in short supply, and may also have been very important when the death, deliberate or accidental, of a large animal produced a greater quantity of fresh meat than could be consumed within a short period. Where family units or households were small, there were also advantages in raising small animals for meat.

The most common small animals raised for food were the domestic birds.

Bones of chickens and geese are common at rural and indeed urban sites, with chicken the most frequently occurring bird species. Goose bones are in general less common in most medieval contexts, although occasionally they were the predominant domestic bird species.

The popularity of goose keeping seems to be related to local environment. Sites with higher percentages of geese (over 40 per cent of the domestic birds) include King's Lynn and Lincoln throughout the medieval period, Oxford in early contexts and Leicester in later contexts (Bramwell 1977; O'Connor 1982; Wilson, B. 1983; Thawley 1981). King's Lynn and Lincoln both lie in regions which are characterized by large areas of low-lying and marshy ground, which provide the kinds of habitat that geese prefer. The fenlands of East Anglia were an important goose-breeding area where very large flocks were kept (Dudley Stamp 1969, 161). There seems to have been a general increase in the exploitation of geese from the Saxon to the early medieval period but some have suggested a decline in the popularity of this bird in the fourteenth and fifteenth centuries, possibly related to a reduction in the amount of wetland as a result of land drainage (Philips 1980, 84). However, at several locations, and notably at King's Lynn and in Northampton, the proportion of geese increased in the later medieval period (Bramwell 1977; 1979).

The limited amount of evidence available also suggests that geese may have contributed a larger proportion of the food eaten in towns than they did in rural areas. This may, in part at least, reflect the environment around those few towns for which there has been a detailed analysis of the domestic bird bones. But for those farmers who were raising animals specifically for the urban market, the advantage of the goose was that it could be driven to market while chickens had to be transported in carts or carried.

Many chickens eaten in the towns may in fact have been raised there. They can be fed on household scraps, but if they are to be good egg producers, a more concentrated food, such as grain is required (Williams 1978, 50). In the later medieval period, when tenement yards began to be built on (Platt and Coleman Smith 1975, 33), a larger proportion of the fowls eaten in the towns may have been bought in from the rural areas. The increase in the proportion of geese in some late urban deposits may be reflection of a decline in local chicken keeping.

Hens and geese seem to have been kept as much for their eggs as for their flesh. This is suggested by the high proportion of the bones of mature birds and the rather low incidence of the bones of young fowl (for example, Levitan 1984a). In some later medieval deposits there is evidence of a change in emphasis in poultry farming, with an increasing proportion of immature birds, suggesting that they were being bred for meat. There are many documentary references to capons (Yaxley 1980, 576; Jones, G. 1983, 41) but the archaeological evidence for the practice of caponization to improve meat yield is somewhat uncertain (West 1982).

Eggs and poultry, which are both comparatively cheap animal protein to produce, are frequently mentioned as rents or pittances (for example, Yaxley 1980, 576; Hockey 1975, 29). In fact eggs and live poultry both seem almost to have been a rural currency. Even the poorest peasant may have been able to raise a few hens and a cock or a gander and geese and the eggs may have been an important component of his protein diet, even though egg productivity seems to have been rather low. A modern breeding set of three geese and a gander should produce at least 100 eggs per year (Williams 1978, 54). At North Elmham Park, 13 geese were kept in 1287–8 but produced only 40 eggs (Yaxley 1980, 576).

Domestic ducks also occur in the species lists of excavation reports, although their bones are seldom very common, and finds of the bones of peafowl are also occasionally noted (for example, Levitan 1984b, 111). Ducks and duck eggs may have made a small contribution to the diet of all classes of the population, but while the peacock appeared at banquets of the wealthy, its role in the medieval diet in general can only have been very minor. Its value almost certainly lay as much in its spectacular feathers as in its palatability (Bond 1984, 127).

The domestic animals are, of course, not the only creatures of the countryside. There are a large number of wild animals, some of which have been exploited by man. The range of wild species to be found in the countryside in the past was not quite the same as that found today. The wolf and the wild boar, which are now extinct, could still be found in England as late as the sixteenth and seventeenth centuries respectively (Corbet and Southern 1977, 311, 409). Others, including the fallow deer, the rabbit and the carp were introduced during the medieval period. Introductions and extinctions were both often a direct result of man's demand for meat. Rabbits were introduced by the Normans, and fallow deer, which may have been present in small numbers in Roman times, do not appear to have been widespread until the eleventh and twelfth centuries (Chapman and Chapman 1975). Pheasants and carp were introduced a few centuries later.

A small group of wild animals, including rabbits, deer and doves were not truly domesticated by men but became what can be termed a 'managed' wild resource. The most important of these was the deer. Bones from three deer species, red, roe and fallow, have been recovered from a wide variety of contexts and in many castles very large numbers of deer bones have been found. They are, however, very rare in most urban contexts. The prevalence of deer bones at these high status sites is entirely in accord with what is known about deer from historical sources. Some of the wild population of the two indigenous wild species of deer, the red and the roe, together with the introduced fallow, were confined in parks. The deer of the parks and the Royal forests were not a resource freely available to the ordinary peasant or even the town dweller. Hunting these animals was a jealously guarded and protected privilege of the upper classes, and a favourite pastime (p. 140).

At some of the high status sites, notably at Barnard, Sandal and Okehampton Castles, the bones of deer were almost as common as those of cattle, sheep and pigs together and these animals appear to have made a large contribution to the meat diet of the castle inhabitants (Jones et al. in press; Griffith et al. 1983; Maltby 1982). They were present in much smaller numbers at Portchester and Bramber Castles (Grant 1985; Westley 1977), but percentages of deer bones at these sites are still considerably higher than in the vast majority of towns and villages. In general, and it must be stressed that the information is not extensive, their remains are most common on sites in the remoter and less populated regions of the north and the west, and slightly less common in the south and the midlands.

Deer were an occasional, if usually illicit, food resource for the poor as well as for the rich (p. 143). Penalties for poaching deer could be extremely high but despite this, significant numbers of deer bones were found in several rural contexts. In early medieval levels at one of the Lyveden tofts, deer remains were more numerous than those of pigs, and an almost complete, but butchered red deer skeleton seems to have been hidden in a well in the fourteenth century (Grant 1975).

There is a rather puzzling aspect to the deer remains which has been reported at several sites (for example, Jones et al. in press; Levitan 1984b). A disproportionate number of the bones identified as deer seem to be the lower limb bones, and not those of the main meat-bearing parts of the body. One explanation for this may be the comparative ease with which these lower limb bones in particular can be distinguished from the same bones of cattle. An alternative and perhaps more plausible explanation is that deer were butchered in the forests where they were killed. The meat, stripped from the main bones of the body, could then be carried back in or with the skin to which the lower limb bones were still attached. The thirteenth-century story of Tristan describes his arrival in a clearing in a wood where hunters have just killed and are about to butcher a deer. Tristan shows them the correct way to butcher and share out the carcass, and tells them to take away the hide (von Strassburg 1960, 78 f.).

In the early post-conquest period, red deer are almost always the most common of the deer species in all types of context, but the fallow deer, with very few exceptions, becomes the most important species in the later middle ages. The success of the establishment of this introduced species is evident. The smaller size of the fallow deer makes it a more suitable animal than the red deer for the confined area of a park. The smallest of the three deer species, the roe deer, is a great deal scarcer than either of the other two species at almost all locations throughout our period.

At several castles with a long occupation sequence, the increase in the proportion of fallow deer bones is paralleled by an increase in the importance of deer in general as a food resource (Grant 1977; Maltby 1982; Jones et al. in press; Griffith et al. 1983). Deer bone proportions drop in castle contexts in the late fifteenth and sixteenth centuries and remain negligible in towns (Grant in press, fig. 2).

The earliest documentary reference to rabbits in Britain is from the Isles of Scilly and is dated to 1176 (Veale 1957, 86). Rabbits are not native to Britain, and they, like the fallow deer, were deliberately introduced. They were initially established on islands, in enclosed areas on heathland, in parks and in forests (Rackham 1986, 47). Some of the artificially created mounds, known as 'pillow mounds', have been excavated to reveal stone-built burrows inside them, thus providing the least ambiguous archaeological evidence for rabbit exploitation (p. 144). Archaeozoologists have rightly been cautious in their analysis of rabbit bones found in archaeological contexts and have frequently ignored them, as the dating of the remains of any burrowing animal by reference to the context in which its bones are found may often be open to question.

Sadler (in press) has reported them in apparently undisturbed eleventh-century deposits in Hampshire, and at Exeter a small number of rabbit bones of twelfth-century date have been found (Maltby 1979, 61). At Okehampton Castle, in the same county, no rabbit bones have been found earlier than the fourteenth century. After this date they were more common here than in the town (Maltby 1982; and see Wilson, B. 1980).

Rabbits were, legally at least, the possessions of the wealthy who built and maintained the warrens and used the rabbits as a source of food and of fur. Attempts to keep the rabbits confined were inevitably unsuccessful and they gradually escaped and began to establish in the wild. It is difficult to assess the scale of the rabbit's contribution to the diet. While those who owned warrens may have eaten a fair amount of rabbit flesh, warrens were not found universally. Although they can live in most types of habitat, rabbits prefer areas of light, dry soil.

Poaching the lord's rabbits also provided some peasants with welcome additions to the meagre meat component of their diet. By the later medieval period, the establishment of the rabbit is reflected in its slightly increased representation in contexts from urban and rural areas, but it seems that it was not until the post-medieval period that this animal was extensively exploited as a food supply for the urban market (Maltby 179, 61; Sheail 1971, 69).

A further 'managed' species was the dove. Again, the importance of this creature is most clearly reflected in the documentary record and in the archaeological evidence for the dovecotes in which the birds were encouraged to nest. Assessing the archaeozoological evidence is difficult, partly because remains of such small creatures are not always well recovered during excavation (p. 5) and partly because of the difficulty of distinguishing the domesticated rock dove (*Columba livia*) from its wild counterpart, the stock dove (*Columba oenas*).

Dovecotes are a feature of many castles, monastic complexes and substantial farms, and many dating from the medieval period survive today. Again, it is difficult, if not impossible, to quantify the amount of protein supplied by these very small creatures. Finds of dove bones are frequently recorded, but they are rarely a major bird species in the bone assemblage. Exceptionally, at the village of Walton, the manor of Faccombe and at the castle at Portchester, dove bones were rather common finds (Bramwell 1976; Sadler in press; Eastham 1985). At Walton, there was a high proportion of bones from immature birds, demonstrating that these birds were eaten in spring and summer and were not just used for food in the winter. At Porchester there was a significant increase in the proportion of dove bones in the fourteenth and fifteenth centuries, and fifteenth-century contexts at the Bishop's Palace in Lincoln included a large number of what were described at feral pigeon bones (Ellison 1975). These may well have been the bones of birds kept in dovecotes, and included many young as well as adults.

Some of the animals utilized for food were truly wild, living their lives separate from man until they were hunted and killed. Species lists from medieval excavations include a wide range of creatures among which are hares, foxes, stoats, weasels and even whales. The bones of many of these animals may have been chance occurrences and their presence does not necessarily imply that they were eaten. Some animals, including the hare, undoubtedly were eaten, especially in rural areas but also in towns (Maltby 1979; Wilson, B. 1980).

Occasional finds of whale bones are most likely to be from accidentally stranded animals, although commercial whaling began in the Bay of Biscay in the twelfth century, rapidly spreading further north (Barrau 1986, 216).

The boar, once an important wild animal, had been deprived of much of its woodland and forest habitat and even in the early medieval period was unlikely to have been found except in remote and densely wooded areas. Brawn made from boars' heads and shoulders was a Christmas dish and boars' heads were a traditional part of the food at large banquets (Wilson, C. A. 1984, 76). However it was probably more often the domestic male rather than the true boar that graced the tables. Certain identifications of the bones of wild boar in archaeological assemblages are extremely rare.

The most common of the wild creatures to be killed for human consumption were not in fact terrestrial mammals, but birds and a range of sea creatures. A review of the published archaeological evidence for birds in medieval contexts has produced a list of over 75 wild species, ranging in size from swans and cranes to pipits and larks and in habitat from coasts, marshes and lakes to moors, woodland and towns. Although few are commonly eaten today, the majority of the many species found on medieval sites could have been used for food. Some, including the hawks, gulls and the scavengers in general are not usually thought to be edible. However claims are made that even rooks are quite palatable when young, and choughs, members of the crow family, were among the game shot in Cornwall as late as the early nineteenth century (Maltby 1979, 73).

The extent to which the bones of even the potentially edible species were in fact the remains of meals is of course uncertain. Butchery marks on the bones of wild birds are rarely reported, although on such small creatures these would not necessarily be expected even when they have been cooked and eaten. Some birds may have been killed as pests (p. 184), but while there is some evidence that at least a small percentage may have been killed and not eaten or may have died from natural causes (for example, Rackham, J. in press), the weight of both the archaeological and the historical evidence shows that wild birds were considered as a source of food and were exploited as such (figure 8.5).

8.5   *Trapping birds, from the marginal illustrations of a fourteenth-century Flemish manuscript showing everyday life (Bod. Lib. MS Bodl. 264 f. 21v).*

The natural wild bird population of the countryside was not a resource freely available for all the population. The restrictions on hunting in woodland applied to birds as well as to boar and deer. At the royal castle of Portchester in Hampshire, licences to capture gamefowl were granted, but only on payment, to 'ceux qi demanderount congée apprendre volata sour la terre nostre soigneur le Roi' (Munby 1985, 289). On common and on waste land birds were a legitimate resource for peasants, but the limited archaeological evidence does not suggest very large-scale exploitation. On the small number of rural sites where bird bones have survived and been recovered, both the number of bird bones found and, perhaps more significantly, the range of species identified is generally low.

However, until we have larger and better-preserved collections from rural sites it would be unwise to assume that we have as yet any real measure of the importance of wild birds in the diet of the poor in the country.

In contrast, large numbers of bird bones have been recovered from urban sites and at many of these a wide range of species has been identified. At Exeter, London, Oxford and Northampton (Maltby 1979; Bramwell 1975; 1979; Wilson, B. 1980) over 15 different wild species were present in medieval contexts and there were over 20 species present at King's Lynn and Lincoln (Bramwell 1977; O'Connor 1982). The species include many of the common game birds as well as the scavenging species such as ravens, crows and jackdaws and the ubiquitous birds of the modern urban environment, the blackbirds, thrushes and sparrows. At Exeter, the predominant species in twelfth- and thirteenth-century contexts was the woodcock, but wildfowl are generally the most common wild bird species.

Tariff lists exist for the London Company of Poulterers from the thirteenth century onwards and show that as well as domestic birds and game birds the poulterers sold a wide range of wild birds including blackbirds, larks and thrushes (Wilson, C. A. 1984). Some of the birds may have been trapped in, or at least very close to, the towns. Others, such as teal, wigeons, plovers, partridges, woodcock and snipe, may have been caught some distance from the town and their inclusion on the tariff lists suggests that there was a well established trade in wild birds, although some town dwellers may have trapped or shot their own birds.

The species found in towns often reflect quite clearly particular aspects of the local environment. Not surprisingly, seabirds are usually found at coastal sites but not at sites very far inland. The birds at King's Lynn could almost all have been caught within a few miles of the town, but included some whose habitats ranged from seashore, estuary, marsh and freshwater to dry ground and woodland (Bramwell 1977). The range of environments suggests that, although the exploitation may have been relatively local in this instance, it still seems to have been fairly intensive.

A feature of the bird remains found at many castles is the number and diversity of the wild bird species. Forty-three wild bird species were represented in late medieval contexts at Baynard's Castle in London, at Okehampton Castle there were over 20, at Portchester Castle 28 and there were 14 even in the relatively small sample from the castle at Baile Hill in York (Bramwell 1977; Maltby 1982; Eastham 1985; Rackham, J. 1978). It has already been noted that at many towns there was also a wide range of bird species, but a further feature of these high status contexts, not generally seen at urban sites, is the high ratio of wild birds to domestic birds. Records show that some estates employed bird catchers and fowlers. Richard de Swinfield, a thirteenth-century bishop of Hereford employed a fowler who set nets in the autumn to catch partridges and other birds (Labarge 1980, 172). It would appear that, to the rich, birds, like fish (below) were an important source of variety in the menu.

There is some indication of an increase in the relative importance of wild birds during the medieval period. At many sites where there is a long occupation, there are higher percentages of wild birds in relation to domestic birds in the later periods (for example Maltby 1979; Levitan 1984b; O'Connor 1982; p. 181). At Portchester and Okehampton Castles this increase continues into the sixteenth century (Eastham 1985; Maltby 1982). During the medieval period in general, the natural wild bird resources seem to have been utilized rather more intensively than in earlier periods. The range of bird species found, and the proportion of wild bird bones, are considerably greater than in any earlier period since the advent of farming.

There were undoubtedly important regional differences in the distribution and exploitation of wild birds and they may have been a particularly valuable resource in marginal areas. Fowling was one way of using the marshland areas that could not be put to productive agricultural use. Regrettably, the archaeological evidence is not yet equal to the task of determining the full extent and nature of regional patterning.

Fish have long been recognised as an important element in the medieval diet, not least because of the restrictions imposed by the Church on the eating of meat. In upper class and prosperous households, freshwater fish ensured not only a continuity of first class protein throughout the year, but also provided a significant part of the required variety in the daily menus. The source of the freshwater fish that supplied the aristocracy, the monks and the nuns was frequently the fishponds that were a common feature of lay and monastic estates. The ponds were often extensive and elaborate constructions that were regularly stocked with fish, often bought from local fishermen and eel trappers. Species kept in Prior More's ponds in Worcestershire in the early sixteenth century were eels, tench, pike, pickerel (small pike), perch, roach and carp. There is every reason to suppose that More was following a traditional and well established practice in the management of his fish ponds, the only hint of innovation being the inclusion of carp which are believed to have been introduced from the continent in the late fourteenth or early fifteenth century (Hickling 1971, 121).

The consumption of freshwater fish from ponds in particular symbolized high status, and monetary values attached to some fish were far in excess of their palatability (C. Dyer pers. comm.). Many of the freshwater fish are thus unlikely to have been a legitimate resource for the rural population, but common rights were held in respect of some fishponds and fisheries. Other fisheries were rented by villeins, and Domesday records renders of large numbers of eels from fisheries and fishermen (for example, Darby and Finn 1967, 111, 188).

Poaching would no doubt have allowed some to enjoy a more varied freshwater fish diet.

Documentary evidence suggests that a wide range of freshwater fish were eaten, including perch, lampreys, pike, roach, tench, dace, chub, trout, ruffe and barbel. Eels are also frequently mentioned and were kept in ponds and caught in rivers, but may also have been caught from the sea to which they return to spawn. The archaeological evidence has as yet relatively little to add to the documentary evidence for the range of freshwater fish consumed. Considerations of survival and recovery affect the interpretation of bone remains from all species, but nowhere are they more acute than when the importance and significance of fish are being assessed. Indeed, where sieving is not a routine part of excavation practice, one may expect only to recover occasional larger fish bones or substantial concentrations. Fortunately an awareness of this problem has led to a much more systematic sieving of at least samples of archaeological deposits, increasing the volume and quality of the evidence available. Despite this recent improvement in recovery techniques, finds of freshwater fish remains have been relatively rare, even on sites where frequent consumption of these fish is suggested by the documentary evidence. The fish bones from Okehampton Castle in Devon include remains from 27 species, none of which was exclusively a freshwater fish, although salmon, eel and sturgeon could have been taken in rivers during their periods of migration (Wilkinson 1982b, 136). Even at the castle of Middleton Stoney in Oxfordshire, almost as far from the sea as one can be in Britain, three of the six fish species represented were marine; eel may have been imported with the sea fish although is perhaps more likely to have been caught locally, and only pike and chubb were certainly taken from fresh waters (Levitan 1984b, 121).

Small numbers of bones from freshwater fish have also been found in urban contexts (Cartledge 1983; O'Connor 1982; Jones, A. 1979; 1984; Wilson, B. 1983; Wheeler 1984). At Abingdon, ten freshwater species were identified in a sieved deposit. This is an unusually large number and may reflect the richness of the Thames as a source of fish (Wilkinson 1982a).

Eel bones are found at many sites and although some are from the conger eel (*Conger conger*), an exclusively marine species, the majority, even at coastal sites are those of the migratory species, *Anguilla anguilla*.

Apart from the eel, the most common of the freshwater fish reported in archaeological contexts is the pike. The pike is one of the largest of the British freshwater fish, commonly growing to over 14 kg. It has a palatable flesh and a widespread distribution, making it a favoured sport fish even today (Wheeler 1969, 167). However, we must not assume that pike was necessarily the most frequently consumed. The small size of most freshwater species is a factor that must be taken into account in explaining their scarcity in archaeological deposits, especially where these deposits have not been sieved.

Archaeological deposits of fish bones are heavily dominated by the remains of marine species, not only at sites near to the coasts but also in inland areas. The range, documented by both archaeological and written evidence, makes it clear that there was a major exploitation of coastal and inshore resources and also of deep-sea fish. At King's Lynn, ten different fish were identified including some, such as cod and haddock, that may have been taken locally, and others such as ling, whose northerly distribution suggests exploitation of more distant waters or importation from northern ports (Wheeler 1977). An even wider range was found in sieved deposits at Great Yarmouth, adding herring, whiting, mackerel and scad to the list for the east coast ports (Wheeler and Jones 1976).

At Okehampton, a castle situated within easy reach of the large coastal towns of Plymouth and Exeter, 25 marine species were identified (Wilkinson 1982b), but at the inland castle site at Middleton Stoney there were only three (Levitan 1984b). Excavations at Exeter itself yielded at least 24 different marine fish but at the landlocked towns of Oxford and Northampton there were only four and five respectively (Wilkinson 1979; Wilson, B. 1983; Jones, A. K. G. 1979). Documentary sources indicate that a range of fresh marine fish was available at inland markets. Pershore Abbey in Worcestershire was buying fresh sea fish at Coventry (Hickling 1971, 120; Andrews 1933, 36). The archaeological evidence, however, suggests that, while in coastal regions many species of fresh sea fish were consumed, those that reached the more inland areas were usually restricted to a smaller number of common species, some of which may have been preserved.

It is clear from documentary evidence that various methods of fish preservation were used extensively. White (salted) herrings and red (smoked) herrings are frequently referred to, and drying was another method used, particularly for large fish such as cod. While examination of the remains themselves cannot generally be expected to distinguish between fresh and preserved fish, there is some evidence for fish processing in the archaeological record. At Taunton most of the bones were from the heads of the fish and there were very few body vertebrae. Wheeler (1984) interpreted the deposit as kitchen waste, but it is possible that the fish were being prepared for preservation. The medieval cod bones from Exeter were dominated by head and tail bones, whereas the bones from post-medieval deposits at the same site were mainly those of the body, some of which had cut marks. Wilkinson (1979) suggests that the post-medieval bones were from fish that had been split and then preserved by drying or salting. These fish may have been brought already preserved from fisheries in distant waters; the medieval deposits may suggest local drying and salting.

While some fish processing may have been carried out at the English ports, it is clear from documentary evidence that during the medieval period there were substantial imports of preserved fish into Britain. Cod were imported already salted or dried from fisheries as far distant as Norway and Iceland. They were transported from the ports by boat and cart and marketed as 'stock fish' (Carus-Wilson 1962–3, 191).

With evidence of extensive importation and the very widespread distribution of several of the common marine species, it is difficult to determine the extent of English exploitation of fishing grounds. Metrical analysis of the cod bones found in deposits at King's Lynn showed two distinct size groupings which Wheeler suggests were the product of two separate fisheries (1977, 408). The smaller fish may have been caught locally during the winter migration of young cod, while the larger fish may have been caught in more distant northern waters or imported.

The archaeological evidence also suggests that while cod and herring were one of the most important catches at northern and east coast ports, hake may have been more important in southern and western ports. This is consistent with the modern distribution of these species (Wheeler 1969, 136). Many of the fish could have been caught with hook and line, but Wheeler (1977) believes that plaice in particular could more profitably be caught in seine nets from small boats. Wilkinson (1979) suggests line fishing, surface net and estuarine traps for the species found in the Exeter deposits.

There is a further marine resource that appears to have been extensively utilized in the medieval period. Marine mollusc shells have been recovered in very large numbers during excavation, although they do not always receive specialist attention. Oyster shells are particularly common, and whelks, cockles, mussels and winkles are also frequently encountered. Oysters did not have the status that they have today and were a relatively cheap food even until quite recent times, only becoming a luxury when pollution radically reduced their distribution.

At the small port of Pevensey, the molluscan species included oysters, whelks, musssels and cockles. Oysters may have been obtained locally from oyster beds in Pevensey Bay and are the most numerous species in all periods. The uniform size and age of the majority of the oysters found at Okehampton Castle suggested that they may have been cultivated and collected in batches (Backway 1982).

Whelks first appear in thirteenth-century contexts, and from that time onwards are almost as common as oysters. One pit dated to the late fourteenth century contained over 13,000 shells (Dulley 1967, 232). Marine molluscs are also very common at inland locations, and occur on sites of high and low status. Oysters, cockles and winkles were found at the palace at Kings Langley in Hertfordshire (Locker 1977, 163) and at Oxford, finds of mussels, oysters, cockles and limpets have been reported (Wilson, B. 1980). Fresh molluscs can be transported more easily than fresh fish as they will survive for some time packed in barrels. At Bramber Castle a feature claimed to be a tank for storing oysters was excavated (Barton and Holden 1977, 34).

The nature of the archaeological evidence itself and the inconsistency of its treatment make it very difficult to trace any changes in freshwater and marine exploitation during the medieval period. Numbers of fish bones at different sites can rarely be usefully compared and there is not yet enough evidence to look in detail at patterns of regional exploitation. However, some broad chronological changes can be charted. There is very clear evidence of a significant increase in the exploitation of fish in the medieval period compared to earlier periods at many sites. For example, at Portchester Castle, situated at the tip of a peninsula, the number of fish bones recovered increased dramatically from the Roman to the medieval period, even though similar methods of excavation were employed for most deposits (Grant 1985). At Exeter, there was not only an increase in the numbers of fish bones recovered, but a twofold increase in the number of species represented from the Roman to the medieval period (Wilkinson 1979).

Food and Religion

The wide range of animal foods consumed in the medieval period – and not all the species eaten have been mentioned here – must be viewed in relation to the attitudes of the Church to food consumption. The theological bases for dietary restrictions are linked with the concepts of both fast and abstinence. The Biblical concept of fasting meant total abstinence from food and drink until after sunset. However, during the medieval period, the fast was permitted to be broken earlier and earlier in the day, until fasting was understood to be the taking of only one meal a day.

Fast days were also days of abstinence, but additional days were for abstinence alone, and so it was this custom rather than that of fasting that had the most effect on diet. The laws regulating abstinence were unwritten and were subject to variations in time and place. This is very important, and meant that the restrictions could reflect, or even influence, local conditions.

In the early church, flesh meat and meat products, together with milk, eggs, butter and cheese were proscribed on days of abstinence. However, local customs and repeated dispensations led to the exception of milk, eggs and milk products by the ninth century (NCE 1967–9, 8.847). Fish and molluscs were not considered to be meat nor, in general, were birds.

By the medieval period, the flesh of most four-legged animals was banned on up to three days a week, and throughout Lent. Some monastic orders, such as the Cistercians, proscribed meat and lard entirely, except for the sick, and even banned eggs and cheese during Lent and Advent (Knowles 1963, 641). The only animal whose flesh was entirely forbidden was the horse, rather against the general principles of the Christian attitude to food. The proscription was issued relatively late, by Pope Gregory III, in 732 (Rau 1968, 100).

The effect of dietary restrictions in the middle ages was to provide an important incentive towards diversification of food resources, particularly towards fish and birds which were exempt from prohibitions. One of the striking features of most medieval bone assemblages in the number and range of fish and bird species present. This diversification was extremely important at a time when the human population was increasing, but there were no major animal improvements (p. 176) and the majority of the domestic animals were required on the land as vital components of the agricultural system rather than in the kitchens. Limiting the amount of meat that was required from domestic animals prevented depletion of the stocks of animals necessary for essential agricultural purposes. The wild animal population provided 'food for free', or at least free from major harmful effects on agriculture.

Meat in any form was not the main component of the diet for the majority of the population. Cereal and vegetable products were the staple foods of all but the very rich, and most peasants would not have expected to eat meat every day, even if it had been allowed. The Church offered believers a justification for this deprivation at the same time as encouraging practices that ensured the continuation of supplies of cereal and vegetable food. In later periods, the restrictions were enforced by secular law (Grant in press).

The total ban on the consumption of horse meat spared this animal for its important role in warfare and as a provider of transport and traction. By limiting the number of horses that were needed, the ban may have prevented expensive grain and oats, food that could be used for human consumption, being inefficiently converted to protein (Grant 1984a, 521; Harris 1986, 96; but see Sahlins 1976, 170–9.)

The dietary restrictions also had an important influence on the organisation of animal husbandry and the provision of food. On the estates of religious orders who adhered to the rule of abstinence, only a very small proportion of the animals kept were slaughtered for home consumption. These would have been to feed visitors, the lay members of the community and those in the infirmary. The majority of surplus animals must have been sold at market, providing an important component in the system of supply and demand.

It seems that the dietary rules were not always strictly adhered to, even in the religious communities. Bones were found in the area of the monks' kitchen and refectory at the Cistercian abbey of Valle Crucis, although it is possible that they were the remains of the meals of lay brothers (Barker 1976). However, it is clear from the scathing remarks in the satirical writings of Wireker and 'Gregory' that the monastic ideals were not universally maintained (Regenos 1959, 106; Colker 1975, 13–15).

Animal Productivity

The productivity of domestic animals can be measured in a variety of ways. For example, it is possible to assess the weight and quality of a wool clip, the milk produced by a cow, the number of live lambs, calves or piglets per breeding female, the number of eggs produced by a hen, or carcass weight at slaughter. For any measure of most of these for the medieval period, we must rely on the documentary record. This generally shows a very low productivity by moderns standards (pp. 29, 164).

Exceptionally, there have been finds of preserved wool, parchment and textiles that have allowed an assessment of wool quality. The results of his examinations of preserved wool have been summarized by Ryder (1983, 472 ff.). He has found a range of fleece types, including a very fine wool, but a 'primitive hairy generalized medium type' predominated. The major change to the modern wool types seems to have occurred after the medieval period, although it seems that longwools first appeared in the fourteenth century.

The measurement of excavated bone remains can give information about the size of animals. Unfortunately, unbroken bones that can be measured accurately are relatively rare since many of the bones have been accidentally broken or chopped into pieces when the carcass was butchered (p. 162).

In the twelfth and thirteenth centuries, most cattle were of a fairly primitive short-horned variety, and were quite small (Armitage 1980, 408). Calculations of shoulder heights give a range of sizes from just under one metre to 1.29 m, with an average of around 1.10 m. In the fourteenth and fifteenth centuries, the majority of the cattle were still of the short-horned variety, but some long-horned animals are also found (Armitage 1980, 408). Shoulder heights range from just over one metre to 1.25 m, with an average size of 1.13 m, which represents little improvement on the earlier period. Although there is evidence for the presence of larger cattle by the fifteenth century, and at some individual sites a small size increase is indicated (Bourdillon 1980, 187), it is only in the sixteenth century that significantly larger cattle become common (see Armitage 1980, 409).

In the early medieval period, the height of sheep ranged from 0.5 to 0.6 m at the shoulder, with a very similar range in the late middle ages and no evidence for any size improvement for this animal. By the sixteenth century, although most of the sheep were still quite small, some larger animals are also found. It is of particular significance that most of the cattle and sheep of the medieval period are considerably smaller than the animals of the Roman and Saxon periods (Armitage 1982, 52; Bourdillon 1979a, 519; Grant 1977, 228).

Possible causes for size changes in animals can be genetic, environmental or a combination of the two. It seems unlikely that a reduction in size in the early medieval period was solely genetic in origin. There is no evidence for the introduction of new smaller stock and the types of animals seem to remain the same. When animal populations become isolated, there is a tendency for a reduction in the gene pool to occur, and a diminution of size often results. However, in the period were are discussing, there seems, from the documentary sources, to have been much movement of animals, with breeding animals sold from one farm to another, which should have prevented excessive inbreeding. The widespread practice of castration may have had a detrimental effect on the genetic constitution of the animals. If the best sheep and cattle were castrated to improve their wool quality and strength and tractability as plough animals, there may have been a loss of some of the 'best' genes.

Environmental factors are likely to have made an important contribution to the size reduction. The expansion of arable in the early medieval period pushed the grazing land to more and more marginal areas, with a consequent adverse effect on animal nutrition and productivity. It will certainly have made sheep the best animals to keep in large numbers, since their nutritional requirements are a great deal lower than those of cattle, but even the sheep will have suffered. Modern hill sheep are smaller, slower growing and have a lower reproductive potential than lowland sheep (Croston and Pollott 1985, 155).

It is rather surprising that there is so little sign of size improvement in the fourteenth and fifteenth centuries, when much of the better quality land was returned to pasture. Low performance caused by poor nutrition is not irreversible. Sheep drafted from hill to upland farms show a marked increase in productivity, and improved nutrition can also increase size in larger animals (Suttie and Hamilton 1983). It is possible that poor management techniques contributed to the failure to improve the animals. Suttie and Hamiltons's study showed that, in order to realize the full genetic potential of the Scottish red deer, it was essential to give supplementary feeding while the animals were young and still growing, particularly in the winter. It is clear that medieval farmers knew how to fatten up older animals for market by giving them extra food (p. 162), but this will only have added extra flesh and fat, and will not have affected their basic size. They may not have realised the importance of giving extra food to young animals (see p. 154) and winter food supplies were probably often scarce throughout the period.

Pigs are usually killed before they are fully grown, so there is very little information available on pig sizes. Such evidence as does exist shows that the pigs of the period were thin, long-legged creatures, a fraction of the size of modern animals (figure 7.2). Again, a size reduction from the Roman period is suggested.

Information on the size of horses is also scarce, since the bones of these animals tend to be found in rather small numbers (p. 160) but a range of sizes can be demonstrated. The bones of some animals are small enough for them to have been donkeys or mules, and few animals reached 1.6 m. The average for the period was around 1.4 m. An analysis of horse bone measurements from sites of different social and economic status failed to demonstrate any size differences that could be related to the different uses to which the horses may have been put.

R. Harcourt has made a general study of horse size, and has attempted to find archaeological evidence for the great medieval war horse. However, this much-discussed animal (Davis 1983) has proved elusive, and Harcourt was not able to prove the existence of an animal of the expected size (pers. comm.).

The overall impression is that the medieval farmers failed, either through ignorance, or lack of resources, to realize the full potential of their animals, and that it was only in the early modern period that real animal improvements can be demonstrated.

Animals and Status

The animal resources available to the peasants were not the same as those available to the lords, and the nature of the inter-relationships that existed between man and animals was dependent on social position. For example, if a peasant kept a horse it was as a working animal. The investment made in food and labour had to be repaid by work done – pulling ploughs and harrows, carting wood, carrying goods to and from the market and many other essential tasks. A lord might keep a horse for sport and for pleasure.

The traditional leisure and sporting pursuits included several that involved animals. Riding horses were important for jousting and were often used with dogs for hunting (figure 8.6). The keeping of dogs for hunting may be reflected in the high percentages of dog bones found at some high status sites (for example Grant 1977; 1985). Deer hunting was an important and popular activity (see p. 140) and very much the prerogative of the upper classes. One of the main animals of the chase, the fallow deer, was actually introduced into Britain (p. 164) and a great deal of time, effort and money was expended on maintaining the parks in which the deer were confined, and ensuring that only those permitted to hunt did so (p. 141). Intensive deer hunting was by no means a long-established tradition in Britain. Bones of deer are in fact extremely rare in archaeological contexts from the Iron Age to the Saxon period, even where there was ample evidence for the presence of deer in the local environment (Grant 1981). In the same period in some parts of Europe the bones of wild animals are often a significant component of faunal assemblages. Even during the medieval period, hunting was probably more important on the continent than it was in England. The fourteenth-century *Le Livre de la Chasse* of Gaston Phoebus is a

8.6 *Hawking, from a late fourteenth-century set of calendarial and astrological pieces (Bod. Lib. MS Rawl. D. 939 (sect. 2)).*

marvellous example of the attention given to the chase in France (Bise 1984). It gives detailed instructions not only for hunting a large number of wild creatures, including deer, boar, rabbits, otters and badgers, but also for the training of huntsmen and the care of hunting dogs. The increase in the importance of hunting in England coincides with important political connections between England and France and may be evidence of a strong foreign influence.

Falconry was another sport on which important resources of time and money were expended (figure 8.6). Nothing shows this more clearly than White's (1951) account of the training of a goshawk. Serious scientific treatises were written on falconry in the medieval period, and falconers were employed in most upper class households. One of the tasks of Bishop Swinfield's fowler was to watch the falcons' eyries in June in order to capture young birds as soon as they were fledged (Labarge 1980, 172). Falcons were also imported from abroad (Carus-Wilson 1962–3, 192). Falconry was not exclusively a sport of the upper classes; priests and yeomen flew hawks, but social position was expressed in a hierarchy of the birds themselves. The true falcon and the noblest hunting bird was the trained female peregrine and peregrines were the birds of princes and nobles. Lesser birds were for lesser beings; merlins were for ladies, goshawks for yeomen and sparrowhawks for priests (Eastham 1977). Bones from falcons have been quite frequently reported. Sparrowhawks and goshawks are the most commonly represented in archaeological deposits and have been found at several castles as well as in some towns. Remains of a peregrine falcon were found at Baynard's Castle in London (Bramwell 1975) but also in urban deposits at Ilchester and Lincoln (Levitan 1982; O'Connor 1982).

The poor were not permitted to hunt deer and were rarely able to support the expense, in time at least, of training and caring for a hawk, neither would they have been able to afford to keep animals that served no utilitarian purpose. Pets may also be viewed as symbols of high status and it is to be expected that at castles, some of the bones of dogs, cats and even songbirds may have been those of pets rather than working or food animals.

The upper classes also reinforced their social position with the food that they ate. The documentary record shows that meat formed a particularly high proportion of their diet when compared to that of the lower classes and that a low value was placed on vegetables and milk products (Dyer 1983, 211). Both the documentary and archaeological records show that the kind of meat that the lords ate often differed from that eaten by the ordinary peasants. Archaeologically, high status sites can in broad terms be characterized by their high proportions of bones from pigs, deer and domestic and wild birds, animals from which meat is the primary rather than a secondary product.

The typical diet of the upper ranks in medieval society seems by modern nutritional standards to have had serious deficiencies in quality (Dyer 1983,

195). Harris (1986) suggests that what he terms 'meat hunger', a craving for animal foods above those from plants, is a world-wide phenomenon, and gives many examples where an apparently disproportionate amount of wealth and energy is spent on acquiring meat. The upper classes of medieval England clearly valued meat highly – they felt strongly enough about their deer in the early medieval period to protect them by penalties of death for poaching.

In modern western society, status, or at least wealth, is often demonstrated in the cuts of meat that are eaten. With a few obvious exceptions, there is comparatively little consumption of meat other than from the common domestic farmyard animals, but the various parts of the animals consumed all have their own values. In the archaeological record of the medieval period, we rarely have clear evidence that particular cuts of meat had different values attached to them. Bones from all parts of the animal and from animals of all ages are found at most locations, including the high status sites, although, exceptionally, Maltby noted that predominantly 'prime joints of meat' were consumed at Okehampton Castle (1979, 153).

What more clearly distinguishes the rich from the poor seems to be the frequency with which the former could afford to eat animals that had not previously served a useful purpose on the farm. The high percentages of pigs in castle deposits suggests that the rich were even prepared to expend other food resources to fatten these animals. The Peterborough Abbey accounts show that there was a considerable expenditure on grain for pig fattening (Biddick 1984, 176). However, an important proportion of the 'high status protein' came from wild or 'managed' animals that had eaten food that was of no significant use to either man or his domestic animals, and at least part of the food that the pigs ate may have also been 'food for free'. Many of the expenses involved in the consumption of 'high status' animals were essentially labour expenses.

The farming economy, with its low productivity (p. 29), could not have supported the rising population of the twelfth and thirteenth centuries if there had been an attempt to raise large numbers of domestic animals exclusively to produce meat. Thus the population in general, and the upper classes in particular, turned to non-domestic animal resources. In the fourteenth and fifteenth centuries, the reduced population and the availability of better grazing land for fattening animals seems to have made it possible to increase the meat available from domestic animals (p. 156). During this later period, the percentages of deer bones increase at several high status sites. As meat became more available for the lower classes of society, the importance of the rarer meats as symbols of status may have increased. There seems to have been an increase in the proportion of domestic bird bones and but also in the relative proportion of wild birds at several sites. While this phenomenon was observed in some urban contexts, it was most marked at high status sites.

There is also evidence of the development of what Goody (1982, 134) calls a 'sumptuary cuisine', which although not sophisticated was certainly 'hierarchical'. The distinction between rich and poor may have begun to lie not only in what they ate, but in how they cooked and ate it. For example, the city of Norwich had to render annually to the king pies of the first fresh herrings (Labarge 1980, 78). The real value and cost of this render lay not so much in the cost of the fish, which would have been comparatively cheap so near the coast, and available even to the poor, but in the ginger, pepper, cinnamon and other rare and extremely expensive imported spices that were used to flavour the pies.

Animals and Employment, Crafts and Trade

The majority of the population of England during the medieval period was involved in farming. The working day of many peasants consisted of a wide range of activities concerned with agriculture and animal husbandry, but the occupations of some were more specialized, and shepherd, oxherd, cowherd and swineherd all appear as occupations in the written record.

Some of the population found employment in activities directly concerned with the provision of food. Butchers were already established as a guild in London by the late twelfth century (Jones 1976, 2) and there are records of butchers selling meat in villages in the late medieval period (Dyer 1983, 207). Bird catchers and fowlers could gain a living for at least part of the year by supplying the urban meat market or as employees of some of the large estates (p. 169). Fishing provided employment not only for the fishermen themselves but also in the creation and maintenance of fish ponds and river fisheries and in the making and repair of boats, nets and traps.

The resource potential of the animals of the English countryside and surrounding waters lay not only in the meat, milk and wool that they provided, but also in the many other byproducts of their carcasses. These included hide, skin, horn, gut and bone from the larger animals, fur from some of the smaller animals, feathers from the birds and oil from fish and whales. Even oyster shells were utilized. At Corfe Castle they were used to level up the ashlar course of the walls (RCHM 1960, 53).

Many animal products were processed locally. Hides were of particular value for leather and although the flesh of horses was not eaten, their hides were used (Oschinsky 1971, 319; Yaxley 1980, 574). At Beaulieu the monks themselves made a small amount of parchment and vellum from the skins of sheep and calves (Hockey 1975, 37). The crudeness and simplicity of many of the bone ornaments and tools found during excavations imply that their manufacture was the result of a home craft rather than an organized industry (MacGregor 1985, 44). However, the bone material from a toft excavated at the village of Lyveden included a large amount of waste from bone working and suggested that the scale of the craft may have been more than was necessary to supply just one household (Grant 1971, 92).

The domestic animals were able to supply a range of raw materials that not only met local needs and provided local employment, but also supplied craft and manufacturing industries within the towns. In small towns in the early medieval period, many of the crafts that became well developed in the later period seem to have been carried out on a smaller scale, and local markets may have acted as collection points for raw materials. Here peasants or the landowners' agents could trade not only the animals but also their byproducts.

The small scale of some of the craft activities was demonstrated by a series of excavations in Bedford. In the collections of animal bones, cattle horn cores were either absent or found in small concentrations, suggested that horn working or possibly glue boiling may have been carried out on a small scale and possibly part-time basis at several locations (Grant 1979a, 288). In the later middle ages, an even more significant part of the products of pastoral farming was for the market rather than for home use (Dyer 1981, 30). Lists of trades and occupations of town dwellers reveal a high proportion based on the manufacture and sale of items that were animal in origin. Of the 28 non-agricultural occupations listed in the leet records for the small town of Tamworth in the fourteenth and fifteenth centuries, 12 are entirely and a further three partly related to animal products (Hilton 1975, 84). Phythian-Adams lists 15 specialist trades directly concerned in the textile and clothing industry and nine that supplied equipment for the trade (1977, 12). Similar numbers of specialists were involved in the leather and food industries.

Crucial to the organization of many of the non-textile crafts may have been the butchery industry, and the butchers' guild was one of the earliest of the craft guilds to be established (Jones 1976, 2). Once the killing of animals was in any was centralized, the abattoirs could become collecting points for carcass byproducts, which could then be sold.

Some particularly prized items were not available in sufficient quantity or quality from local resources and were imported. One example is processed fish oil which was imported with preserved fish through the east coast ports (Carus-Wilson 1962–3, 190). It was used for lighting and in leather manufacture – the shoemaker at Beaulieu Abbey was supplied with herring dripping in addition to lard, for softening shoe leather (Hockey 1975, 38). At Baynard's Castle, a fragment of elk antler must have been imported from abroad, probably from northern Europe, as raw material for tools or ornaments (Armitage 1977; MacGregor 1985, 37).

Animals were important not only as the source of the raw materials for many trade and manufacturing industries, but also as the means of transport for both the raw materials and the finished goods. Some goods were moved over very long distances, and specially trained pack animals made this possible (figure 10.4).

Animals as Pests

Animals are not universally beneficial to man. They are sometimes a threat to human welfare. Some animal species have probably been regarded as pests ever since the earliest days of farming. Foxes will readily kill small farmyard animals such as chickens and lambs, and remains of foxes found in archaeological deposits may be those of animals killed to protect the farmyard stock, although some of these animals may have been hunted for sport. Wolves still lived wild in England during the medieval period, but they are believed to have become extinct at the beginning of the sixteenth century and are only likely to have been a threat in remoter areas (Corbet and Southern 1977, 311). Some of the bird species recorded may also have been killed as pests. The larger birds of prey such as marsh harriers will take young lambs, and wood pigeons, rooks, crows and starlings can do considerable damage to crops. The predatory fish however could be put to human advantage. Prior Moore stocked his fishponds with pike and eel to thin out excessive numbers of small fry while they themselves grew fat (Hickling 1971, 120).

Small wild animals such as mice, rats and shrews are serious pests where food is being stored. Many granaries of the medieval period were raised above ground level to prevent small creatures from getting in. Another strategy adopted by the farmer and the housewife was keeping cats. The Countess of Leicester in the thirteenth century purchased a cat as soon as she and her household moved house (Labarge 1980, 184). Cat bones are found in archaeological contexts in both town and country. At the castle at Middleton Stoney and in deposits within the medieval town of Southampton, there were very large numbers of cat bones of twelfth- and thirteenth-century date (Levitan 1984b; Bourdillon 1979b). Occasionally, cut marks on the bones of cats suggest that the fur had been removed, but the animals were probably most valuable as ratters and mousers. The particular concentrations of bones at these sites may be chance occurrences reflecting rubbish disposal.

Animals can also be harmful to growing crops. Overgrazing by domestic animals can lead to soil erosion and the loss of topsoil and soil fertility. Domestic animals need to be carefully controlled to prevent them from straying onto cultivated land and, where pasture and arable were adjacent, this required the construction and maintenance of field boundaries and adequate human supervision. Both deer and rabbits can, and did, cause considerable damage to crops. In the fourteenth century, the reeve of Lighthorne, in Warwickshire, made several complaints about the devastation of crops by the lord's rabbits (Dyer 1981, 14). It is ironic that animals introduced to supply food became a threat to existing food supplies when not properly controlled. Deer, goats (figure 8.7) and pigs can have a devastating effect on woodland resources, and dogs were often the subject of complaints in the manor courts because they harassed sheep and pigs (C. Dyer pers. comm.).

8.7   *A goat, a stag and a doe from a late twelfth-century bestiary. The goat is eating a branch of a tree*
(Bod. Lib. MS Bodl. 602 f. 17v).

Some animals posed a much more dangerous and immediate threat to man. The disease that was, in most people's opinion, responsible for the death of a large proportion of the population of Europe was bubonic plague, which is carried by a flea that lives on the black rat (see p. 208). The dramatic reduction of the population that resulted from the major epidemics had important consequences for the organization of agriculture and animal husbandry in the fourteenth and fifteenth centuries (p. 156).

Close contact with domestic animals can also have adverse effects on human health. Anthrax, tuberculosis, trichinosis and brucellosis can all originate from the animal population and the misunderstanding of the mechanisms of disease transmission and ignorance of the importance of hygiene exposed many to serious risk of disease and death.

Conclusions

The fields, pastures, woods, fens, marshes, heaths and moorlands that were the land of medieval England, and its rivers, ponds and seas supported a wide range of animals that was one of the country's major resources. Domestic livestock were economically the most important creatures, and provided not only food, but also agricultural labour, fertilizer and a range of other products that were utilized at home or could be exchanged or sold for cash. But the wild animals of the countryside were also an essential part of the economy. In fact, in comparison with earlier agricultural societies, the English medieval population greatly intensified its use of wild animals for food. Hunting and trapping wild animals were ways of gaining benefit from the natural environments, such as marshes, poor quality heathland and woodland, that were of limited value for domestic animals or crops, thus expanding the area of useful land. The two native wild deer species, the red and the roe, together with the introduced fallow deer and the rabbit were semi-domesticated, or at least 'managed'. Keeping these animals in enclosed parks, or in the case of rabbits, in specially constructed warrens, ensured that hunting expeditions had a much better chance of success than if the animals had been truly wild.

Much of the pressure for this expansion of resource exploitation must have been the increase in population during the twelfth and thirteenth centuries (p. 191). In earlier periods, domestic animals seem generally to have adequately supplied the food needs of the population, but the expanded arable land which was necessary to increase production of cereals and other vegetable food required regular ploughing and manuring, and wool was a vital product for the domestic and the international markets. Meat production thus often had to take a secondary role in the animal husbandry, but almost all animals were eventually eaten, including elderly animals that has been used for traction or had given many fleeces. Butchery evidence suggests that when they were killed, little of their carcasses was wasted (p. 162).

The attempt to use the available resources to the full was not entirely successful. The inability to bring about domestic livestock improvements, or even to maintain the value of the legacy handed down to them, can be seen as a failure by the agricultural population to realize the full benefits of its most important animal resource. In order to feed the increasing population, it was also necessary to start importing significant amounts of foodstuffs, mainly in the form of fish. Of course, an animal product, wool, was one of the export goods that allowed the possibility of participating in international trade.

If an expanding population provided the stimulus for an increased use of wild or semi-wild animals for food, there is little evidence for any decline in their importance as a result of the marked decrease in population numbers in the fourteenth century. In fact, in the later medieval period, a rise in the proportion of deer bones has been noted at some castles. There is a more general increase in bird bones but in particular a rise in the proportion of wild birds at the higher status sites. At this time these animals may have been valued even more as symbols of status than as necessary protein, since animal meat became a more widely available resource for all levels of society. Previously, pigs had been the only large domestic animal where the main aim of the husbandry had been the production of meat, but in this later period, this role began to be usurped by sheep and especially by cattle. The area and the quality of the land used for pasture increased, horses gradually replaced cattle for traction and the demand for meat rose on the urban market. The nature of the cattle husbandry began to change; a much higher proportion of the animals were now reared specifically for meat. Sheep husbandry remained one where both wool and meat were important products, but while pork seems to have declined in importance, lamb and, especially, mutton were providing an increased proportion of the diet by the end of our period (figure 8.2).

The broad trends of the archaeological record for animal husbandry obscure the many local variations and specializations that must have existed. The modern distribution of domestic animals shows large regional differences (Coppock 1964, 155), even though much food eaten by these animals is in the form of concentrates or imported food. Geology, soil type, climate and topography all put constraints on farming systems although these are rarely so severe as to allow no element of human choice, and practices such as transhumance allow the possibility of maximizing the available resources of an area (p. 217).

For early periods, differences in animal husbandry have been related to local topography and geology (Grant 1984a; King 1984). Attempts to identify regional patterns in the archaeological record for the medieval period have so far been unsuccessful although this may be largely due to a shortage of appropriate information. A significant proportion of the archaeological evidence for the rural economy consists of the remains of animals eaten in the towns but raised some considerable distance away and in a range of different environments. Animals may have been bred in one environment, raised in another and finally fattened for slaughter in a third (Thirsk 1957, 69; see p. 217). If more material from rural sites is recovered in the future it may be possible to map more closely the responses of the farmers to local conditions.

9

Human Resources

Richard Smith

In their approaches to the population of medieval England scholars in the fields of economic and social history have been primarily concerned with demographic quantities and in particular with the way in which growth and decline in numbers affected the exploitation of other, mainly inanimate resources. Somewhat less interest has been shown in people themselves although much ink has been spilt on the appropriation of men by men within the framework of such institutions as slavery and serfdom. There is a need to broaden the conventional treatment by considering behaviour that influenced fluctuations of medieval English populations. In doing this we must consider the question of regional variations in the intimate relationships between human, animal and inanimate resources rather than succumb to what has been termed the 'lure of aggregates' at the national level. The 'quality' of those populations as indicated by health and nutrition, and their value as human capital in terms of their productive capabilities as opposed to their needs as consumers, will be given some attention and in so far as we can regard the medieval human population as a potentially 'renewable' resource, we should assess its reproductive efficiency.

The role of population had figured prominently in the debate over the large-scale forces driving the processes of social and economic change and hence resource exploitation in this period (Aston and Philpin 1985). The ideas of Malthus have been both used and, very frequently, misused by the protagonists. Portrayed incorrectly by some historians as a demographic determinist, Malthus is more correctly regarded as an advocate of the view that population processes are to be seen as unequivocally 'secondary to economic resources' (Schofield and Wrigley 1986, 2). Medievalists have, however, given far greater attention to the more pessimistic aspects of Malthus's thoughts; they stress that demographic growth would come to outstrip resources and lead on inevitably to the operation of the 'positive' check as mortality rose in order to bring the relationship between agricultural and human resources back to an equilibrium (Bolton 1980, 56). In later editions of his *Essay* Malthus came to place increased emphasis upon the working of the 'preventive' check which involved an adjustment of fertility primarily through variations in the age and incidence of marriage (Wrigley 1986; Schofield 1986). These aspects of Malthus's thinking are rarely mentioned in the debates among medievalists. Furthermore, Malthus did not suppose that these adjustments would occur instantaneously because of the operation of what he termed 'interrupting causes' that he believed would 'not be remarked by superficial observers' (Malthus 1798, 30–6). Such arguments will receive some assessment, as will those of the school that regards mortality in pre-industrial societies as autonomously determined. The most sophisticated advocate of this position is Lee (1973; 1986), who sees both medieval and early modern English society distinguished by long and deep swings in population numbers, largely the product of the exogenous shifts in mortality, which served to determine the supply of labour power and hence the living standard.

The 'Lure of Aggregates': National Demographic Estimates

Unfortunately the evidence needed to test such thought-provoking theories is barely adequate. Medieval registration of vital events for, or censuses of, complete populations just do not exist or have not yet come to light. While demographic data come high on the list of historians' basic requirements when writing of medieval society, councils and parliaments '. . . rarely discussed population except in terms of fighting men or the numbers who managed to escape taxation' (Coleman 1976, 97). Even evidence that might be said to bear in a general way on population seems to have been poorly understood. For instance, when in March 1371, Parliament granted the King a subsidy of £50,000 it was to be levied at the cost of 22s and 3d on each parish. Such an estimate suggests a view that there were 45,000 parishes in England rather than the actual 9,000-odd, even though the information had been available in the subsidy returns held in the Exchequeur. The true number was subsequently discovered because within a few months the levy was raised to 116s per parish.

Nevertheless documentary sources available to English medieval historians, in contrast to their colleagues in continental Europe, permit the construction of plausible national population totals for a few individual years; Domesday Book and the Poll Taxes are sources for the estimation of national demographic totals for 1086 and 1377 respectively.

Domesday Book does not purport to be a head count, nor does it cover the whole of England; it omits the northern counties and is incomplete in its record for Lancashire. Important towns such as London, Winchester, Bristol and Southampton do not appear, nor do priests except in six counties. But what is most troublesome is that Domesday Book, while a quite remarkable resource inventory, is a list of tenants and not a register of population. Does the Domesday record include sub-tenants, and were the tenant land holdings occupied by just one or a number of households? Russell (1948, 51–4) argued that Domesday Book recorded all the landholders and that there was only one household for each holding.

However, doubt now exists over the completeness of the tenant-count in Domesday as in some areas King William's survey omitted about half the population (Walmsley 1968, 73–80). The compilers of the survey were principally interested in the demesne resources of estates and in particular, what such an estate was worth. Thus, if peasants paid rent, their contributions were likely to have been included in the total value. How generally such an argument can be applied across all English counties in Domesday is impossible to say. A rather different interpretation has been applied to other areas of the country where it is proposed that persons with no demesne connections whatsoever stood the best chance of being recorded (Harvey, S. P. J. 1976, 196).

We need next to consider the question of the social units to which these tenants belonged. Did each tenant represent a complete household or was he a member of a larger co-residential group? Even if Russell's (1948, 47) view that recorded Domesday Book tenants represented household heads is accepted, there are problems in estimating the mean household sizes to be used. Russell (1948; 1958; 1969; 1985) has always insisted on a low figure of 3.5 persons per household, while now majority opinion would prefer a group of 4.5 to 5.0. The spectrum of opinion leads to estimates of English population totals that range from as few as 1.1 to as many as 2.25 millions. Such estimates, of course, make no allowance for unenumerated tenants. Consequently some authorities would argue for a Domesday population of more than 2.5 millions (Hallam 1981, 247). Demographic estimates from Domesday Book may therefore lead to margins of error of 100 or 150 per cent.

Comparable exercises in informed 'guesswork' have been undertaken on the Poll Tax of 1377. In theory, there should be more confidence in the results of these calculations because those liable for tax were clearly specified; they were all lay persons with the exception of genuine paupers over the age of 14. The returns indicate that 1,386,196 taxpayers were netted in 1377 (Russell 1948, 146). Once again any estimate of total population from this evidence depends upon assumptions made on the age structure of the population, an assessment of the degree of evasion by eligible taxpayers and an estimate of those ineligible to pay. Using varying estimates of those under 14 of 33 to 50 per cent and levels of evasion and ineligibility of 5 to 25 per cent results in calculations of English population totals in 1377 of between 2.2 and 3 millions (Hatcher 1977, 13–14).

While making due allowance for all the margins of error there is apparently little evidence to show any net gain in population size from the late eleventh to the late fourteenth centuries. Of course, the demographic situation in 1377 was the product of changes that had occurred very largely in the course of the preceding

30 years with major epidemics of plague in 1348–49, 1360–62, 1369 and 1375. Current estimates of tenant deaths in manorial records suggest that by 1377 population may have fallen to a level some 40 to 50 per cent below that of 1348 when it most likely stood at 5 to 6 milions (see pp. 208–9). This level was not necessarily a maximum, for in certain parts of the country there had been substantial loss of population since the late thirteenth century (see pp. 192–3). Yet in other communities the population rose continuously until 1348–49. None the less there is every reason to accept an English population in 1300 of over 6 million. This was at least twice the level of the most expansive estimates for 1086 and was not to be attained again until the second half of the eighteenth century.

The most recent estimates for the early sixteenth century were produced using a variety of techniques and source materials. Parish registers, tax and muster returns have been used to show that England in the 1540s had a total population of between 2.8 and 3.1 million (Wrigley and Schofield 1931, 563–9). Such evidence suggests a national population in the 1540s that may have been little different from a widely favoured total for 1377.

Measuring Rates of Demographic Change

Population totals, estimated with considerable margins for error, hardly constitute the most stable foundations for an evaluation of long-term demographic behaviour. Do these estimates provide us with any sense both of the volatility of the population or of those 'oscillations' in numbers to which Malthus referred? Many continental scholars use a model of the whole pre-industrial epoch in which historical change is seen as a repetitive cycle, 'the respiration of an organism', periodically reaching a demographic ceiling. For France the ceiling is specified as a population total of *c*.20 million reached in 1300 and again in the seventeenth century (Le Roy Ladurie 1981, 1–27). The intervening period is interpreted as one that was ecologically and demographically 'near-stable', in contrast to the twelfth and thirteenth centuries which experienced 'real expansion'. Many would wish to interpret developments in England along similar lines, although account should be taken of the genuine possibility of oscillations in the preceding millennia on the scale of those occurring after 1300 (Dyer 1982, 33; Campbell 1981b, 123).

Our consideration of population dynamics between 1086 and 1540 has been confined to a review of the major cross-sectional snapshots that permit an enumeration of the population for an individual year. In using the term 'oscillation' we may be exaggerating the degree of regularity of the changes. In seeking to chart demographic movements over time most commentators have used indirect evidence such as movements in rents, prices and wages (Postan 1966, 561–70; 1973, 186–213; Blanchard 1970, 427–45). Others have used the size of agricultural holdings, the ratios of arable to pasture and evidence of the expansion, desertion and shrinkage of rural settlements (Taylor 1983). Such evidence can be ambiguous and capable only of suggesting, never conclusively proving, demographic trends. Because of the customary nature of prices and wages in particular, sequences based on them are unlikely to show short-term demographic change.

Continuous series of statistics reflecting population totals survive for only individual localities and for relatively short periods. There are none the less some remarkable recently discovered data for 13 Essex manors (Newton 1969, 543–6; Poos 1985, 515–30). They stretch from the late thirteenth into the early sixteenth centuries, and concern the totals of resident adult males registered in the proceedings of leet and manorial courts. In theory, all males of 12 and over who resided in the frankpledge jurisdiction (a community-based organ for policing and providing surety for good conduct) for at least a year and a day were required to be sworn into 'tithings'; in each of the Essex manors frankpledge jurisdiction was performed within a number of tithings each containing from five to twelve males (Poos 1985, 518). The tithing-members each paid annually a penny or a halfpenny and it is therefore possible to regard those sums of tithingpenny as a count of the resident adult males.

The figures in figure 9.1, taken from a selection of the better-documented manors, suggest that the decades around 1300 display no clear trend in population numbers. However, in the years of harvest deficiency between 1315 and 1317, there was a noticeable decline in numbers. The mean loss of resident males was approximately 15 per cent, in line with estimates using different evidence in other parts of the country (Poos 1985, 521; Kershaw 1973b, 11). The following three decades are marked by a sustained decline of almost 30 per cent until 1348–9, when population appears to have fallen by approximately 45 per cent. This death rate is corroborated in the court proceedings of other manors in the same area of Essex (Fisher 1943, 13–20). The scale of population decline may have been exaggerated, as local administration was temporarily thrown into disarray in the plague year itself and took some time to return to normal. The speed with which the adult population in some localities recovered to levels only 15 per cent below the pre-plague total suggests that a rise in fertility could not have been responsible, and immigration may have been a contributory factor. A temporary boost to fertility associated with a 'marriage boom' following the plague would not affect population totals of males over 12 years until after 1361. However, by the late 1360s population resumed the marked fall apparent in the decades preceding 1348–9, until the early decades of the fifteenth century. All manors stagnated for the remainder of the fifteenth century and growth is only once again apparent in the 1520s. After 1538 the tithingpenny totals can be compared with the parish registers and would appear to be in agreement. The series confirm that by the beginning of the sixteenth century population levels

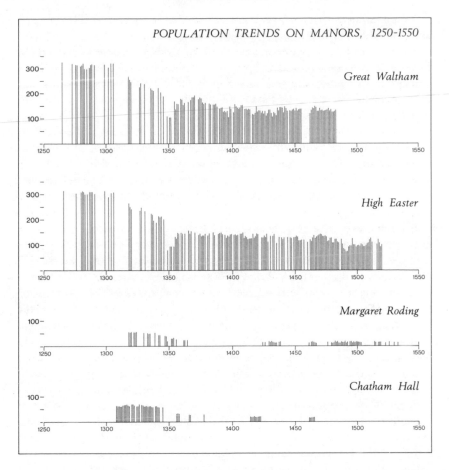

9.1 *Population trends on selected English manors 1250–1550*
(source: Poos 1983).

were well under one-half of those of two centuries earlier and that recovery coincided with the arrival of a systematic parochial registration of baptisms, burials and marriages. The vast bulk of the decline in numbers was confined to a period extending from 1315 to 1370, much of which occurred before plague became a factor. Decline seems to have been especially precipitous and growth, when it eventually got under way, seems to have been equally rapid. The evidence of the Essex manors rests quite comfortably with the national picture reconstructed from the chantry certificates and a sample of post-1538 parish registers which shows growth between the 1520s and 1540s at a rate of 0.8 per cent per annum (Wrigley and Schofield 1981, 568–9). The growth rate for the first quinquennium of the parish register era (1541–6) is estimated by Wrigley and Schofield (1981, 569) to be 0.86 per cent per annum.

Such rapid rates of population growth could rarely have been encountered at the national level for any sustained period since the thirteenth century, and direct demographic evidence is in very short supply for that earlier period when many of the economic signs suggest population growth was widespread. One data set, directly analogous with the tithingpenny series for late medieval Essex, relates to the Somerset manor of Taunton held by the Bishop of Winchester (Titow 1961, 218–23), but gives figures that err by under-estimating resident adult males at any given time. The resident male population more than doubled, from 506 in 1209 to 1359 in 1311, the year of its maximum value, but the rate of increase was much greater in the first two-thirds of the century than it was thereafter. The annual rate of growth between 1209 and 1268 was 1.3 per cent and only 0.5 per cent from 1269 to 1311. We would, however, be rash to suppose that everywhere in the early thirteenth century experienced growth in excess of 1 per cent per annum. Taunton's profile may well represent one of a number of chronologies of demographic change in post-Conquest England.

Other patterns have been suggested, but they are based on problematic techniques of estimation, such as the use of the numbers of males appearing in the proceedings of manorial courts. In Halesowen (Worcs.) adult male population totals show an annual rate of growth between 1270 and 1315 of 0.8 per cent, and while there was a 15 per cent drop in numbers between 1315 and 1321 (cf. Poos 1985, 521), growth was resumed again in the period from 1321 to 1349, but at only 0.4 per cent per annum (Razi 1980, 27–32). A similar technique has been used on the less complete court rolls from the Huntingdonshire manor of Broughton which showed a decline in the number of adult males at an annual average rate of 0.4 per cent from 1280 to the arrival of plague in 1349 (Britton 1977, 132–43). Another common method is to compare tenant numbers of manors at Domesday with those recorded in a later source such as the Hundred Rolls of 1279 or a manorial survey (Harley 1958). Hallam (1965, 197–222), using such an approach, found growth rates in the Lincolnshire silt fens from 1086 to 1300 varying between sixfold and sixty-twofold, which contrasts with a slower rate for the rest of the county.

Local ecological conditions and earlier settlement histories seem to lead to divergent experiences over quite short distances. In 1086 on the south Essex manor of Havering 87 tenants are recorded occupying a little over 2,000 ha; in 1251 the number of tenants had risen to 368, and by 1352/3 to 493 (McKintosh 1986, 126–30). McKintosh argues that population in 1352/3 stood at between 1,500 and 1,750, slightly below the 1,800 to 2,000 of 1251. Having made an allowance for a plague mortality of 33 per cent in 1348–49 she concludes that there was 'considerable growth after 1251'. Havering had been a lightly populated manor at Domesday and over 1,200 ha had been assarted between

1086 and 1251 with a further 400 ha added over the course of the following century.

The two manorial case studies of Halesowen and Havering suggest substantial net population growth in the later thirteenth and early fourteenth century. They are both communities distinguished by their relatively low population densities. In Halesowen a population at its maximum of close to 1,000 persons utilized 4,000 ha of land and at Havering in 1250 less than 2,000 persons had access to 2,000 ha of land, with a more diversified economy. Ratios of land to labour were more favourable than on the Essex manors of Great Waltham and High Easter (Poos 1985) and the Huntingdonshire manor of Broughton. Taunton (Titow 1962) seems to display a pattern intermediate between that of Halesowen and Havering on the one hand and the central Essex manors and Broughton on the other; those were anciently settled and lacking large reservoirs of land into which twelfth- and thirteenth-century colonisers could move. Taunton grew demographically, although increasingly slowly, until the second decade of the fourteenth century.

Another measure of population trends pioneered by Thrupp (1965), uses the numbers of surviving sons who are alive at their father's death to compute a replacement rate or ratio. It shows that, with the exception of the decade of agrarian crisis between 1310 and 1319, Halesowen families in the pre-plague period were able not only to replace themselves from generation to generation, but also to produce a surplus of offspring to maintain population growth (Razi 1980, 32–4).

Campbell (1984, 95–6), using replacement rates and the record of tenant numbers listed in surveys, concluded that on the Norfolk manor of Coltishall population growth took place until the Black Death struck in 1349, in spite of tenant-to-land ratios of almost 0.4 per ha and a population density approaching 200 per square km. Until the arrival of bubonic plague well over 60 per cent of fathers were survived by at least one son and demographic growth was assured (Campbell 1984, 98). In marked contrast, well before 1315 in the north Suffolk manors of Redgrave and Rickinghall, only 50 per cent of men had surviving sons as their heirs (Smith, R. M. 1984a, 49). Similarly, at Great Waltham and High Easter there was no detectable demographic growth before 1315, and marked decline in numbers between 1320 and 1348 (Poos 1985, 522; Smith, R. M. 1984a, 54).

It is evident that many English rural communities experienced turning points in their demography in the thirteenth and fourteenth centuries, but there was much variety in the timing and intensity of the shifts. We know more about the turning points between 1250 and 1349 than in earlier or later centuries. We have seen that the upturn in Essex was delayed until well into the sixteenth century, but we know little about the dates at which population decline ceased in the fifteenth century, or about the depth of the demographic trough. For the period after 1086 it is doubtful if the rapid growth rates over 0.5 per cent per annum found in the thirteenth century can be projected back to 1086. There are signs in the economy to suggest that continuous growth was unlikely. Although the scale of the seigneurial retrenchment in the mid-twelfth century is frequently disputed, few historians would doubt its existence (Bridbury 1978; Postan 1978). Economic change shows in contracting demesnes and a decline of labour services as well as the leasing-out of manors by lords (Miller 1966; 1971). In fact these 'tell-tale signs' are reminiscent of those of the late fourteenth century when a shrinkage of population is indisputable (Postan 1973, 186–213). Although the twelfth-century retrenchment occurs in the troubled context of Stephen's reign and is an ambiguous indicator of demographic decline, it is hardly evidence of a society with growing demand for land and produce (Hatcher 1981, 34).

The Spatial Distribution of People

Discussion of population geography is limited to three major cross-sections in the late eleventh, the late fourteenth and early sixteenth centuries. The Domesday survey suggests that the north with 1.5 to 2 inhabitants per square km was the most sparsely settled part of England. This is largely because the land was relatively infertile and inaccessible, as well as because of the devastation by Norman and Scottish armies (see figure 9.2). However, Miller and Hatcher (1978, 32) argue that between 1086 and the late thirteenth century, 'starting from low bases we find that these upland communities recorded the highest rates of growth in England'. The data presented by Russell (1948, 313) suggest that the population of Yorkshire in 1377 was seven times as large as it had been in 1086.

Darby (1977, 92–4) concluded that the median population density of Domesday England, excluding Lancashire and the four northernmost counties, was 2.5 per square km. The highest densities were almost invariably found south of a line from the Humber to the Severn. Exceptions are of course found in the marshlands, the areas of poor soils, coarse sands and gravels such as the Brecklands, the New Forest, the Dorset heathlands and the uplands of the south west. Within these regions were districts later to be royal forests such as Savernake in Wiltshire. There were especially dense concentrations of population in east Kent, coastal Sussex and the southern parts of the Lincolnshire wolds. The highest densities of all were those in East Anglia where parts of north-east Norfolk record over eight persons per square km, implying population densities of at least 39 persons per square km.

Certain scholars advocate caution in accepting such data at their face value; Sawyer (1976, 2–4; 1978, 136–8) warns against interpreting areas devoid of settlement in Domesday as if they were uninhabited. He shows that 400 places in Kent with churches are recorded in eleventh-century sources, of which 159 are

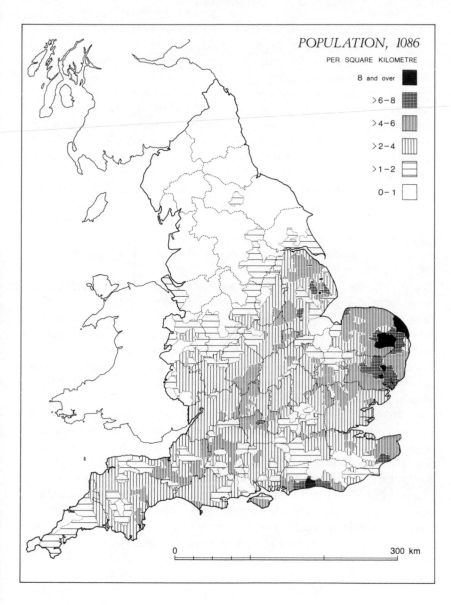

9.2   *Population in 1086*
(source: Darby 1977).

not even mentioned in Domesday Book. The Kentish Weald, like that of Sussex and Surrey, was an area of dispersed settlement with churches serving many separate farms and hamlets. The character of the Domesday inquest, with its tendency to focus upon estates rather than places, may well have depressed recorded population densities in areas of dispersed settlement.

Further doubts are raised by S. P. J. Harvey (1976, 196–8) who suggests that in areas such as the eastern counties, with numerous autonomous smallholders who would tend to be enumerated separately, a particularly complete inventory of tenants was achieved. Consequently the true differential in population density between the east of England and elsewhere is exaggerated, and estimates of population growth up to the later thirteenth century are too high for communities outside Eastern England.

However, the population geography derived from the Poll Tax of 1377 is very similar to that revealed by Domesday Book, even when due allowance is made for the possible shortcomings of the eleventh-century survey (Pelham 1936, 232; Baker 1973, 191).

The 1377 data demonstrate a contrast between those thinly populated areas north and west of a line drawn from York to the eastern border of Dorset, and those areas of higher densities to the south and east. This is a pattern highly reminiscent of the Domesday Survey, although there are differences, in particular the emergence of relatively high population densities in Bedfordshire, Northamptonshire, Leicestershire and Rutland. Similarly high population density in the Holland division of Lincolnshire linked this area to the still thickly peopled counties of Norfolk and Suffolk.

A large block of the east midlands, East Anglia and south-east England reached taxpayer densities in excess of 20 per square km, but the population density of Cambridgeshire, for example, is grossly distorted with the northern peat fenland very sparsely inhabited and most of the population resident within the southern, 'upland' area (Smith, C. T. 1965, 150).

Few areas of England in 1377 had population densities that exceeded 39 persons per square km. Despite the reduction in absolute population totals from their late thirteenth-century levels, the pattern may well have continued to reflect the earlier spatial arrangement. There were obviously substantial regional variations in population densities. The rich silt fens of south Lincolnshire were crammed with people, as they had been in the 1260s and 1270s (Hallam 1961, 73–7), and in Essex there was a thickly peopled belt in the central and northern parts of the county extending south from East Anglia (see figure 9.4). Taxpayer densities here frequently exceeded 20 per square km. Great Waltham which had by 1377 fallen to almost one-third of its population in 1300 still recorded 26 taxpayers per square km (Poos 1983, 36). In 1300 there would have been between 106 and 116 persons per square km, a level close to that prevailing at the time of the first census in 1801.

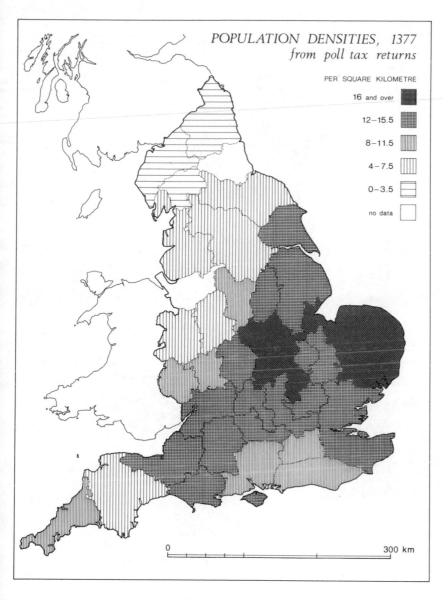

POPULATION DENSITIES, 1377
from poll tax returns

PER SQUARE KILOMETRE

16 and over

12–15.5

8–11.5

4–7.5

0–3.5

no data

0   300 km

9.3   *Population densities from the 1377 poll tax returns*
(source: Baker 1973).

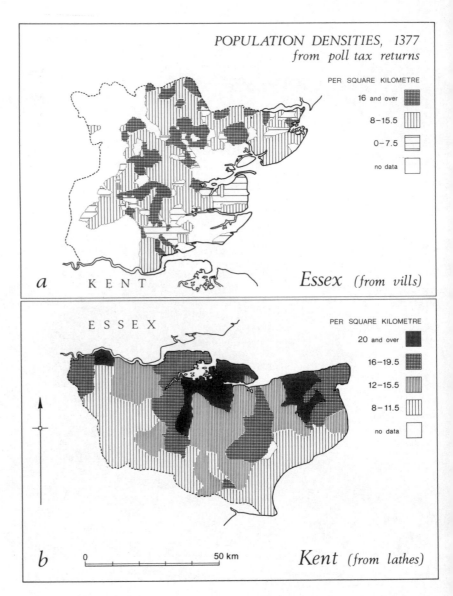

POPULATION DENSITIES, 1377
from poll tax returns

PER SQUARE KILOMETRE

16 and over

8–15.5

0–7.5

no data

a K E N T *Essex (from vills)*

E S S E X

PER SQUARE KILOMETRE

20 and over

16–19.5

12–15.5

8–11.5

no data

b 0 50 km *Kent (from lathes)*

9.4 *Poll tax population densities in 1377: evidence from English vills and lathes.*

In north-east and east Kent population densities were frequently in excess of 27 to 30 per square km, in marked contrast to the comparatively lightly populated parts of the downland parishes in the north-west of the county and the Weald, where fewer than 8 taxpayers per square km could be found (see figure 9.4).

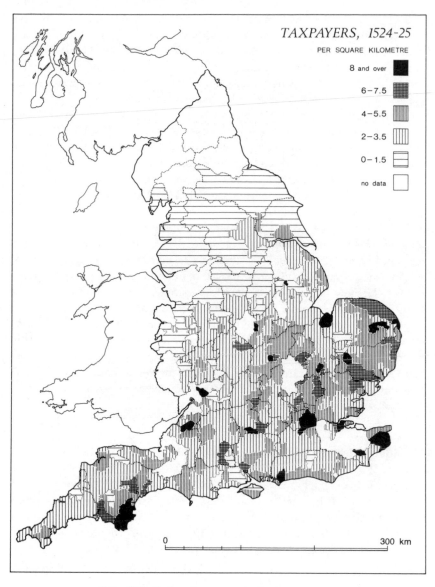

TAXPAYERS, 1524–25

PER SQUARE KILOMETRE

8 and over

6 – 7.5

4 – 5.5

2 – 3.5

0 – 1.5

no data

0   300 km

9.5   *Distribution of taxpayers in England 1524–25*
(source: Sheail 1972).

By 1377 rural areas with more than 39 persons per square km had become relatively rare, and by the 1520s these densities had fallen still further as national population had probably declined by an additional 700,000. The lay subsidy returns of 1524 and 1525 provide an indication of regional demographic patterns (Sheail 1972, 111–26; see figure 9.5) although they omit certain sections of the population. In the north of England substantial proportions of the population included in the other regions were excluded from taxation altogether (Hoskins 1976, 19; Campbell 1981a, 147–8). The east midlands, while still forming part of the more densely populated areas of the country, is no longer as prominent as it was in 1377. We also have a clearer sense that it was the eastern rather than western parts of Norfolk that contained the bulk of that county's population, confirming the patterns at the time of the Poll Tax. The most densely inhabited areas of Essex and Suffolk had come to be the cloth-producing communities in and around the valley of the river Stour. A similar diversification of economic activities in the mining and textile areas of Devon and Cornwall may have facilitated increased population densities here relative to other areas of England. A move away from agriculture and towards industry may also have increased relative densities in parts of Somerset, Gloucestershire and Wiltshire. The taxation data suggest that the south-western, eastern and south-eastern areas of England had increased their share of the population in the later middle ages, whereas between 1086 and the early fourteenth century it was the marshlands in the east and most of the north of England that had shown the highest demographic growth rates. However, the evidence deriving from taxation provides a questionable basis for measuring population and must be regarded with special caution.

Identifying the Malthusian 'Checks' between 1250 and 1348

The spatial demographic changes outlined above tend to treat northern and western regions of England as economically 'marginal' to the traditional 'core' area of the English economy, the south-east. The evidence of the spread of settlement and relatively rapid demographic growth within the 'margins' suggests to some that the thirteenth century was a period of demographic growth and that an increase in numbers was exceeding the capacity of the land to maintain living standards. Agricultural historians have debated the extent to which the process of demographic growth led to the use of poor quality soils with attendant loss of fertility and falling crop yields (p. 230). Demographic historians have considered the extent to which the cultivators themselves were punished for their 'reproductive success' or implied lack of demographic prudence. As with yield ratios or land abandonment, mortality has been employed as an indicator of the well-being of the nation's human capital. Commenting on the critical late thirteenth and early fourteenth centuries, Miller and Hatcher have stated that 'at birth even the children of gentry and noble families might on average have expected a life span of no more than 22–28 years' (Miller and Hatcher 1978, viii). Postan and Titow (1973, 150–85) also considered the relationship between heriots, that is death duties, usually the tenant's best animal, levied on the holdings of customary tenants, and grain prices. They showed that years of high prices such as 1258, 1272, 1289, 1297 and above all 1309–19 saw marked rises in the numbers of recorded deaths, especially among the poorer, animal-deficient tenants. Other studies can confirm such associations of heriots and prices in many other parts of England (Kershaw 1973b), but views do differ about the extent to which years of high prices invariably led to significant rises in mortality (for example, Campbell 1984; Hallam 1981).

Postan and Titow (1973, 159–64) attempted to go further and made efforts to compute crude death rates and life expectancies. In the early fourteenth century they suggest that the crude death rates on some manors (Taunton in Somerset, Fareham, Waltham and Meon in Hampshire and Wargrave in Berkshire) approached 70 to 75 per 1000. The reproductive capacity of most societies, as reflected in the birth rate, generally does not exceed 55 per 1000, thus such high levels of mortality would inevitably lead to severe demographic decline. What is more, a crude death rate of this order is equivalent to an expectation at birth of only 15 years. Doubts surround the methods of calculation which may have exaggerated the index of mortality (Ohlin 1974, 73–7).

Postan and Titow (1973, 181–3) also attempted to calculate life expectancies of tenants on entry into property. The interval between accession to land at age 20 and death declined from 24 years in the 1240s to 20 years or less in the first half of the fourteenth century. At Halesowen, Razi (1980, 34–45) calculated a life expectation at birth of 25 years for the period 1270–1349, which, while far less severe than Postan and Titow's estimate, is still suggestive of very harsh mortality. What is more, the evidence seems to suggest very considerable discrepancies between the life expectancies of tenants at age 20; the more substantial 'well-documented tenants' who died between 1300 and 1348 lived on average a further 30.2 years after entering land; poor tenants (those holding under a quarter virgate) lived a further 20.8 years; those almost destitute such as cottagers survived a further 10 years. It is, however, unclear whether the discrepancies are exaggerated because the poor were obliged to wait longer to acquire land than the sons of the better-off tenants (Poos and Smith 1984, 140–4).

Expectations of life at 20 of only 25 years imply male expectations of life of 18–22 years. However the calculation of expectations of life at birth from adult mortality is problematic. Work on European historical populations (Ohlin 1974, 68–9; Schofield and Wrigley 1979, 61–95) has shown that although societies might have adult mortalities that are comparable, their associated infant and child mortality rates may not be, and adult expectancies may underpredict life expectancy at birth by as much as ten years. Nor can it be assumed that life expectancy at age 25 for tenants-in-chief of the crown, estimated as 24.5 in 1250–1348 (Russell 1948, 178–88), is necessarily suggestive of infant mortality less than that of more humble levels of the population. We know from later centuries that among the upper classes infant mortality may have been considerably greater than among the masses because of the former's reluctance to breast feed and their use of wet nurses (Smith, R. M. 1978, 213).

The exceedingly low medieval life expectancies at birth are perhaps eight to ten years lower than comparable measurements for rural parishes in late Elizabethan and early Jacobean England, when real incomes were low (Wrigley and Schofield 1981, 230–1). Razi argues that the population of Halesowen, notwithstanding high mortality, managed an annual rate of growth of almost 0.5 per cent for much of the period from 1270 to 1348. This implies gross reproduction rates considerably in excess of those for sixteenth-century England – in short, a 'high pressure' demographic system in which high mortality is counterbalanced by high fertility. Accepting these basic demographic inter-relationships suggests that the turning point in demographic growth most likely derived from a severe rise in mortality. 'Positive checks' served therefore in this argument as the prime demographic determinant. Miller and Hatcher (1978, 244) view the period from 1315 to 1349 as one where 'the increased death rate may have reduced, however marginally, the intensity of consumer demand, and done something to damp down both competition for land and for employment by stabilizing or thinning the number of competitors'.

High death rates intensified by phases of harvest failure are of course central to Postan's model of demographic–economic change (Postan 1975, 33–4). Differential mortality contingent upon the intensification of social differences is fundamental to Razi's argument. In this approach the survival chances of the smallholders are poor. The strategies of social reproduction displayed by richer tenants is achieved largely through the colonization by the sons of wealthy tenants of holdings vacated by cottagers and smallholders who sold out or died without surviving offspring. This model implies far greater variation across the rural social strata in life expectancy than in fertility. It is reminiscent of Darwin's view of the animal world when he wrote of the gaps in the 'economy of nature' formed 'by thrusting out weaker ones' (Keynes 1983, 359–60). Adam Smith also thought that it was 'among the inferior ranks of people that the scantiness of subsistence can set limits to the further multiplication of the human species' by 'destroying a great part of the children which their fruitful marriages produce' (1863, 36).

Of course, the medieval demographer is restricted in his evaluation of Adam Smith's argument by not being able to study infant and child mortality. Evidence is however available for the mechanisms by which economic constraints on fertility served to limit demographic growth in the late thirteenth and early fourteenth centuries. There has been some interest in the possibility that birth-control by *coitus interruptus* became more common at the turn of the thirteenth century in a context of 'poverty, increasing numbers and concern about the problem' (Biller 1982, 20) in Western Europe. Texts written by churchmen, in their subject matter and tone, suggest the church's preoccupation with a widespread social problem. Unfortunately, the demographic data needed to identify such activities among the English medieval rural populace are hardly adequate for the task.

Homans (1941, 121–59) portrayed marriage among the customary tenantry of medieval England as unavailable to males until they had gained property, and he saw impartible inheritance as limiting the marital opportunities of male siblings of the designated heir. He showed that marriage was far from universal as they waited to inherit or, in some cases, met their side of a maintenance contract supporting their elderly parent(s).

Razi (1980, 50–7) and Britton (1976, 2–7) have established that non-inheriting sons in the thirteenth and fourteenth centuries did acquire property without waiting for their fathers to die or to retire. In Broughton 23 per cent of resident families between 1288 and 1340 had more than one son who managed to acquire property (Britton 1976, 4). Of the 290 Halesowen families who had two or more sons, in 140 cases two or more siblings are observed holding land simultaneously (Razi 1980, 57). Homans's distinctions between areas of England practising impartible and partible inheritance now seem to have been overdrawn and there were substantial divergences of theory from practice (Smith, R. M. 1984a, 46–52).

It has been argued that different inheritance practices exerted very distinctive effects on demographic behaviour. Impartible inheritance has been claimed to help sustain larger holdings and also to result in higher marital fertility through fewer marriages, and the permanent emigration of celibate males and spinsters. Partible inheritance is supposed to have led to a reduction in the size of holdings, higher levels of nuptiality and possibly lower marital fertility. Partible areas should therefore have had relatively high rural population densities and growth rates, since in principle all the male offspring could remain to marry, whereas impartible areas would have revealed lower population densities and near stationary demography as the landless either remained celibate or emigrated (Berkner 1976, 71–4).

It was not the death or retirement of an individual's father that mattered but any death or retirement. For many men would die or retire without direct offspring. In fact in stationary populations 40 per cent of men would be without sons and only approximately 28 per cent would have had two or more sons (Wrigley 1978, 235–54; Goody 1976, 86–98; Smith, R. M. 1984a 44–5). The prospects for 'surplus sons' of course deteriorated markedly when the population was growing, but there were always some opportunities for them in a system of impartibility through inheritance within a wider kin group, marriage to an heiress, or through leasing and purchasing land from men lacking heirs. Britton's and Razi's demonstration of successful acquisition of land by younger sons is not incompatible with impartibility, nor is it at odds with Homans's rule that marriage without land was socially unacceptable (Homans 1941, 144–59). It is not therefore necessarily the case that social practices would be fundamentally different in communities practising impartible and partible inheritance, especially if population growth was minimal. Surplus sons might move to holdings of other men just as co-heirs might rationalize their inheritances and avoid physical partition through sale by one sibling to another, and subsequent entry of the 'seller' into the land market (Smith, R. M. 1984b, 194).

The potential for fragmentation of holdings was obviously greater in areas of partible inheritance during periods of population growth. There were no obvious connections between inheritance practices and demographic growth rates. For example, customary tenants on the Suffolk manors of Redgrave and Rickinghall practised partible heritance (Smith, R. M. 1984a, 49), but between 1260 and 1320 demographic trends were similar to those on the Essex manors of Waltham and Easter where single-heir inheritance was the custom. Hallam (1958, 350–1) has suggested that multigeniture in the Lincolnshire Fens fostered particularly heavy concentrations of people. It is, however, difficult to observe any consistent association between partible inheritance and especially high levels of nuptiality between 1250 and 1349.

We have no clear sense of what these differing inheritance practices implied for female marriage chances. The evidence from the listings of the Prior of Spalding's serfs in Weston and Moulton (Hallam 1958) suggests that of the females over the age of five between 36 and 48 per cent and between 23 and 50 per cent respectively were married. For men the estimates lie between 32 and 50 and between 29 and 48 per cent respectively. There are good reasons for assuming that the marriage proportions for males and females fell between the two extremes (Smith, R. M. 1983a, 120–4). These listings omit those who were not serf land holders (that is, unattached labourers and servants), the least likely to be married.

Titow (1962, 7–9) has drawn attention to the effect of the pressure of demand for land on patterns of widow remarriage in rural communities. On the Bishop of Winchester's manor of Taunton from 1260 and 1315 between one-fifth and one-third of recorded villein marriages involved a widow remarrying, under the pressure of demand for land. Here the holding of the dead husband passed to the widow. Similar proportions are found among the villeins of the Cambridgeshire manor of Cottenham, even though the widow in theory forfeited her holding if she remarried (Smith, R. M. 1983b, 123–6; Ravensdale 1984, 218–20). However, in the early years of the fourteenth century remarriage with land seems to have been the dominant form of property transfer among the Cottenham villeinage. Between 1300 and 1320 approximately half the recorded marriages were of widows with land, but by 1348 only 25 per cent of recorded marriages were of this nature. The decline in the remarriage of widows continued after 1350, and was associated with an increasing incidence of retirements of widows and surrenders of holdings to the use of others who may or may not have been kin.

Over the course of the fourteenth century entry into marriage seems to have become easier with declining pressure of population on resources. In the late thirteenth and fourteenth century, lightly populated areas with less demand for land, such as on the manor of Thornbury in the unhealthy marshes of Severnside, experienced lower levels of widow remarriage (Franklin 1986).

Geographical variations and chronological fluctuations of the kind we have just described are to be expected in a society in which entry into marriage was conditional upon economic independence on the part of the newly married. In the late sixteenth century, the evidence suggests that a high proportion of all marriages were remarriages; this period has in common with the early fourteenth century severe 'land hunger' and falling living standards (Smith, R. M. 1979, 95).

Historical demographers working on English society after 1538 have shown that late female marriage and the muted fertility levels associated with it are central to an understanding of how demographic growth rates could be effectively depressed. Hajnal (1965) originated the phrase 'European Marriage Pattern' to describe a regime in which mean marriage ages for both sexes were relatively late and substantial numbers of men and women never married at all. This pattern created comparatively low upper levels of fertility and unless growth rates were to diverge greatly from zero per cent per annum these fertility rates had to co-exist with moderate levels of mortality (Wrigley 1987).

Estimates of life expectation at birth and older ages made by Postan, Titow and Razi for the century before the Black Death would imply fertility levels one to one and half times higher than those found in Elizabethan England. Razi (1980, 45–71) does indeed argue that the Halesowen peasants practised a 'non-European' pattern of marriage, using three major lines of argument. His denial of Homans's view that impartible inheritance severely hindered the marriage prospects of non-inheriting siblings relates primarily to male marriage chances, and therefore bears little on the critical issue of female marriage.

Attempting an estimate of generational length and thus marriage age, Razi shows that some men married at 20, but his findings are dependent upon the acceptance of his methodology and the assumption that the legal age of majority is indistinguishable from the age of property acquisition (Razi 1980, 83; Smith, R. M. 1986b, 170–2; Poos and Smith 1984, 146–8; Williams 1984, 12–14).

Razi also argues that the high levels of extra-marital pregnancy prevalent among Halesowen females before 1349 suggest a high level of fertility associated with a casual attitude to marriage. To measure illegitimacy he (1980, 64–71) employs a controversial definition of *leyrwite*, which he interprets to mean an extra-marital pregnancy rather than an extra-marital fornication.

High levels of illegitimacy are not necessarily the hallmark of an early-marrying society, although there is in early modern England a remarkable inverse relationship between the illegitimacy rate and marriage age and proportions never marrying (Smith, R. M. 1986a, 78–98). In this period a particular variant of the European marriage pattern was firmly in place. As in the consideration of widow remarriage, a broader comparison with ostensibly non-European marriage systems would show that low illegitimacy and early and near-universal female marriage usually co-existed.

Demographic Trends 1350–1530: the 'Golden Age of Bacteria'?

While the debate on demographic behaviour at the turn of the thirteenth century is in its pioneering stage a consensus is unlikely, but there is a measure of agreement as to what forces were responsible for generating change after 1349.

In 1348, the Black Death, a plague epidemic of particularly ferocious character, arrived in England, having moved swiftly across Europe (Biraben 1975, 87–91). Historians differ in their estimates of the death toll in England, but some calculations suggest that 25 to 40 per cent of the population perished (Hatcher 1977, 21–5). Further epidemics, in particular those of 1361, 1369 and 1375, also exacted a sizable death toll. The frequent recurrence of plague throughout the fifteenth century made it a major determinant of national demographic trends. It is not surprising that one historian should define this period as the 'golden age of bacteria' (Thrupp 1965, 118).

However, Morris (1977, 37–48) has argued that clinical bubonic plague could develop secondary pneumonic complications, thereby facilitating transmission of bacilli by droplet infection between humans. Pneumonic plague mortality thus might have been exceptionally severe with little participation from the indigenous rat population, especially in the epidemic of 1348–9 (Poos 1981, 229). Twigg (1984) has offered another 'heretical' interpretation of the cause of death in 1348–9 which, because of the speed of the disease's transmission, he prefers to see as an air-borne pathogen, constituting Europe's first exposure to anthrax. But since anthrax is a disease which strikes both man and beast, this theory is undermined by the absence of detectable abnormal mortality among demesne livestock (Campbell 1985, 314).

If there still remains room for doubt as to the cause of mortality in 1348–9, there is an emerging consensus concerning its scale. Tenant deaths at Waltham and High Easter in Essex suggest a probable mortality rate of around 50 per cent (Poos 1983, 107–13). This level of mortality is confirmed for Halesowen, for Cottenham in Cambridgeshire, and for the manors of the Bishop of Worcester

(Razi 1980, 98–110; Ravensdale 1984, 198; Dyer 1980, 218–43). The detailed investigations of tenants imply a very infectious form of disease which seems to have killed indiscriminately, placing large and smallholders at equal risk (Poos 1983, 114–15; Ravensdale 1984, 199). England's population was dealt a blow of enormous force with loss of life on a scale that has not since been experienced.

Opinions differ concerning the role of the plague as a demographic agent over the course of the following 150 to 175 years. Hatcher (1977, 15–25) argues that plague became endemic in England in the late fourteenth and fifteenth centuries, and also suggests that after 1375 England experienced at least 15 outbreaks of plague and of other epidemic diseases of national or extra-regional proportions. This pattern of fifteenth-century epidemic mortality appears to be borne out by extensive analysis of wills from Norfolk, Suffolk, Hertfordshire and London in the period 1430–80 (Gottfried 1977, 127–8). Peaks in mortality coincide with periods of epidemic disease reported in the narrative sources for the period.

The seasonal pattern of deaths has been used as a basis for arguing the case that late medieval plague was endemic. In bubonic plague, the seasonal pattern is determined by biological factors affecting rats and fleas, their feeding habits and reactions to changes in temperature and humidity. Bubonic plague therefore tends to be a disease of the late summer and early autumn; Gottfried's evidence partly accords with a seasonal pattern of high autumn indices throughout the fifteenth century, although it is possible that the method he uses to interpret the evidence could have helped to create such an effect.

However analysis of deaths of manorial tenants at Waltham and High Easter displayed a late winter–spring peak very similar to that found among deaths of the tenants-in-chief (Poos 1983, 121–3, 129–34).

Hatcher (1986) has recently demonstrated that among the monks of Christchurch, Canterbury there was a particularly severe mortality regime in the second half of the fifteenth century, the years 1457, 1471 and 1485 being outstanding. Perhaps 25 to 30 per cent of the monks died from plague, although over the period of particularly low life expectancy from 1485 to 1507 tuberculosis is the cause of death most frequently identified. Hatcher stresses how well cared for were the monks, which tempts one to perceive the English population as in the vice-like grip of a mortality regime that paid little attention to the state of individual well-being.

No rational observer would wish to underestimate the extent to which the nation's demographic fabric was undermined by these outbreaks of disease in the century and a half from 1349. However, there is now a steady accumulation of evidence indicating that demographic growth had faltered in many communities for more than two generations before the arrival of plague in 1349, warning against the acceptance of any one single factor as the explanation of fourteenth-century demographic change. Furthermore, recovery may have been a good deal swifter and earlier in many parts of Europe than in England (Smith, R. M.

forthcoming). We have no reason to suppose that such differences derived solely from geographical variations in the severity of epidemic disease.

It is useful to consider certain conditions that held in the seventeenth century. That period saw a substantial deterioration in life expectancy, but it would seem that fertility reacted to that change in a perverse manner. Indeed the response of fertility exacerbated the effects of lowered life expectancy upon national rates of population growth when rising real incomes and labour shortages should have made marriage and household formation easier. In the fifteenth century rising mortality and real wages also prevailed. What was their impact on fertility?

It is sometimes stated that changes in fertility could not have had any significant influence on the rate of population growth because fertility was already high and incapable of rising higher. Hatcher (1977, 56–7) adopts the view that because in the later middle ages women already married at or close to puberty they had no opportunity to enhance their reproductive activity by marrying even earlier, and Hajnal (1965, 116–20) has argued that in the later fourteenth century England most likely possessed a pattern of non-European marriage. To support this view, he uses Russell's (1948, 148–53) analysis of the 1377 Poll Tax returns to show that 60 to 70 per cent of women over the age 14 were married.

However, we can detect many factors, especially tax evasion and exemption on grounds of poverty, which are likely to have eroded the numbers of unmarried women recorded on the tax lists (Smith, R. M. 1979, 1983a; Fenwick 1983). It can be argued that under 60 per cent of women were married, suggesting a marriage regime of decidedly 'European' character.

The significance of servants in late-marriage regimes has recently been recognised by Hajnal (1982). Service was a stage in the life-cycle of young persons between the natal hearth and their household of marriage. In Rutland in 1377 20 per cent of households contained them (Smith, R. M. 1981) and comparable proportions occur in Gloucestershire in 1381 (Hilton 1974, 112–13; 1975, 76).

Agrarian service in early modern England reached its maximum extent in periods of labour shortage, (that is in the late seventeenth and early eighteenth centuries), when there was a move away from grain farming towards pastoral activities. In periods of rising wages and low prices farmers were likely to prefer a dependable, live-in full-time labour force, hired on annual contracts, especially if livestock were kept. Servant-keeping was also practised on a large scale in the late fourteenth century and it may have increased still further as the population contined to fall and wages rose (Kussmaul 1981, 97–119). This institution may have served to keep young adults out of marriage since for live-in labour, celibacy was a pre-requisite.

The occupational evidence in the 1381 Poll Tax for both urban and rural communities indicates a substantial number of single women working in trades that might be thought to have been male preserves, such as smithing, tanning, carpentry and tiling (Smith, R. M. forthcoming). They are a feature of towns, most of which were numerically dominated by women. For instance, most towns had between 90 and 95 men for every 100 women over the age of 14 or 15 years, and this figure is likely to be a maximum because of the tendency of women to evade, or frequently to be exempted from, tax (Goldberg 1986; in press). In the post-Black Death era periods of quite acute labour shortage resulted in a high level of female migration to towns. Urban employment for women provided them with opportunities outside marriage; it also had the effect of concentrating them geographically, which reduced their marriage chances.

These enquiries into female employment may provide a key to the explanation of why a worsening in life expectancy at least before 1450 was exacerbated in its effects by the diversion of women from marriage into the labour force (Penn 1987).

Conclusion

Identification of the driving forces behind medieval rural demographic growth remains elusive. While reasons were given as to why the exact extent of demographic growth between 1086 and 1300 may have been exaggerated because of the under-enumeration of the eleventh-century population, growth did occur to such an extent that numbers doubled. Some would stress the role of a set of endogenous technological changes associated with the advent of the stirrup, the heavy plough, horsepower, the shift from two to three course rotation, and the introduction of legumes in agriculture (Langdon 1986a, 288–9). Others, however, following Boserup (1965; 1981), reverse the causal relationship and suggest that agricultural intensification resulted from demographic growth. These arguments about the relationship between population and rural resources regard demographic growth as fundamentally exogenous. Boserup herself believes that populations waxed and waned in the past largely because of shifts in mortality. She writes (1981, 94–5) 'that the decline and stagnation of population in most of the first millennium AD was due to the ravages of major epidemics . . .' and suggests that the slow growth between the ninth and fourteenth centuries was a return to a 'normal' pattern.

Malthus, in contrast to Boserup, did see both mortality and fertility as endogenously determined (Wrigley 1983). Lee (1973, 1986) however characterized pre-industrial England as possessed of a demographic system that was driven by exogenously determined mortality which in turn affected the supply of manpower and set the level of real incomes per capita. Fertility ultimately responded to these mortality-induced real income changes much in the way proposed by Malthus. This approach sees the growth in population between the tenth and the late thirteenth centuries in terms of major improvements in the disease environment but brought to a halt by a fall in fertility and a rise in mortality as harvests failed more frequently and numbers pressed on agrarian resources. Such variations as there were in the chronology across England might have depended on the particular local circumstances which may help to explain why certain places continued to register demographic growth well into the fourteenth century and others exhibited stagnation and decline long before.

Lee's (1986) theory can explain demographic decline in the later middle ages as exogenously determined mortality rose once again driving numbers down and wages up to such a degree that eventually a positive fertility response engendered population growth. There is still much to do to identify what might be perceived as Malthusian 'interrupting causes' that stood in the way of the immediate recovery of demographic equilibrium. Did a set of medieval institutions work to delay the onset of fertility decline in the later thirteenth century when economic conditions were deteriorating for the broad mass of the population? What features for example, of the lord–tenant relationship could have served to stimulate fertility or to minimize its reduction? What features of serfdom were pro-natalist in their effects? Did the growth of direct cultivation of demesnes enhance the demand for wage labour and thereby fertility? Did the growth of grain farming and the relative decline in livestock husbandry within the peasant sector reduce the incidence of agrarian service? Conversely, what features of later medieval society served to lower fertility when mortality itself worsened? It is likely that the European Marriage Pattern was firmly in place, together with other necessarily attendant features of the social structure such as a system of life-cycle service, limited sex-segmentation of the labour force, a set of legal institutions that provided a reasonably secure environment within which women could be independently economically active and a degree of geographical mobility for both sexes. We may thus have identified those institutions that were catalytic in securing both a decline in nuptiality as real incomes rose and its intensification as living standards passed their peak after 1450. Such speculative thoughts are still compatible with a mortality-driven model of demographic change, but a model within which there is a larger place for institutions and their reactions to the demographic shifts so created.

10

The Medieval Countryside: Efficiency, Progress and Change

Grenville Astill and Annie Grant

Efficiency and Productivity

Earlier discussion has emphasized the relatively low levels of plant and animal yields (pp. 29, 164, 176). Useful as modern figures are as a point of reference, the productivity of medieval land, plants and animals cannot be judged solely by the standards of contemporary western agriculture. Dramatic increases in the productivity of land in recent times have only been made possible by mechanization, intensive use of artifical fertilizers and improvements in animal and plant breeds that were not possible with contemporary knowledge of the mechanisms of reproduction and inheritance. What is of interest is whether yields were as good as they could have been, given the resources and knowledge available at the time. This is inevitably a more difficult question to answer, but we can approach it by looking at three of the elements that have led to modern 'success'. Firstly, there is mechanization, principally affecting crop rather than animal husbandry. The main advantages of some form of mechanization in the cultivation of land are clear. Ploughing, for example, increases the depth of soil that can be turned and the speed with which the operation may be carried out. Limitations on the potential for mechanization at any point in time include the legacy of the past and current technological skills. Langdon's assessment here of agricultural equipment concludes that 'tool development during the middle ages tended to stagnate, at least in relation to the periods which preceded or followed (p. 107), although some developments in plough technology can be charted (p.89).

In other spheres of technology some have claimed greater progress. Gimpel's view is that 'the Middle Ages introduced machinery into Europe on a scale no civilization had previously known' (1977, 1). The most common and ubiquitous of these machines was the mill, which harnessed the power of wind, rivers and even the tides and used it not only for the grinding of corn, but for a wide range of other processes, including metal working, water pumping, cloth fulling and beer making. However, many of the technological developments in mill mechanisms had been made long before the medieval period and there was a substantial legacy of technological knowledge handed down to the medieval engineers. Their main contribution to agriculture seems to have been in the application and adaptation of existing knowledge. The importance of this contribution should not, however, be minimized. There is impressive evidence of water engineering, not only in marsh- and fenlands but also in the wet claylands, which enabled these inhospitable lands to be colonized.

Animals were another essential source of power in our period. Cattle had been used for heavy traction since prehistoric times, but by our period the invention of the rigid collar also made it possible for horses to pull heavy loads (Langdon 1986a, 8). Despite the horse's qualities of strength, stamina, longevity, versatility and tractability, there was a widespread prejudice against the use of horses in agriculture, justified principally by the increased expense of keeping them in preference to oxen (Oschinsky 1971, 319; Langdon 1982). By the fifteenth century, however, there was a significant increase in the use of horses for ploughing. This is consistent with a modest increase in crop yields, although it is not clear if there was any causal relationship (Langdon 1986a, 278).

It is difficult to assess the influence that the availability of raw materials had on the development of technology, but it does not seem to have been a major limitation. Most machines, tools and implements were made of wood and iron. While iron was expensive, it was obtainable, and even in the later medieval period large timbers still seem to have been available (p. 54).

The second important element, the replenishment of the nutrients taken from the soil by the growing of crops, was clearly understood. Animal manure, lime and marl were all used in attempts to improve fertility and soil condition (p. 26). Practices such as the folding of sheep on arable land and the carting to the fields of manure produced by stalled animals were adopted, although inevitably much was lost for crop husbandry when animals grazed pastureland and pigs were driven into forested areas to forage. Vast quantities of human and animal manure were produced in the towns, and some industrial waste and butchery debris could also be used as fertilizer. Although there are records of the carting of such debris from the towns to the surrounding fields and even of the purchase of urban muck, much was dumped inappropriately and wastefully, causing nuisance, health risks and pollution (Keene 1982, 28; Sabine 1934).

The major problem however seems to have been that the balance of crops and animals in many parts of England was such that there was just not enough manure produced to fertilize the cultivated land adequately (p. 31). It has been suggested that regular manuring would have been possible only for the land nearest to the settlements, and even there we do not know if the quantities available were really sufficient to maintain an optimum level of fertility. The islanders of St Kilda in the nineteenth century are recorded as having taken infinite pains to utilize all possible sources of fertilizer for their fields, yet, despite the laborious digging in of fertilizer and meticulous hand weeding, the yields of the plots declined dramatically as they became overworked until the crops were 'scarcely worth the trouble of lifting' (Steel 1975, 89).

Archaeobotanical evidence has suggested that weed infestation may have been a significant problem in the medieval period (p. 114), although the appearance of a new type of weeding tool shows that some attention was given to this problem (p. 99; figure 2.4), and fallowland was ploughed to kill weeds (p. 20). The addition to muck heaps of manure, vegetable matter and weedy straw used for animal bedding may have constantly recirculated the weed seeds back on to the fields. Further attempts to improve soil fertility have been documented for the later medieval period, including the sowing of legumes or grass on land previously left fallow (Dyer 1981, 28). The grass was first grazed by livestock and then ploughed in. However, there is little direct evidence to show whether there were any real improvements in yields as a result (Dyer 1981, 30).

The third element that is important in ensuring success in farming lies in the crops cultivated and the animals kept. The main field crops being grown at the end of the medieval period were very little different from those that were cultivated at the start of our period. The major changes in the range and type of crops grown in the pre-modern era seem to have occurred in the first millennium BC and the yields obtained from these crops in Roman times may have been greater than in our period (Jones 1981, 97–110, 114). Although related to modern cereals, the varieties grown in these early periods are 'primitive' strains, whose productivity could not be expected to match that of the modern hybrids. However, experiments in the growing of primitive cereals using simple agricultural techniques have shown that it is possible to produce yields far higher than those documented for classical Europe and medieval England (Reynolds 1981, 24–36; Jones 1981, 114).

Archaeological evidence for the domestic livestock has demonstrated a significant reduction in animal size, and thus productivity, at least in relation to meat yield, from the Roman to the medieval period, and yet in the early modern period there was an increase that cannot be entirely accounted for by the introduction of new breeds (Armitage 1982). Poor animal nutrition may have been at least as important a determinant of animal size as their genetic potential (p. 177).

We cannot blame the medieval farmers for misunderstanding the mechanisms of genetic inheritance. False notions about conception and breeding have been confidently expressed in very recent times (Stebbings 1982, 29). However, the failure to bring about livestock improvements cannot be entirely excused on the grounds of ignorance. Some of the general principles of animal breeding were understood. For example, attempts were made to improve local sheep stock by bringing in rams from other areas (p. 29). However, we must also acknowledge that the most highly valued product of sheep farming was not meat but wool. Animals were not valued for their conformation, but the quality of their wool, and some of the fleeces produced by English sheep were valued on the international market as the best obtainable.

The attitudes and motivations of the human population have a significant effect on productivity, particularly in farming systems that are labour intensive. One must question the efficiency of a system where many of the resources of skill and knowledge lay in the hands of the peasantry, but many of the profits of their endeavours were taken from them by the landowners.

We are left with a slightly depressing picture of medieval agricultural progress and productivity, which suggests that opportunities for improvement may have existed but were not taken up. There was, however, a series of small-scale agricultural innovations in the later middle ages that laid important foundations for the Agricultural Revolution. The new practices, which included the growing of more legumes, intensive animal folding on fields, thicker sowing of seed corn and a greater emphasis on spring-grown cereals, have in the past been regarded as having little impact, but recent work suggests that they led to greater productivity (Campbell 1983a; Dyer 1981; Langdon 1986a).

Precautions against Failure

Real and often insuperable difficulties for the medieval farmer lay in the natural hazards of climate and plant, animal and human disease which were even more difficult to counteract or compensate for than they are today. The early decades of the fourteenth century were noted for their bad weather and many harvests failed to ripen, yields were even lower than usual and the incidence of 'murrains' in animal flocks and herds increased. This was followed by the devastating epidemics of plague in the human population. The effects of the crop failures and animal diseases were largely simple, direct and mostly immediate – there was a substantial drop in food production and in the many byproducts of farming, resulting in starvation and also rising prices for a wide range of goods. Recovery, however, could in some circumstances be relatively rapid. As long as there was sufficient seed corn available, a poor harvest in one year could be followed by a very good one (Kershaw 1973b, 15). However, in times of acute hardship, peasants were forced to eat their seed corn and their plough animals, leaving them then in a hopeless position (Hanawalt 1986, 112).

The most common cause of animal death was recorded as 'murrain'. In reality, this term is likely to have been used to describe many different diseases recognized by modern veterinary medicine (p. 154). Attempts were made to control, cure and prevent animal disease, some of which were not without some beneficial effect, despite a fundamental ignorance of the causes of most diseases. For example, animals that died of murrain were burnt, and their heads placed on stakes to tell travellers to avoid the area. Today, farms with foot and mouth disease are sealed off, and the affected animals slaughtered and buried. However, the medieval farmer did not know about disinfection, nor that the disease could be spread by carrion crows feeding on the infected carcasses (Hartley 1979, 83).

Estate records show a massive reduction in flock size in the early years of the fourteenth century, but also a relatively rapid return to earlier levels. For example, at Bolton Priory the size of the sheep flock fell by two-thirds in 1315–16, but had recovered half of that loss within the following six years (Kershaw 1973a, 80). However, such rapid growth would not have been possible merely by reproduction within the flock and there must have been much redistribution of sheep in this period.

The effects of the losses to the human population were perhaps far more complex and, in addition, recovery was extremely slow (p. 191). Increased human mortality rates in the fourteenth century affected not only total population levels, but also family size, and thus the ratio between workers and consumers. The effects of changing family size are not clear-cut. When there is plenty of opportunity for productive employment, large families may be at an advantage. However, when such opportunties are limited, smaller families may be more viable.

What mechanisms were employed to try to counteract endemic low productivity and the more catastrophic losses resulting from disease and bad weather? One solution to the problem of low yields is to increase the area under cultivation and this seems to have been a strategy adopted in the early part of our period. However, the consequent decrease in the amount of good pasture land available for grazing may have encouraged overgrazing and increased the vulnerability of the animal population to disease (p. 154). Any reduction in animal numbers will have reduced the amount of manure available.

Another strategy adopted seems to have been a diversification of exploited resources. There was not only an expansion of arable land onto areas that had previously been used for pasture, but also an increased exploitation of marginal land. But resources were also over-used, and attempts were made to prevent this by such practices as 'stinting' (p. 31) or even the total exclusion of some animals from woods in an attempt to ensure regeneration of these valuable areas (p. 133).

Transhumance is an ancient solution to the problem of feeding animals where pasture is restricted or seasonal. The classic transhumance, the movement of animals in the spring from the plain to upland grazing is associated with a mediterranean climate or mountainous regions, but transhumant movements can also be in the reverse direction or involve no significant change of altitude at all (Brisbarre 1978, 49). There was considerable movement of animals in England in our period, not only in the classical tradition from valley to upland areas in the summer, but also from manor to manor, to marshland areas, and to wooded areas for sheep and cattle grazing and the autumn feeding of pigs, in order to maximize the use of the natural assets of these areas (p. 29).

The exploitation of different environments allowed access to a range of resources, but there were some measures taken that were more directly concerned with spreading the risks of failure. The division of open fields into blocks of strips meant that landholdings were widely distributed over all the soil types, drainage conditions and aspects of each cultivated area. In most regions a range of crops was grown, including some that were autumn- and some that were spring-sown (p. 112). This not only decreased the risk of complete crop failure, but also spread the labour requirements more evenly through the year – very important when it became scarce in the post-Black Death era. The change to an agricultural economy with a larger pastoral element can be viewed as a solution to the shortage of manpower in the later medieval period as animal husbandry is less labour intensive than crop growing, and the labour requirements are more evenly distributed. A feature of the archaeological evidence for animals in the medieval period that has already been stressed is the vastly increased range of animals utilized for food (p. 170). The domestic animals are the same as those of the previous millennium, but there is a much more intensive exploitation of domestic birds and of a range of wild animals.

Diversification seems to have been one strategy adopted to try to spread the risk of failure, but in some areas, especially those where the topography and climate did not allow the same range of land use, an alternative strategy, that of specialization, was adopted. The large-scale sheep farming, particularly associated with the religious communities in the northern counties, is the obvious example and was particularly effective in areas where a relatively sparse population had access to large amounts of land. However, there was rarely, if ever, complete reliance on a single agricultural product and even where there were very large sheep flocks the other domestic animals were also kept and a range of crops was grown. Some resources, previously widely available, did become scarce by the later part of our period. For example, as local timber supplies were exhausted, communities became dependent on outside supply (pp. 40, 137; figure 7.4). Specialization can only be effective when there is a well-developed system of exchange or an established market economy (pp. 31–3). As a strategy for survival, it is clearly very vulnerable, both to failures in production and to fluctuations in market value. A buffer can be provided if the product can be stored and storage is possible in many different ways. The keeping of animals as a source of food may have disadvantages in terms of the energy loss at their higher trophic level, but they do have the advantage over seasonal vegetable products in that as long as they can be kept alive, even if only in a thin and mangy state, they may be rapidly fattened up with a sudden flush of grass or the surplus from an unexpectedly good harvest.

Live animals could serve as stores of food, but it was also possible to preserve their meat by salting, drying or smoking. Salting is one of the most suitable methods in a damp climate, but the procurement of salt in most inland areas depended on there being something to give or sell in exchange. Salting was a very common method of preservation for fish – here there is the advantage that the source of the food and the means of its preservation are one and the same. One of the major salt-producing regions of England was the area around the Wash, and there is evidence of considerable expansion of the industry in the twelfth century, both for home use and to supply the demands of the North Sea fisheries (Carus-Wilson 1962–3, 187). By the thirteenth century the home demand could not be satisfied by native salt production and it became necessary to import French salt, produced along the Atlantic coast (Wilson, C. A. 1984, 38).

Storage of cereal products creates difficulties: they are highly susceptible to bacterial and fungal decay and infestation by insects and small animals; they are bulky and require a considerable investment in sound structures for good preservation. The storage facilities in most peasant tofts were limited (p. 56), and prior claims had to be made for essential items such as seed corn, winter fodder for animals and agricultural equipment. When an agricultural surplus was produced it was usually sold rather than stored. There is, however, evidence in some excavated tofts of the later medieval period for an increase in the number

10.1   *Caldecote, Hertfordshire. The excavation of a fifteenth-century toft. The house is in the centre with a large barn on each side. Inside the barn on the left is a corn-drying kiln. The scale has one foot divisions*
(photo G. Beresford).

and size of outbuildings, unrelated to any apparent change in the size of the household, together with, in some examples, corn drying kilns (figure 10.1; Astill 1983, 232–4). Thorough drying of the corn in these kilns would enable it to be stored for a longer period so that it could either be sold at the best price or saved for eating in years when harvests were poor.

Most of the methods of preservation available for animal and plant foods would not allow indefinite or even very long-term storage, but they were none the less important in allowing the possibility of distributing the products of farming more evenly throughout the year. And they allowed the produce to be traded over long distances – this was particularly important for fish, which was both imported from distant Scandinavian and Icelandic ports and exported from England to other European countries (Carus-Wilson 1962–3).

The storage of non-perishable goods, such as wool or cloth, does not present the same problems as that of most foodstuffs, but it does require an investment in sound buildings, to guard against theft as well as to keep the products dry. Participation in international trade spreads the risks of local or even national failure and was only made possible by the production of surpluses of goods with a high market value. Wool in particular, grain, salt and increasingly cloth were major export goods. The profitability of this international exchange may not always have had a direct effect on the nutrition levels of the peasantry. Food goods continued to be traded even when there were shortages at home, and one of the major imports was wine, a luxury for the better off (Miller and Hatcher 1978, 82; Carus-Wilson 1962–3, 189). However, other important imports were fish and fish products, which provided a significant component of the diet of all levels of society. Within the human population, misfortunes such as infant and child mortality or infertility could be alleviated by adoption or the hiring of servants to do the work essential to the economic viability of the family unit (p. 210).

Seasonality

Hardship and shortages can often be prevented or at least minimized if they can be predicted. The weather, a major cause of disaster, can rarely be accurately predicted even with all the technological advantages of the modern world. None the less, attempts seem always to have been made to predict at least short-term fluctuations and many agricultural communities have a set of beliefs and superstitions concerning future weather.

What can be predicted with greater accuracy is the effect of the changing seasons within the year, and the management of the rural resources and the traditions and customs of the farming year were strongly tied to the seasonal shifts in availability of food and other rural products. The labours of the months are a common theme in illustrations and sculpture, depicting, for example, ploughing in March, driving the pigs into the woods in October and killing them in November (figures 5.6 and 10.2). The leanest time of the year was the winter, and so during the autumn preparations were made to ensure a supply of food for this period. Those with sheep and cattle had to decide which animals could be kept through the winter, and the rest, fattened up on the last of the summer grass, the harvest waste and any surplus grain, were sold, slaughtered for immediate consumption or preserved (for example, Webb 1854, 19). A large proportion of the pigs may have been killed after fattening at the end of the autumn, and their salted or smoked meat was one of the main sources of protein in the winter months. It was in the winter months too that many of the wild animals, particularly birds, were caught. Several birds commonly found are either, like wild geese, migratory species, only visiting England in the winter, or are easier to catch out of the breeding season. Hunting scenes are often portrayed as a December activity.

Although archaeological deposits often build up over a long period of time and seasonal accumulations can rarely be detected, it is likely that many of the bones of wild creatures represent the remains of winter meals. The increased

10.2 *Pig killing, from a twelfth-century calendar illustrating the occupations of the months. The monogram is for November (Bod. Lib. MS Auct. D. 2. 6 f. 6).*

exploitation of these animals may have been an attempt to increase general food production, but it may also be viewed as a particular response to the problem of seasonal shortages. However, hunting was not exclusively a winter occupation, but provided supplements to the food produced by farming at other times of the year (Labarge 1980, 76).

Fluctuations in food supply over the course of the year also resulted in surpluses. At harvest time in a good year a superabundance of food could be produced. If adequate facilities existed, much of this could be stored as an insurance against lean times in the future, but these frequently were not available, especially for the peasantry, and the harvest feast was a means of dealing with the surplus, allowing the lord to offer a reward to his villeins at minimum cost and reinforcing community solidarity at the same time. Other feast days existed throughout the year, often with traditional food associations which reflect the abundance of particular products. At harvest time, geese, fattened on the stubble, were slaughtered, and pancakes are associated with shrovetide, which falls when milk and eggs are at their most plentiful.

In bad years, the traditional feasts could put an additional strain on already stretched resources and, although they may be viewed as an extravagance at such times, they had important ritual meaning and those associated with baptisms, weddings and deaths in particular were important for maintaining status (Hanawalt 1986, 111).

Demands for labour were also seasonal. Peak times, such as lambing, calving and shearing, but more especially ploughing, sowing and harvesting required the marshalling of the forces of all family members, and often the hiring in of extra labour. With the post-Black Death decline in population, shortages of manpower made these seasonal demands more difficult to satisfy.

Status and Inequality

The countryside was home to a divided society. The inequalities that existed between lords and peasants were seen in every aspect of their lives – in their living conditions, the food that they ate, the leisure they had to enjoy and even in their family size, and several authors in this book have made specific reference to these differences (figure 10.3; pp. 21, 127, 140, 178). Nor were resources evenly distributed among peasants. There were wide differences in peasant wealth, seen in the amount of land, livestock and equipment they held and reinforced by variations in soil fertility and topography on their holdings (p. 30).

The feudal system maintained an unequal distribution of resources by, as Dyer has expressed it, 'transferring wealth in the form of goods, labour and cash upwards, from the peasant producers to the aristocracy' (p. 23). The peasants

10.3 *A medieval banquet, from a fourteenth-century Flemish manuscript
(Bod. Lib. MS Bodl. 264 f. 73v).*

had not only to maintain their own families, but in effect also those of their
lords. The discrepancies that existed between the upper and lower levels of
society were probably at their greatest when resources were most stretched, for
the lord was buffered from the worst effects of shortages by the peasantry and the
labour, goods, rents and fines he could extract from them, and by those reservoirs
of food and other produce such as the parks, which he reserved for his exclusive
use. However, he was not immune from hardship, and disputes between lord
and peasants and between lord and lord highlight the competition that developed
during times of scarcity (p. 23).

During the latter part of our period, some of the differences between the
standards of living of lords and peasants became less marked. The greater
purchasing power of the peasants in the post-Black Death era together with the
growth of the market economy led to a more equal distribution of resources – for
example, there was a notable increase in meat consumption by the peasantry
(p. 21).

Regions

Many contributors to this book have considered the ways that resources differed from one part of the country to another. The theme is worth exploring a little further: can distinctive regions be explained by agricultural practice or by the dominant influence of a region's resources?

Most contributors here argue that the need for communities to provide for their own subsistence required that they should practise both grain and livestock farming, no matter where they lived. There were certain basic similarities in cereal farming; the medieval agricultural treatises rarely mention variation in conditions under which crops had to be grown and techniques of, for example, stock raising, marling or manuring differed little on estates spread over the country (Mate 1985). Despite the variety of field systems, traditionally regarded as an example of regional traits, there appears to have been little functional difference between them (Campbell 1981b, 116). The topography and soil type of a region seem to have been primarily responsible for determining the types of livestock reared, or the types of cereal: deer for example were kept mainly in the north and west and oats was the preferred grain in the south-west, barley in East Anglia (pp. 111–12, 165.)

While the subsistence needs of agricultural communities may have tended to homogenize farming practice, major differences between regions can be seen in the relative importance given to arable and pasture, and this underlay the well-known division of the British Isles into 'highland' and 'lowland' zones (Fox 1932; Fowler 1978). Recent work has developed this classification and identified smaller, yet no less distinctive, blocks of countryside – the *pays*. At least three basic types of *pays* have been suggested, defined by the land use, which is assumed to reflect the differences in geology, soil, topography and climate. There were those areas which had a dominance of either pasture in a woodland environment or in the open uplands, and those which were primarily geared towards cereal cultivation. Geographers were impressed with the consistent similarities between settlement, farming and social structure in these *pays* (Everitt 1977; Slater 1979). Thirsk's discussion has been most influential (1967a, 1–112), but claims only to outline the situation in the sixteenth century. Many argue here that the essential characteristics of these *pays* were clearly visible in the medieval period (p. 19), but others warn us that the pronounced differences only appear with increasing agricultural specialization from the late fourteenth century. To a certain extent the concept of a region has to be flexible, as it is bound to change in size and character with time (Everitt 1977), but nevertheless exploitation of most of the resources discussed in this book can only be assessed by taking a regional perspective.

The geographical attributes, for example topography and soil type, have been used to explain the regional variations in field systems, including the most recent discussion of two- and three-field systems. Fox notes the coincidence of two-field systems with areas of less fertile soils (1986, 542). Others, however, choose to emphasize human factors in their explanation of regional variations. Campbell has argued that prevailing social conditions in East Anglia, such as the independence of the peasantry, or the strength of local lords, have to be taken into account. In Norfolk, for example, there is a good correlation between regularly arranged field systems and areas of strong manorialism (Campbell 1981b, 28).

While Langdon found that a 'physical' explanation was sufficient to explain why some regions in England preferred to use horses rather than oxen for agricultural work, there were enough non-correlations for him to suggest that factors such as social structure, or the predominant type of tenure, were also important. It should be said, however, that until the fifteenth century there was in some cases as much variation between social groups within one region as between different areas (Langdon 1986a, 273).

While economic historians are increasingly considering social factors, demographers prefer to explain variations in population growth as primarily a result of the prevailing geographical conditions. In the broad periods of demographic growth between the late twelfth and mid-fourteenth centuries there is generally a higher growth rate in the north and west of England, the traditional highland zone. More detailed work shows that for different parts of the country there are different chronologies for population change. Smith regards these patterns as essentially a comment on the physical attributes of the areas. Demographic growth tended to slow down first in those parts of England that were 'anciently settled' and intensively worked long before the twelfth century. In regions which still had potential for colonization, later growth was still possible. There were some areas, however, such as east Norfolk, which had a high population and yet were still able to support a high growth rate.

The factors which distinguished *pays* were also fundamental in determining the residential and working arrangements of the medieval rural communities. Pastoral regions supported a settlement form which was designed to give maximum control of animals, and this can be seen in both seasonally and permanently occupied sites. Tracks, at one place constricting, at another funnelling out, allowed a high degree of management where dispersed settlements meant that there were few neighbours to help. The lack of crofts and the stability of the settlements in upland pasture areas also mark this settlement form out from other, more arable, regions of medieval England. Dispersed forms of settlement may be more common throughout the country than was previously thought, but we must avoid the temptation to assume that hamlets in lowland areas were like those in the uplands. To do so might be to misunderstand the reasons which determined the character of the upland settlements; they were disposed to cope with a farming regime that was solidly based on animal management. Regional variation in the arrangements of settlements between regions is probably more important than differences in building type for there are fewer *functional* differences than is commonly supposed. The longhouse, for example, is found in most areas, not just the pastoral regions of England, nor is it merely one stage in the evolution of the 'farm'. This building form indicates instead the importance the peasantry placed on the animals which did agricultural work, whether horses or oxen (pp. 44–50, 58).

Inter-regional Contact

The *pays* usually reflected the character and range of resources that were available in individual villages. Despite the strip arrangement of some parishes and manors which enabled the exloitation of differing types of land (for example p. 22), no single property was completely self-sufficient. There was often a need to travel quite extensively to obtain basic necessities, and in the course of doing this to cross the geographical boundaries of particular regions.

For the higher nobility and the major monastic houses the process of exchange of raw materials was part and parcel of the everyday running of their estates. There was much travelling between properties, whether by officials or by lords and their retinues, and this is reflected in the distribution of certain archaeological material. Pottery which normally circulated within a region can also be found in isolated pockets hundreds of kilometres away, brought there by one of the baggage trains in the course of perambulating the estate (Moorhouse 1983).

The expedients adopted to avoid the dangers of an introverted farming regime were not only those of the upper echelons of medieval society. The benefits were realized by peasants and gentry but, because they did not have the advantage of widespread estates, they relied on the market to provide the means by which to overcome these regional limitations. From their earliest pre-Domesday beginnings markets were in a sense antithetic to the concept of the region because they were often sited on the edge of several geographical zones. They were able to perform a function similar to that of the widespread estates, in redistributing materials from a wide area.

How did regions respond to shifts in the economy? The major trends in particular should have had an effect on the countryside: firstly the increasing pressure on diminishing resources in the late twelfth and thirteenth centuries, and secondly the release of this pressure from the mid-fourteenth century, and the consequent reorientation of the economy. The most obvious result of the late twelfth- and thirteenth-century trends was the increase in cereal production in virtually all regions. We have for example the cultivation of oats in traditional pastoral areas like the Peak or Dartmoor (pp. 21, 45). Within the arable areas of England the midlands may have experienced most pressure, resulting in careful management of the agricultural resources, perhaps as late as the thirteenth century, or more likely three or four centuries before. In some pastoral areas the most dramatic pointer to increasing exploitation – the change from shieling to permanent, mixed, farm — had occurred by the tenth century (p. 43). The twelfth-century use of a site may thus represent a reoccupation, and not the first, or most intensive, farming of the uplands.

From the mid-fourteenth century we see a widespread shrinking and desertion of settlements. This is far more noticeable in the core arable areas such as the midlands than in the pasture areas. Areas on Dartmoor, for example, continued to be farmed, although over a reduced area, until *c.*1500 (p. 82). In the midlands there was a change in the organization of the farms, associated with the 'crewyard', a result no doubt of the increasing emphasis on pastoralism. In areas where there was still an emphasis on cereal growing, a trend towards larger holdings and more investment in the construction of more and larger barns may point to a desire to take advantage of the market (Astill 1983, 233–4).

Despite the abundant documentary evidence for widespread colonization and assarting in the twelfth and thirteenth centuries, and the increasing trend to pastoralism from the mid-fourteenth century, the essential agricultural character of the regions remained the same.

Change in the Countryside: Market, Population or Climate?

In his search for the origins of the English farming regions, Hoskins suggested a critical role for the market in what he thought was the formative period, the fourteenth and fifteenth centuries. He characterized this time as one of low market activity, when the inhabitants of a region were thrown back on their own resources, and in doing so established the individuality of their region (Hoskins 1954, 7). More recent work has confirmed his observations, but has reversed his reasoning. The late middle ages is seen as a period of innovation in agricultural practice which made the land more productive. Particular regions began to specialize in the production of crops for which they were most suited, thus making the *pays* more distinctive: as a result agricultural equipment also became more distinctive from region to region (p. 105).

Accentuation of regional differences was possible because of the high level of market activity. It has been argued that areas could only have specialized in particular products if the provision of foodstuffs could be guaranteed from other areas so, contrary to Hoskins' view, it was the *increased* velocity of exchange that was responsible for regionalization.

Rural communities became more actively involved in marketing from the thirteenth century (figure 10.4). We have mentioned the need to buy in some

10.4   *A pack horse arriving at an inn, from an early fifteenth-century manuscript*
(Bod. Lib. MS Bodl. 264 f. 245v).

materials, but there was a stronger need to be able to sell surplus in order to
obtain cash not only to settle fines and rents but also to pay for goods and services
(Britnell 1981, 209–21). This is confirmed by the huge increase in the volume,
and no doubt the speed of circulation, of coin in the thirteenth century (Metcalf
1977, 7). Langdon has argued that the increased use of the horse for drawing
vehicles enabled the peasant to visit more markets more often (Langdon 1984).
Increased exposure to the market place also meant that the peasant became more
aware of urban demand, for example for meat. One of the side effects of the
increased use of horses for agricultural work was that more cattle could be sold
for meat consumption, and this change is confirmed by the occurrence of
increased numbers of juvenile cattle bones in towns (p. 156). The high level of
wages which existed in the fourteenth and fifteenth centuries may have been
responsible for an increased consumption of meat, particularly in towns. Given

this, it is appropriate to regard the market's response as important in fostering the shift from arable to livestock husbandry in this period.

Specialization in production also enabled some regions to become industrialized. Increased local demand for metals and clothing, and the failure of traditional markets to meet it, stimulated the metal industries in Somerset and Devon and textile manufacture in Essex and Suffolk. This diversity of the local economy in such regions facilitated an increased population growth, which again contributed to the distinctiveness of the areas (p. 202).

While the market may have fostered an increased regionalization in farming practice, its influence can have been neither sustained nor continuous. In the course of the later fourteenth and fifteenth centuries trade seems to have declined and there is some evidence to suggest that a rationalization of markets took place, with the weakest ones failing, as for example in Staffordshire, Derbyshire and Nottinghamshire (Palliser and Pinnock 1971; Coates 1965; Unwin 1981). Excavations within small market towns suggest a contraction in this period (Astill 1985), and further evidence comes from pottery, a low cost item sold at markets. Increased production and a wider distribution caused the potter to leave the sale of his pots to traders in the larger centres, who acted as middlemen (Astill 1983, 219–30). The middleman may also have short-circuited the web of small markets and taken over their trade. He seems to have been increasingly important in the sale of wool and grain during this period. The contact between local rural communities may well have been maintained by middlemen, at least until the revival of the small market town in the sixteenth century.

The market, then, could have helped to bring about change in the medieval economy, but its influence cannot be regarded as constant. We have not only the lesson of the later fourteenth and fifteenth centuries, but also that of the twelfth when access to centres of exchange was much more limited. Often of course the growing complexity of the market is a response to other forces for change within rural society. The money supply, for example, can be seen as an important determinant in periods of inflation, most notably between 1180 and 1220 (Harvey, P. D. A. 1973), and in helping to explain periods when the market was apparently sluggish, as in the later fourteenth century (Astill 1983, 239–42).

No one would deny the critical importance of change within the human population. The basic features of a demographic profile, birth, fertility and mortality, directly affected the labour/land ratio, and had repercussions throughout the economy. There is general agreement about the major shifts in medieval population. What is less clear is their significance. Some see population growth as a result of peasant prosperity and technological advances that enabled an expansion of the cultivated area. Others, and it must be said the majority, argue that the population grew and outstripped resources. The result was a reduction in yields and eventually subsistence crises. Population decline, accentuated by outbreaks of plague, was responsible for the improved land/labour ratios from the mid-fourteenth century. Conditions, however, did not allow an increase in the population until the early sixteenth century (Postan 1975, 35–8, 41–4, 135–59).

It is difficult to assess the influence of population change when so little is known about medieval demography. The overriding concern with the growth and decline in numbers over the whole country needs to be balanced by more attention to trends within regions and events within families. The role of mortality in population change has been emphasized, but increasingly the effect of low fertility is being investigated especially in the later middle ages. Smith considers whether the impact of 'institutions' was important. What effect for example did the lord–tenant relationship or direct demesne cultivation have on family size (p. 212)? Future work should consider whether the ways in which resources were exploited could have had a demographic effect.

The primacy of demographic processes in determining the medieval economy has recently been challenged from a different point of view. Brenner has restated and augmented Marxist arguments for the importance of the class struggle as a determinant (Brenner 1976). Few Marxist historians would deny the importance of class conflict, but some would choose to give more weight than does Brenner to other aspects of the productive process in feudal society. For example, in order to understand the 'mode of production' it is necessary to consider the 'forces of production', that is the available natural resources, the capacity of the existing technology and the labour force; and whether these 'forces' changed in the course of the medieval period and in turn affected the relationship between the owners of the means of production and the producers (Hilton 1985, 6–9).

A consideration of the indirect evidence for change, for example the expansion of the cultivated area and the role of technology, is necessary for this kind of approach. It is normally assumed that the extension of the arable landscape, especially on to what is sometimes called marginal land, was a direct result of population expansion. In some parts of the country this course of action was just not available to the majority of the population simply because all the available land was being exploited. This was certainly the case in much of the champion areas of the midlands (for example Dyer 1980, 84–112). In other parts expansion was possible, although often because of the technological capabilities of the communities.

The abandonment of cereal cultivation on 'marginal' lands is often thought to have been caused by a decline in soil fertility. This argument is based on the abundant data for declining yields, particularly in the late thirteenth and early fourteenth centuries. The trend is to be seen on manors located in a variety of *pays*, and not just on the uplands. Postan and others, however, believe that the loss of soil fertility was most severe on the marginal and late colonized lands.

Their abandonment took place while there was still a high population, and thus precipitated a subsistance crisis (Postan 1975, 67–79).

It is necessary to examine this view that 'marginal' land, often upland, was the first to be exhausted. One of the major causes of soil infertility was the lack of a regular source of manure which had been exacerbated by the declining stock of animals because of the scarcity of pasture. This shortage would have been felt most keenly where the resources of particular manors were fully stretched, that is in the belt of champion country. The upland soils are of couse thinner, and often more acid, than elsewhere in England, but a particular farming technique, the infield–outfield system, was designed to cope with the problem (p. 63).

The fertility of the infield would have been mantained by animal manure and the uplands were the one area of the country which did not suffer from shortage of this resource for they were traditionally pastoral, and the arrangement of the settlements demonstrates this, whether on Dartmoor or the Peak (figure 10.5; p. 45). A case could therefore be made that, although some marginal lands had the poorest soils, the availability of land could allow a shifting type of agriculture to be practised on the outfield, with intervals between cultivation to let the soil recover, while the fertility of the infields was maintained with animal manure. There is also the possibility that the upland soils were not as poor as we tend to assume. Postan has argued that the cultivation of oats is often a good pointer to marginal land (1975, 57), but it is noticeable that the cereals most commonly

10.5 *Houndtor, Devon. This settlement, on the fringes of Dartmoor, demonstrates the increased exploitation of 'marginal' land in the twelfth to fourteenth centuries (photo: G. Astill).*

grown on the edge of Dartmoor were not oats but rye and barley (Maguire et al. 1983, 94–5; Austin et al. 1980, 54). A programme of soil analysis, especially of soils sealed by dated medieval field boundaries, is needed to solve this critical issue (for example Maguire et al. 1983, 57–68).

We are not of course claiming that cereal cultivation was as efficient or as productive in the uplands as it was elsewhere: traditionally pastoral areas were only brought into cultivation when there was an imperative to increase production and suitable environmental conditions prevailed. An important component of these conditions was climate and this invites us to consider its role in influencing change.

Climatic change is not a fashionable explanation for the trends in the medieval economy. Some historians, for example, have failed to find correlations between climatic variations and agricultural change, and have therefore discounted the effect of long-term change in the former (Titow 1972, 24; Kershaw 1973b, 7–8; Le Roy Ladurie 1972). Parry however has argued that crop yields are affected more by *weather* than by long-term climatic change, and therefore historians are not comparing like with like: they are comparing short-term changes in the weather with long-term economic change (1978, 20–3). There has also been a failure to realize that the impact of climate is regional with the greatest effect on those areas which are 'marginal', and clearly some assessment of these areas is necessary (Parry 1985).

Archaeologists have claimed that some alterations within medieval settlements, such as the cutting of ditches and creation of building platforms, were provoked by increasing wetness after the mid-thirteenth century. However such evidence is often not sufficiently well dated to be used in this way, and other data would tend to discount the role of climate (Beresford and Hurst 1971, 121–2; Beresford, G. 1975, 50–4; Wright 1976). The relationship between settlement change, including desertion, and climate is not well understood, and archaeologists' attempts have been regarded as crude and unconvincing (Parry 1978, 144–5). The relationship between land use and climate is much better understood, and it is here that archaeological and environmental fieldwork can make an effective contribution.

Climatologists have identified a 'warm epoch' between *c*.1150 and 1250 when winters were milder and wetter, and summers drier and warmer than today. The increase in temperature has been shown to have had a dramatic effect on the limits of cultivation in the uplands of south-east Scotland, and it has been suggested that as much as a third of Britain's moorland would have been capable of growing crops (Parry 1985, 45). The intake of moorland for cultivation can be seen in Cornwall, Devon and Derbyshire, where pollen analysis shows cereal cultivation in the twelfth and thirteenth centuries in some areas on land above the level at which it would be possible to grow cereals today. Since summer temperatures are the major constraint on the limits of crop cultivation in the uplands, such evidence might suggest that amelioration of the climate, occurring at the time of population growth, encouraged the cultivation of moorland. We do however have evidence of the intensive use of these areas before and after the warm epoch and Lamb has argued that there was a 'warming phase' in the 900s which was preparatory to the warm epoch (Lamb 1977, 435). The later abandonment of cultivation is more difficult to explain in climatic terms unless it marks a slow response to a gradual drop in temperature.

It is difficult to advance further, given the limited data. At present we are merely noting environmental and economic coincidences, and we need to develop our enquiry to see if they are related. One explanation for the abandonment of cultivation is hinted at in some soil profiles recently examined on Dartmoor. They may be important because they seem to mirror the findings for that other period when the moor was extensively used, the Bronze Age (Balaam et al. 1982, 256–60). It seems that the actual process of field construction and cultivation could have substantially altered the surface drainage of the areas. The soils examined show increasing podsolization, and the accumulation of peat which would gradually have reduced the areas available for cultivation. The problem of surface drainage may also have been exacerbated by the warm epoch when there was a succession of mild, but moist winters. Abandonment of the fields may thus have been related to both the intensification of land use and the climatic trends. This clearly needs to be tested by further work.

While the land-use history of the uplands may have been influenced by long-term climatic change, it is difficult to see how the lowlands could have been affected. Here the role of climate has been accepted as minor: the short-term changes, for example those between 1315 and 1322, are seen as triggering a crisis which was deeply founded in the economic and social structure of medieval England (Kershaw 1973b). The one area which perhaps may have been affected by long-term climatic change was vine growing, but even this is difficult to demonstrate. Vine growing in England was labour and capital intensive, and the struggle may have been abandoned when the market guaranteed a reliable supply of wine from Gascony (Le Roy Ladurie 1972, 14–16; pp. 33, 103).

Conclusion

We have attempted to look at the countryside of medieval England from a series of different points of view, but with a unified and fairly specific objective: our examination has been primarily of the *resources* of the countryside, particularly the human, animal and plant resources. In presenting and then attempting to integrate the differing perspectives of historians, archaeologists and environmentalists we hoped both to deepen and expand knowledge of the medieval past. We may, in some small measure, have succeeded, but we have certainly raised more questions than we have resolved. The countryside did, and still does, offer an enormous complexity of opportunities and constraints for the human population that inhabits it. It is both changed by, and changes, that population in an intricate web of stimuli and responses. We have been forced by the limitations of currently available evidence and of our knowledge and understanding to fragment the whole into more easily accessible parts. Further integration of the differing approaches is necessary but not sufficient. We must also widen our perspective to look, for example, at rural industry and trade. In particular we must examine more carefully the complexity of the interactions between the human population and the natural world, in an attempt to provide a more complete and coherent view of human society in the past.

Bibliography

Documents

Bodleian Library, Suffolk rolls, no. 21.
Cambridge University Library, Ely Dean and Chapter, 7/15/11/2/15.
Longleat manuscript 9654.
Shropshire Record Office, 334/2.
Shropshire Record Office, 1224/1/9.
Staffordshire Record Office, D. (W.) 1734/2/1/599.

Books and articles

Addyman, P.V. 1964: A dark age settlement at Maxey, Northamptonshire. *Medieval Archaeology* 8, 20–73.

Addyman, P.V. 1976: Archaeology and Anglo-Saxon society. In G. Sieveking, I.H. Longworth and K.E. Wilson (eds), *Problems in Social and Economic Archaeology*. London, 309–22.

Alcock, N.W. and Smith, P. 1972: The longhouse: a plea for clarity. *Medieval Archaeology* 16, 145–6.

Alcock, N.W. and Laithwaite, M. 1973: Medieval houses in Devon and their modernization. *Medieval Archaeology* 17, 100–25.

Allen, D. 1979: Excavations at Hafod y Nan Griafolen, Brenig Valley, Clwyd, 1973–74. *Post-Medieval Archaeology* 13, 1–59.

Allison, K.J. 1957: The sheep–corn husbandry of Norfolk in the sixteenth and seventeenth centuries. *Agricultural History Review* 5, 12–30.

Allison, T.M. 1904: The flail and its varieties. *Archaeologia Aeliana* third series 2, 94–125.

Ambros, C. 1980: The mammal bones. In P. Wade-Martins, Fieldwork and excavation on village sites in Launditch Hundred, Norfolk. *East Anglian Archaeology* 10, 158–9.

Amherst, A.M.T. 1894: A fifteenth-century treatise on gardening by 'Mayster Ion Gardener'. *Archaeologia* 54, 157–72.

Andrews, F.B. 1933: The compotus rolls of the monastery of Pershore. *Transactions and Proceedings of the Birmingham Archaeological Society* 57, 1–94.

Applebaum, S. 1972: Roman Britain. In H.P.R. Finberg (ed.), *The Agricultural History of England and Wales* I.I. Cambridge, 3–277.

Armitage, P. 1977: The Mammalian Remains from the Tudor Site of Baynard's Castle London. A Biometrical and Historical Analysis. Unpublished PhD thesis, Royal Holloway College / British Museum of Natural History, London.

Armitage, P. 1980: A preliminary description of British cattle from the late twelfth to the early sixteenth century. *The Ark* 7, 405–13.

Armitage, P. 1982: Developments in British cattle husbandry. *The Ark* 9, 50–4.

Astill, G.G. 1983: Economic change in later medieval England: an archaeological review. In T.H. Aston, P.R. Coss, C.C. Dyer and J. Thirsk (eds), *Social Relations and Ideas: Essays in Honour of R.H. Hilton*. London, 217–47.

Astill, G.G. 1985: Archaeology and the smaller medieval town. *Urban History Yearbook 1985*, 46–53.

Aston, M. 1985: *Interpreting the Landscape*. London.

Aston, T.H. and Philpin, C.H.E. (eds) 1985: *The Brenner Debate: Agrarian Class Structure and Economic Development in Pre-industrial Europe*. Cambridge.

Atkin, C.W. 1971: Herefordshire. In H.C. Darby and I.B. Terrett (eds), *The Domesday Geography of Midland England*. Cambridge, 57–114.

Atkin, M. 1985: Some settlement patterns in Lancashire. In D. Hooke (ed.), *Medieval Villages*. Oxford, 171–85.

Ault, W.O. 1972: *Open-field Farming in Medieval England*. London.

Austin, D. 1978: Excavations in Okehampton Deer Park, Devon, 1976–78. *Devon Archaeological Society Proceedings* 36, 191–239.

Austin, D. 1985: Dartmoor and the upland villages of the south-west of England. In D. Hooke (ed.), *Medieval Villages*. Oxford, 71–80.

Austin, D. (forthcoming): *The Deserted Medieval Village of Thrislington, County Durham: Excavations 1973–4*. London.

Austin, D., Daggett, R.H. and Walker, M.J.C. 1980: Farms and fields in Okehampton Park, Devon; the problems of studying medieval landscapes. *Landscape History* 2, 39–58.

Austin, D. and Walker, M.J.C. 1985: A new landscape context for Houndtor, Devon. *Medieval Archaeology* 29, 148–52.

Ayers, B. and Murphy, P. 1983: A waterfront excavation at Whitefriars Street Car Park, Norwich, 1979. *East Anglian Archaeology* 17, 1–60.

Backway, C. 1982. Oyster shells. In R.A. Higham, J.P. Allan and S.R. Blaylock, Excavations at Okehampton Castle, Devon. Part 2 – the Bailey. *Devon Archaeological Society Proceedings* 40, 138–44.

Baker, A.R.H. 1973: Changes in the later middle ages. In H.C. Darby (ed.), *A New Historical Geography of England before 1600*. Cambridge, 186–247.

Baker, A.R.H. and Butlin, R.A. 1973: Conclusion: problems and perspectives. In A.R.H. Baker and R.A. Butlin (eds), *Studies of Field Systems in the British Isles*. Cambridge, 619–56.

Balaam, N., Smith, K. and Wainwright, G. 1982: The Shaugh Moor project: fourth report – environment, context and conclusion. *Proceedings of the Prehistoric Society* 48, 203–78.

Bamford, H. 1985: *Briar Hill Excavations 1974–1978*. Northampton.

Barker, G. 1976: Diet and economy at Valle Crucis: the report on the animal bones. *Archaeologia Cambrensis* 125, 117–26.

Barker, P. and Lawson, J. 1971: A pre-Norman field-system at Hen Domen, Montgomery. *Medieval Archaeology* 15, 58–72.

Barley, M.W. 1961: *The English Farmhouse and Cottage*. London.

Barrau, J. 1986: *Les Hommes et Leurs Aliments*. Paris.

Barron,W.R.J. (ed.) 1974: *Sir Gawain and the Green Knight*. Manchester.

Barton K.J. and Holden, E.W. 1977: Excavations at Bramber Castle, Sussex 1966–7. *Archaeological Jounal* 134, 11–79.

Beresford, G. 1971: Tresmorn, St Gennys. *Cornish Archaeology* 10, 55–72.

Beresford, G. 1975: *The Medieval Clay-land Village: Excavations at Goltho and Barton Blount*. London.

Beresford, G. 1977: Excavations of a moated house at Wintringham in Huntingdonshire. *Archaeological Journal* 134, 194–286.

Beresford, G. 1978: Excavations at the deserted medieval village of Caldecote, Hertfordshire. *Hertfordshire's Past* 4, 5–10.

Beresford, G. 1979: Three deserted medieval settlements on Dartmoor: a report on the late E. Marie Minter's excavations. *Medieval Archaeology* 23, 98–158.

Beresford, M.W. 1957: *History on the Ground: six studies in maps and landscapes*. London.

Beresford M.W. and Hurst, J.G. 1971: *Deserted Medieval Villages*. Guildford.

Beresford, M.W. and St Joseph, J.K. 1979: *Medieval England, an Aerial Survey* second edition. Cambridge.

Berkner, L.K. 1976: Inheritance, land tenure and peasant family structure: a German regional comparison. In J. Goody, J. Thirsk and E.P. Thompson (eds), *Family and Inheritance: Rural Society in Western Europe 1200–1800*. Cambridge, 71–95.

Biddick, K. 1984: Pig husbandry on the Peterborough Abbey estate from the twelfth to the fourteenth century AD. In C. Grigson and J. Clutton-Brock (eds), *Animals and Archaeology: 4. Husbandry in Europe*. Oxford, 161–78.

Biddle, M. 1961–2: The deserted medieval village of Seacourt, Berkshire. *Oxoniensia* 26–7, 70–201.

Biller, P.P.A. 1982: Birth control in the west in the thirteenth and early fourteenth centuries. *Past and Present* 94, 3–26.

Biraben, J.-N. 1975: *Les Hommes et la Peste en France et dans les Pays Européens et Mediterranéens* 1. Paris.

Birrell, J. 1969: Peasant craftsmen in the medieval forest. *Agricultural History Review* 17, 91–107.

Birrell, J. 1982: Who poached the king's deer? A study in thirteenth-century crime. *Midland History* 7, 9–25.

Bise, G. 1984: *Le Livre de la Chasse de Gaston Phoebus, Comte de Foix*. Geneva.

Blanchard, I.S.W. 1967: Economic Change in Derbyshire in the Late Middle Ages, 1272–1540. Unpublished PhD thesis, University of London.

Blanchard, I.S.W. 1970: Population change, enclosure and the early Tudor economy. *Economic History Review* 23, 427–45.

Blith, W. 1653: *The English Improver Improved* third edition. London.

Bolton, J.L. 1980: *The Medieval English Economy 1150–1500*. London.

Bond, J. 1981: Woodstock Park under the Plantagenet kings: the evolution and use of wood and timber in a medieval deer park. *Arboricultural Journal* 5, 201–13.

Bond, J. 1984: The documentary evidence. In S. Rahtz and T. Rowley, *Middleton Stoney*. Oxford, 125–7.

Bond, J. n.d.: The Park before the Palace: the evolution of Woodstock Park up to 1704. Unpublished typescript.

Boserup, E. 1965: *The Conditions of Agrarian Growth*. London.

Boserup, E. 1981: *Population and Technology*. Oxford.

Bourdillon, J. 1979a: The animal bone from Hamwih – some comparisons. In M. Kubasiewicz (ed.), *Archaeozoology*. Szczecin, 515–24.

Bourdillon, J. 1979b: Animal bone. In J.S.F. Walker, Excavations in medieval tenements on the Quilter's Vault site in Southampton. *Proceedings of the Hampshire Field Club and Archaeological Society* 35, 207–12.

Bourdillon, J. 1980: Town life and animal husbandry in the Southampton area, as suggested by the excavated bone. *Proceedings of the Hampshire Field Club and Archaeological Society* 36, 181–91.

Bowen, H.C. and Fowler, P.J. 1962: The archaeology of Fyfield and Overton Downs, Wiltshire. *Wiltshire Archaeological Magazine* 58, 98–115.

Bradshaw, R.H.W., Coxton, P., Greig, J.R.A. and Hall, A.R. 1981: New fossil evidence for the past cultivation of hemp (*Cannabis sativa* L.) in eastern England. *New Phytologist* 89, 503–10.

Bramwell, D. 1975: Bird remains from medieval London. *The London Naturalist* 54, 15–20.

Bramwell, D. 1976: Report on the bird bones from Walton, Aylesbury. In M. Farley, Saxon and medieval Walton, Aylesbury: excavations 1973–4. *Records of Buckinghamshire* 20, 287–9.

Bramwell, D. 1977: Bird bone. In H. Clarke and A. Carter, *Excavations at King's Lynn 1963–1970*. London, 399–403.

Bramwell, D. 1979: The bird bones. In J.H. Williams, *St Peter's Street, Northampton*. Northampton, 333–4.

Brandon, P.F. 1971: Demesne arable farming in coastal Sussex during the later middle ages. *Agricultural History Review* 19, 113–34.

Brenner, R. 1976: Agrarian class structure and economic development in pre-industrial Europe. *Past and Present* 70, 30–75.

Bridbury, A. R. 1978: The farming out of manors. *Economic History Review* 31, 503–20.

Brimblecombe, P. 1982: Early urban climate and atmosphere. In A.R. Hall and H.K. Kenward (eds), *Environmental Archaeology in the Urban Context*. London, 10–25.

Brisbane, M. and Clews, S. 1979: The East Moor field systems, Altarnun and North Hill, Bodmin Moor. *Cornish Archaeology* 18, 33–56.

Brisebarre, A.-M. 1978: *Bergers des Cévennes*. Paris.

Britnell, R.H. 1977: Finchingfield Park under the plough, 1341–42. *Essex Archaeology and History* 9, 107–12.

Britnell, R.H. 1981: The proliferation of markets in England, 1200–1349. *Economic History Review* 34, 209–21.

Britnell, R.H. 1983: Agriculture in a region of ancient enclosure, 1185–1500.

Nottingham Medieval Studies 27, 37—55.

Britnell, W. 1975: An interim report upon excavations at Beckford, 1972—4. *Vale of Evesham Research Report* 5, 37—55.

Britton, E. 1976: The peasant family in fourteenth-century England. *Peasant Studies* 5, 2—7.

Britton, E. 1977: *The Community of the Vill: a Study in the Family and Village Life in Fourteenth-century England.* Toronto.

Brothwell, D.R. 1981: Disease as an environmental parameter. In M. Jones and G. Dimbleby (eds), *The Environment of Man: the Iron Age to the Anglo-Saxon Period.* London, 231—47.

Brown, R.A., Colvin, H.M. and Taylor, A.J. (eds) 1963: *The History of the King's Works* 2. London.

Cal. Pat. Rolls: *Calendar of Patent Rolls* 1891—1916 45 volumes. London.

Campbell, B.M.S. 1981a: The population of early Tudor England: a reinterpretation of the 1522 muster returns and 1525 lay subsidies. *Journal of Historical Geography* 7, 145—54.

Campbell, B.M.S. 1981b: Commonfield origins — the regional dimension. In T. Rowley (ed.), *The Origins of Open-field Agriculture.* London, 112—30.

Campbell, B.M.S. 1983a: Agricultural progress in medieval England: some evidence from eastern Norfolk. *Economic History Review* 36, 24—46.

Campbell, B.M.S. 1983b: Agricultural productivity in medieval England: some evidence from Norfolk. *Journal of Economic History* 48, 379—404.

Campbell, B.M.S. 1984: Population pressure, inheritance and the land market in a fourteenth-century peasant community. In R.M. Smith (ed.), *Land, Kinship and Life-cycle.* Cambridge, 87—134.

Campbell, B.M.S. 1985: Review of G. Twigg, 'The Black Death: a Biological Reappraisal.' *Journal of Historical Geography* 11, 313—14.

Campbell, B.M.S. (in preparation): *Towards an Agricultural Geography of Medieval England.* Cambridge.

Cantimpratensis, T. 1973: *Liber de Natura Rerum* 1. New York.

Cantor, L.M. 1965: The medieval parks of south Staffordshire. *Transactions and Proceedings of the Birmingham Archaeological Society* 80, 1—9.

Cantor, L.M. 1971: The medieval parks of Leicestershire. *Transactions of Leicestershire Archaeological and Historical Society* 46, 9—24.

Cantor, L.M. 1982: Forests, chases, parks and warrens. In L.M. Cantor (ed.), *The English Medieval Landscape.* London, 56—85.

Cantor, L.M. 1983: *The Medieval Parks of England: a Gazetteer.* Loughborough.

Cantor, L.M. and Hatherly, J. 1979: The medieval parks of England. *Geography* 64, 71—85.

Cartledge, J. 1983: Mammal bones. In B. Ayers and P. Murphy, A waterfront excavation at Whitefriars Street Car Park, Norwich, 1979. *East Anglian Archaeology* 17, 30—2.

Carus-Wilson, E. 1962—3: The medieval trade of the ports of the Wash. *Medieval Archaeology* 6—7, 182—201.

Chapelot, P. and Fossier, R. 1985: *The Village and House in the Middle Ages.* London.

Chapman, D. and Chapman, N. 1975: *Fallow Deer.* Lavenham.

Charles, F.W.B. with Charles, M. 1984: *Conservation of Timber Buildings*. London.

Clanchy, M. 1979: *From Memory to Written Record. England 1066–1307*. London.

Clark, H.M. 1960: Selion size and soil type. *Agricultural History Review* 8, 91–8.

Cleere, H. and Crossley, D.W. 1985: *The Iron Industry of the Weald*. Leicester.

Coates, B.E. 1965: Markets and fairs in medieval Derbyshire. *Derbyshire Archaeological Journal* 85, 92–111.

Coggins, D., Fairless, K.J. and Batey, C.E. 1983: Simy Folds: an early medieval settlement site in Upper Teesdale. *Medieval Archaeology* 27, 1–27.

Coghill, N. (tr.) 1960: *Geoffrey Chaucer: the Canterbury Tales*: Harmondsworth.

Coleman, O. 1976: What figures? Some thoughts on the use of information by medieval governments. In D.C. Coleman and A.H. John (eds) *Trade, Government and Economy in Pre-industrial England: Essays Presented to F.J. Fisher*. London, 96–112.

Colledge, S.M. 1981: A report on the micro- and macroscopic plant remains from 'The Crown' car park site in Nantwich (including a preliminary list of Coleopteran remains). Ancient Monuments Laboratory Reports 3347.

Colledge, S.M. 1983: The plant remains. In M. Carver (ed.), Two town houses in medieval Shrewsbury. *Transactions of the Shropshire Archaeological Society* 61, 62–3.

Colker, M.L. (ed.) 1975: *Analecta Dublinensia*. Cambridge, Mass.

Collis, J. 1983: Field systems and land boundaries on Shaugh Moor and at Wotter, Dartmoor. *Devon Archaeological Society Proceedings* 41, 47–62.

Coppock, J.T. 1964: *An Agricultural Atlas of England and Wales*. London.

Corbet, G.B. and Southern, H.N. 1977: *The Handbook of British Mammals*. Oxford.

Corran, H.S. 1975: *A History of Brewing*. Newton Abbot.

Croston, D. and Pollott, G. 1985: *Planned Sheep Production*. London.

Cunliffe, B.W. 1971: *Excavations at Fishbourne 1961–69* 1. London.

Cunningham, W. 1905: *The Growth of English Commerce and Industry* I fourth edition. London, 570–6.

Dahlman, C.J. 1980: *The Open Field System and Beyond*. Cambridge.

Darby, H.C. 1936: *A Historical Geography of England*. Cambridge.

Darby, H.C. 1940: *The Medieval Fenland*. Cambridge.

Darby, H.C. 1973: Domesday England. In H.C. Darby (ed.), *A New Historical Geography of England before 1600*. London, 39–74.

Darby, H.C. 1977: *Domesday England*. Cambridge.

Darby, H.C. and Finn, R.W. (eds) 1967: *The Domesday Geography of South-west England*. Cambridge.

Daumas, M. (ed.) 1969: *A History of Technology and Invention* 1. New York.

Davis, R.H.C. 1983: The medieval warhorse. In F.M.L. Thompson (ed.), *Horses in European Economic History: a Preliminary Canter*. Reading, 4–20.

Demians D'Archimbaud 1981: *Les Fouilles de Rougiers. Contributions à l'Archéologie de l'habitat rural médiéval en pays mediterranéan*. Paris.

DeWindt, E.B. 1976: *The Liber Gersumarum of Ramsey Abbey*. Toronto.

Dodgshon, R.A. 1980: *The Origin of British Field Systems*. London.

Donaldson, A.M., Jones, A.K.G. and Rackham, D.J. 1980: Barnard Castle, Co. Durham. A dinner in the Great Hall: report on the contents of a fifteenth-century drain. *Journal of the British Archaeological Association* 133, 86–96.

Donkin, R.A. 1960: The Cistercian settlement and the English royal forest. *Citeaux* 11, 1–33, 117–32.

Drewett, P. 1982: The archaeology of Bullock Down, Eastbourne, East Sussex. The development of a landscape. *Sussex Archaeological Society Monograph* 1.

Drury, P.J. 1981: Medieval 'narrow rig' at Chelmsford and its possible implications. *Landscape History* 3, 51–8.

Duby, G. 1968: *Rural Economy and Country Life in the Medieval West*. London.

Dudley, D. and Minter, E.M. 1962–3: The medieval village at Garrow Tor, Bodmin Moor, Cornwall. *Medieval Archaeology* 6–7, 272–94.

Dudley Stamp, L. 1969: *Man and the Land*. London.

Dulley, A.J.F. 1967: Excavations at Pevensey, Sussex, 1962–6. *Medieval Archaeology* 11, 209–32.

Dyer, C.C. 1980: *Lords and Peasants in a Changing Society*. Cambridge.

Dyer, C.C. 1981: Warwickshire Farming, 1349–c.1520: preparations for agricultural revolution. *Dugdale Society Occasional Paper* 27. Oxford.

Dyer, C.C. 1982: History and medieval village studies. *Medieval Village Research Group* 30th Annual Report, 33–4.

Dyer, C.C. 1983: English diet in the later middle ages. In T.H. Aston, P.R. Coss, C.C. Dyer and J. Thirsk (eds), *Social Relations and Ideas: Essays in Honour of R.H. Hilton*. London, 191–214.

Dyer, C.C. 1984: Evidence for helms in Gloucestershire in the fourteenth century. *Vernacular Architecture* 15, 42–5.

Dyer, C.C. 1985: Power and conflict in the medieval village. In D. Hooke (ed.), *Medieval Villages*. Oxford, 27–32.

Dyer, C.C. 1986: English peasant buildings in the later middle ages. *Medieval Archaeology* 30, 19–45.

Dyer, C.C. (in press): Changes in diet in the later middle ages. *Agricultural History Review*, 36.

Dyer, C.C. (forthcoming): *Standards of Living in the Later Middle Ages. Social Change in England*, c.1200–1520. Cambridge.

Eastham, A. 1977: Birds. In B.W. Cunliffe, *Excavations at Portchester Castle. Vol. III: Medieval, the Outer Bailey*. London, 233–7.

Eastham, A. 1985: Bird bones, In B. Cunliffe and J. Munby, *Excavations at Portchester Castle. Volume IV: Medieval, the Inner Bailey*. London, 261–9.

Ellison, A. 1975: The animal remains. In H. Chapman, G. Coppack and P. Drewett, Excavations at the Bishop's Palace, Lincoln. 1968–72. *Lincolnshire History and Archaeology* Occasional Paper, 33–7.

Everitt, A. 1977: River and wold: reflections on the historical origin of regions and *pays*. *Journal of Historical Geography* 3, 1–19.

Everitt, A. 1979: The wolds once more. *Journal of Historical Geography* 5, 67–78.

Faull, M.L. and Moorhouse, S.A. 1981: *West Yorkshire: an Archaeological Survey to AD 1500* 3. Wakefield.

Fenton, A. 1973–4: Sickle, scythe and reaping machine. *Ethnologia Europaea* 7, 35–47.

Fenton, A. 1976: On the mapping of carts and waggons in Europe. *Ethnologia Europaea* 9, 1–13.

Fenwick, C.C. 1983: The English Poll Taxes of 1377, 1379 and 1381: a Critical

Examination of the Returns. Unpublished PhD thesis, London School of Economics.

Field, R.K. 1965: Worcestershire peasant buildings, household goods and farming equipment in the later middle ages. *Medieval Archaeology* 9, 105–45.

Finberg, H.P.R. 1954: An early reference to the Welsh cattle trade. *Agricultural History Review* 2, 12–14.

Finberg, H.P.R. 1969: *Tavistock Abbey. A Study in the Social and Economic History of Devon* second edition. Newton Abbot.

Fisher, J.L. 1968: *A Medieval Farming Glossary of Latin and English Words*. London.

Fitter, A. and Smith, C. (eds) 1979: *A Wood in Ascam: a Study of Wetland Conservation*. York.

Fleming, A. and Ralph, N. 1982: Medieval settlement and land use on Holne Moor, Dartmoor: the landscape evidence. *Medieval Archaeology* 26, 101–37.

Fowler, P.J. 1963: The archaeology of Fyfield and Overton Downs, Wiltshire. *Wiltshire Archaeological Magazine* 53, 342–50.

Fowler, P.J. 1976: Buildings and rural settlement. In D.M. Wilson (ed.), *The Archaeology of Anglo-Saxon England*. Cambridge, 23–48.

Fowler, P.J. 1978: Lowland landscapes: culture, time and *Personality*. In S. Limbrey and J.G. Evans (eds), *The Effect of Man on the Landscape: the Lowland Zone*. London, 1–11.

Fowler, P.J. 1983: *The Farming of Prehistoric Britain*. Cambridge.

Fowler, P.J., Musty, J.G. and Taylor, C.C. 1965: Some earthwork enclosures in Wiltshire. *Wiltshire Archaeological Magazine* 60, 52–74.

Fowler, P.J. and Thomas, A.C. 1962: Arable fields of the pre-Norman period at Gwithian, Cornwall. *Cornish Archaeology* 7, 61–111.

Fox, A. 1958: A monastic homestead on Dean Moor, South Devon. *Medieval Archaeology* 2, 141–57.

Fox, C. 1932: *The Personality of Britain*. Cardiff.

Fox, H.S.A. 1975: The chronology of enclosure and economic development in medieval Devon. *Economic History Review* 28, 181–202.

Fox, H.S.A. 1981: Approaches to the adoption of the midland system. In R.T. Rowley (ed.) *The Origins of Open-field Agriculture*. London, 64–111.

Fox, H.S.A. 1986: The alleged transformation from two-field to three-field systems in medieval England. *Economic History Review* 39, 536–48.

Franklin, P. 1986: Peasant widows 'liberation' and remarriage before the Black Death. *Economic History Review* 39, 186–204.

Franks, J. 1977: Plant remains. In H. Clarke and A. Carter, *Excavations in King's Lynn, 1963–1970*. London, 410–11.

Fussell, G.E. 1933: The breast plough. *Man* 33, 109–14.

Fussell, G.E. 1952: *The Farmer's Tools: the History of British Farm Implements, Tools and Machinery AD1500–1900*. London.

Fussell, G.E. 1959: The evolution of farm implements: 4. Field drainage. *Land Agents' Society Journal* 58, 361–72.

Fussell, G.E. 1966: Ploughs and ploughing before 1800. *Agricultural History* 40, 177–86.

Gardner, P., Haldon, R. and Malam, J. 1980: Prehistoric, Roman and medieval settlement at Stretton-on-Fosse: excavations and salvage 1971–76. *Transactions of the*

Birmingham and Warwickshire Archaeological Society 90, 1–35.

Gillam, J.P., Harrison, R.M. and Newman, T.G. 1973: Interim report on excavations at the Roman fort of Rudchester, 1972. *Archaeologia Aeliana* 1, 81–6.

Gimpel, J. 1977: *The Medieval Machine*. London.

Gingell, C. and Gingell, J. 1981: Excavation of a medieval 'Highworth Circle' at Stratton St Margaret. *Wiltshire Archaeological Magazine* 61–75.

Goldberg, P.J.P. 1986: Female labour, service and marriage in the late medieval urban north. *Northern History* 22, 18–38.

Goldberg, P.J.P. (in press): Women and work in two English medieval towns: a study in social topography. In R.M. Smith (ed.), *Regional and Spatial Patterns in Past Populations*. Oxford.

Goodall, I.H. 1980: Ironwork in Medieval Britain: an Archaeological Study. Unpublished PhD thesis, University College, Cardiff.

Goodall, I.H. 1981: The medieval blacksmith and his products. In D.W. Crossley (ed.), *Medieval Industry*. London, 51–62.

Goodridge, J.F. (tr.) 1959: *Piers the Ploughman. William Langland*. Harmondsworth.

Goody, J. 1976: *Production and Reproduction: a Comparative Study of the Domestic Domain*. Cambridge.

Goody, J. 1982: *Cooking, Cuisine and Class*. Cambridge.

Gottfried, R.S. 1977: *Epidemic Diseases in Fifteenth-century England: the Medical Response and the Demographic Consequences*. Leicester.

Grant, A. 1971: The animal bones. In G.F. Bryant and J.M. Steane, Excavations at the deserted medieval settlement at Lyveden. *Northampton Museums and Art Gallery, Journal* 9, 90–3.

Grant, A. 1975: The animal bones. In. J.M. Steane and G.F. Bryant, Excavations at the deserted medieval settlement at Lyveden. *Northampton Museums and Art Gallery, Journal* 10, 152–7.

Grant, A. 1977: The animal bones. In B.W. Cunliffe, *Excavations at Portchester Castle. Volume III: Medieval, the Outer Bailey and its Defences*. London, 214–38.

Grant, A. 1979a: The animal bones from Bedford. In D. Baker, E. Baker, J. Hassall and A. Simco (eds), Excavations in Bedford 1967–1977. *Bedfordshire Archaeological Journal* 13, 286–8.

Grant, A. 1979b: The animal bones. In J. Hassall, St John's Street. *Bedfordshire Archaeological Journal* 13, 103–6.

Grant, A. 1979c: The animal bones. In E. Baker and A. Simco, Cauldwell Street. *Bedfordshire Archaeological Journal* 13, 70–2.

Grant, A. 1981: The significance of deer remains at occupation sites of the Iron Age to the Anglo-Saxon period. In M. Jones and G. Dimbleby (eds), *The Environment of Man: the Iron Age to the Anglo-Saxon Period*. Oxford, 91–108.

Grant, A. 1982: The use of tooth wear as a guide to the age of domestic ungulates. In B. Wilson, C. Grigson and S. Payne (eds), *Ageing and Sexing Animal Bones from Archaeological Sites*. Oxford, 91–108.

Grant, A. 1983: The animal bones. In J. Hassall, Excavations in Bedford, 1977 and 1978. *Bedfordshire Archaeology* 16, 51–2.

Grant, A. 1984a: Animal husbandry in Wessex and the Upper Thames Valley. In B. Cunliffe and D. Miles (eds), *Iron Age Communities in Central Southern Britain*. Oxford, 102–18.

Grant, A. 1984b: The animal husbandry. In B.W. Cunliffe, *Danebury, an Iron Age Hillfort in Hampshire*. London, 496–548.

Grant, A. 1985: The large mammals. In B.W. Cunliffe and J. Munby, *Excavations at Portchester Castle. Volume IV: Medieval, the Inner Bailey*. London, 244–56.

Grant, A. 1987: Some observations on butchery in England from the Iron Age to the medieval period. In *La Découpe et le Partage du Corps à travers le Temps et L'Espace*. Anthropozoologica, premier numéro spécial. Paris, 53–8.

Grant, A. (in press): Food, status and religion in England in the middle ages: an archaeozoological perspective. *L'Animal dans l'Alimentation Humaine: les Critères de Choix*. Anthropozoologica, second numéro spécial, Paris.

Gras, N.S.B. 1915: *The Evolution of the English Corn Market*. Cambridge, Mass.

Gras, N.S.B. 1918: *The Early English Customs*. Harvard.

Gray, H.L. 1915: *English Field Systems*. Cambridge, Mass.

Green, F.J. 1979a: Medieval Plant Remains: Methods and Results of Archaeobotanic Analysis from Excavations in Southern England with Special Reference to Winchester and Urban Settlements of the 10th–15th Centuries. Unpublished M Phil thesis, University of Southampton.

Green, F.J. 1979b: Plant remains. In C.M. Heighway, A.P. Garrod and A.G. Vince, Excavations at 1 Westgate St, Gloucester. *Medieval Archaeology* 23, 186–207.

Green, F.J. 1982: Problems of interpreting differentially preserved plant remains from excavations of medieval urban sites. In A.R. Hall and H.K. Kenward (eds), *Environmental Archaeology in the Urban Context*. London, 40–6.

Green, F.J. 1984: The archaeological and documentary evidence for plants in the medieval period in England. In W. van Zeist and W.A. Casparie (eds), *Plants and Ancient Man*. Rotterdam, 99–114.

Greig, J.R.A. 1981: The investigation of a medieval barrel-latrine from Worcester. *Journal of Archaeological Science* 8, 265–82.

Greig, J.R.A. 1982: Garderobes, sewers, cesspits and latrines. *Current Archaeology* 85, 49–52.

Greig, J.R.A. 1983: Plant foods in the past: a review of the evidence from northern Europe. *Journal of Plant Foods* 5, 179–214.

Greig, J.R.A. 1986: Archaeobotany of the Cowick medieval moat, and some thoughts on moat studies. *Circaea* 4(2), 43–50.

Greig, J.R.A. (in press a): Some evidence of the development of grassland plant communities. In M.K. Jones (ed.), *Archaeology and the Flora of the British Isles*. Oxford.

Greig, J.R.A. (in press b): From lime forest to heathland – 5,000 years of change at West Heath Spa. In D. Collins and D. Lorrimer, *Excavations at West Heath, Hampstead, London*.

Greig, J.R.A. (in preparation a): The medieval (thirteenth- to fourteenth-century) plant remains from Chester, Hunters Walk.

Greig, J.R.A. (in preparation b): Tenby Merchant's House; the pollen from an AD sixteenth-century latrine pit in S.W. Wales.

Greig, J.R.A. (in preparation c): Pollen analyses of sewage from the seventeenth- to eighteenth-century latrine of the Provost of Oriel College, Oxford.

Greig, J.R.A. (in preparation d): Plant remains from the site of Shrewsbury Abbey.

Greig, J.R.A. (in preparation e): Pollen diagram from Cookley, Worcestershire.

Greig, J.R.A. (in preparation f): Plant remains from medieval pits at Watergate Street, Chester.

Greig, J.R.A., Girling, M.A. and Skidmore, P. 1982: The plant and insect remains. In R. Higham and P.A. Barker, *Hen Domen, Montgomery: a timber castle on the Welsh border* 1. London, 60–71.

Greig, J.R.A. and Osborne, P.J. 1984: Plant and insect remains at Taunton Priory. In P. Leach, *The Archaeology of Taunton: Excavations and Fieldwork to 1980.* Bristol, 160–5.

Grieve, M. 1984: *A Modern Herbal.* Harmondsworth.

Griffith, N.J.L., Halstead, P.L.J., MacLean, A. and Rowley-Conwy, P.A. 1983: Faunal remains and economy. In P. Mayes and L.A.S. Butler, *Sandal Castle Excavations 1964–73.* Wakefield, 341–8.

Grigg, D.B. 1980: *Population Growth and Agrarian Change: an Historical Perspective.* Cambridge.

Grigson, G. (ed.) 1984: *Thomas Tusser: Five Hundred Points of Good Husbandry (1580 edn).* Oxford.

Haigh, D. and Savage, M. with Molyneux, N. 1976–7: A Roman villa at Pounce Hill, Radford Semele 1974. *Transactions of the Birmingham and Warwickshire Archaeological Society* 88, 114–17.

Hajnal, J. 1965: European marriage patterns in perspective. In D.V. Glass and D.E.C. Eversley (eds), *Population in History: Essays in Historical Demography.* London, 101–46.

Hajnal, J. 1982: Two kinds of pre-industrial household formation system. *Population Development Review* 8, 449–94.

Hall, A.R. 1981: A cockle of rebellion, insolence, sedition . . . *Interim* 8, 5–8.

Hall, A.R. 1986: The fossil evidence for plants in medieval towns. *Biologist* 33, 262–7.

Hall, A.R., Jones, A.K.G. and Kenward, H.K. 1983: Cereal bran and human faecal deposits; some preliminary observations. In B. Proudfoot (ed.), *Site, Environment and Economy.* Oxford, 85–104.

Hall, A.R. and Tomlinson, P.R. 1984: Dyeplants from Viking York. *Antiquity* 58, 58–60.

Hall, D. 1981a: The origins of open-field agriculture – the archaeological fieldwork evidence. In T. Rowley (ed.), *The Origins of Open-field Agriculture.* London, 22–38.

Hall, D. 1981b: The changing landscape of the Cambridgeshire silt fens. *Landscape History* 3, 37–47.

Hall, D. 1982: *Medieval Fields.* Aylesbury.

Hall, D. 1985: Late Saxon topography and early medieval estates. In D. Hooke (ed.), *Medieval Villages.* Oxford, 61–70.

Hallam, H.E. 1958: Some thirteenth-century censuses. *Economic History Review* 10, 340–61.

Hallam, H.E. 1961: Population density in medieval Fenland. *Economic History Review* 14, 71–81.

Hallam, H.E. 1965: *Settlement and Society: a Study of the Early Agrarian History of South Lincolnshire.* Cambridge.

Hallam, H.E. 1981: *Rural England 1066–1348*. London.

Hanawalt, B.A. 1986: *The Ties That Bound: Peasant Families in Medieval England*. Oxford.

Handley, H. 1840: On wheel and swing ploughs. *Journal of the Royal Agricultural Society* 1, 149–7.

Harcourt, R.A. 1969: The animal remains. In D.G. and J.G. Hurst, Excavations at the medieval village of Wythemail. *Medieval Archaeology* 13, 201–3.

Harcourt, R.A. 1975: The dog bones. In B.W. Cunliffe, *Excavations at Portchester Castle. Volume I: Roman*. London, 406–8.

Harley, J.B. 1958: Population and agriculture from the Warwickshire Hundred Rolls of 1279. *Economic History Review* 11, 8–18.

Harris, M. 1986. *Good to Eat*. London.

Hart, C.R. 1981: *The North Derbyshire Archaeological Survey to AD1500*. Chesterfield.

Hartley, D. 1979: *Lost Country Life*. New York.

Harvey, B. 1977: *Westminster Abbey and its Estates in the Middle Ages*. Oxford.

Harvey. J., 1974: *Early Nurserymen*. Chichester.

Harvey, M. 1981: The origin of planned field systems in Holderness, Yorkshire. In T. Rowley, (ed.) *The·Origins of Open-field Agriculture*. London, 184–201.

Harvey, M. 1982: Regular open-field systems on the Yorkshire Wolds. *Landscape History* 4, 29–39.

Harvey, N. 1972: Plough team, sickle and flail. *Agriculture* 79, 222–6.

Harvey, N. 1980: *The Industrial Archaeology of Farming in England and Wales*. London.

Harvey, P.D.A. 1965: *A Medieval Oxfordshire Village*. Oxford.

Harvey, P.D.A. 1973: The English Inflation of 1180–1220. *Past and Present* 61, 3–30.

Harvey, P.D.A. 1976: *Manorial Records of Cuxham, Oxfordshire*. Oxfordshire Record Society 50.

Harvey, P.D.A. 1984: *Manorial Records*. British Records Association, Archives and the User, 5.

Harvey, S.P.J. 1976: Evidence for settlement study: Domesday Book. In P.H. Sawyer (ed.), *Medieval Settlement*. London 195–9.

Harvey, S.P.J. 1985: Taxations and the ploughland in Domesday Book. In P.H. Sawyer (ed.), *Domesday Book: a Reassessment*. London.

Harwood Long, W. 1979: The low yields of corn in medieval England. *Economic History Review* 32, 459–69.

Hatcher, J. 1970: *Rural Economy and Society in the Duchy of Cornwall 1300–1500*. London.

Hatcher, J. 1977: *Plague, Population and the English Economy 1348–1530*. London.

Hatcher, J. 1981: English serfdom and villeinage: towards a reassessment. *Past and Present* 90, 3–39.

Hatcher, J. 1986: Mortality in the fifteenth century: some new evidence. *Economic History Review* 39, 19–38.

Haudricourt, A.G. and Delamarre, M. J.-B. 1955: *L'Homme et la Charrue à travers le Monde*. Paris.

Havinden, M.A. (ed.) 1965: *Household and Farm Inventories in Oxfordshire, 1550–1590*. Historical Manuscripts Commission, London.

Havinden, M.A. 1968: Agricultural progress in open-field Oxfordshire. In W.E.

Minchinton (ed.), *Essays in Agrarian History* I. New York, 147–59.

Hawkes, S.C. and Gray, M. 1969: Preliminary note on the early Anglo-Saxon settlement at New Wintles Farm, Eynsham. *Oxoniensia* 34, 1–4.

Hayfield, C. 1984: Wawne, East Riding of Yorkshire: a case study in settlement morphology. *Landscape History* 6, 41–67.

Hickling, C.F. 1971: Prior More's fishponds. *Medieval Archaeology* 15, 118–23.

Higgs, J.W.Y. (ed.) 1977: *English Rural Life in the Middle Ages*. Bodleian Picture Book No. 14. Oxford.

Higham, N. 1980: Dyke systems in northern Cumbria. *Bulletin of the Board of Celtic Studies* 28, 142–52.

Hillman, G.C. 1982: Crop husbandry at the medieval farmstead of Cefn Graeanog; reconstruction from charred remains of plants. In R.S. Kelly, The excavation of the medieval farmstead of Cefn Graeanog, Clynnog, Gwynedd. *The Bulletin of the Board of Celtic Studies* 29, 901–6.

Hillman, G.C. (in press): Some poorly digested medieval meals: mineralized plant remains from a latrine excavated at Usk, 1976.

Hilton, R.H. 1974: Some social and economic evidence in late medieval English tax returns. In S. Herbst (ed.), *Spoleczenstwo, Gospordarka, Kultura; Studia Ofiarowan M. Malowistowi w Czterziestolencia pracy Nankowej*. Warsaw, 111–28.

Hilton, R.H. 1975: *The English Peasantry in the Later Middle Ages*. Oxford.

Hilton, R.H. 1983: *A Medieval Society. The West Midlands at the End of the Thirteenth Century* second edition. Cambridge.

Hilton, R.H. 1985: Introduction. In T. Aston and C. Philpin (eds), *The Brenner Debate*. Cambridge, 1–9.

Hilton, R.H. and Rahtz, P.A. 1966: Upton, Gloucestershire, 1959–1964. *Transactions of the Bristol and Gloucestershire Archaeological Society* 85, 70–146.

Hockey, S.F. 1975: *The Account Book of Beaulieu Abbey*. Camden Society, London.

Holden, B. 1985: The deserted medieval village of Thomley, Oxfordshire. *Oxoniensia* 50, 215–38.

Holden, E.W. 1963: Excavations at the deserted medieval village of Hangleton, Part I. *Sussex Archaeological Collections* 101, 54–181.

Homans, G.C. 1941: *English Villagers of the Thirteenth Century*. London.

Hooke, D. 1978: Early Cotswold woodland. *Journal of Historical Geography* 4, 333–41.

Hoskins, W.G. 1954: Regional farming in England. *Agricultural History Review* 2, 3–11.

Hoskins, W.G. 1955: *The Making of the English Landscape*. London.

Hoksins, W.G. 1976: *The Age of Plunder: King Henry's England 1500–1547*. London.

Hurst, J.G. 1979: *Wharram. A Study of Settlement on the Yorkshire Wolds* 1. London.

Hurst, J.G. 1984: The Wharram Research Project: results to 1983. *Medieval Archaeology* 28, 77–111.

Hurst, J.G. 1986: The medieval countryside. In I. Longworth and J. Cherry (eds), *Archaeology in Britain since 1945*. London, 197–236.

Hurst, J.G. and Hurst, D.G. 1964: Excavations at the deserted medieval village of Hangleton, part II. *Sussex Archaeological Collections* 102, 94–142.

Hurst, J.G. and Hurst, D.G. 1969: Excavations at the medieval village of Wythemail. *Medieval Archaeology* 13, 167–203.

Hutchinson, G.E. 1974: Attitudes towards nature in medieval England: the Alphonso and Bird psalters. *Isis* 65, 5–37.

Ingram, A. 1977: *Shepherding Tools and Customs*. Aylesbury.

Jackson, D.A. 1976: Two Iron Age sites north of Kettering, Northamptonshire *Northamptonshire Archaeology* 11, 71–99.

Jenkins, J.G. 1961: *The English Farm Waggon*. Reading.

Jones, A.K.G. 1979: The fish bones. In J.H. Williams, *St Peter's Street, Northampton*. Northampton, 335.

Jones, A.K.G. 1984: The fish bones. In T.P. O'Connor, Selected groups of bones from Skeldergate and Walmgate. *The Archaeology of York* 15.1. London, 48–51.

Jones, G. 1983: The medieval animal bones. In D. Allen and C.H. Dalwood, Iron Age occupation, a middle Saxon cemetery, and twelfth- to nineteenth-century urban occupation: excavations in George Street, Aylesbury, 1981. *Records of Buckinghamshire* 25, 31–49.

Jones, G. and Milles, A. 1984: Charred plant remains. In W. Britnell, A fifteenth-century corn drying kiln from Collfryn, Llantsantffraid, Deuddwr, Powys. *Medieval Archaeology* 28, 190–3.

Jones, J. and Watson, N. (in press): The early medieval waterfront of Redcliffe, Bristol: a study of environment and economy. In N. Balaam and V. Straker (eds), *Studies in Palaeoeconomy and Environment 'in South-western England*. Oxford.

Jones, M. 1981: The development of crop husbandry. In M. Jones and G. Dimbleby (eds), *The Environment of Man: the Iron Age to the Anglo-Saxon Period*. London, 95–128.

Jones, P. 1976: *The Butchers of London*. London.

Jones, R., Sly, J., Rackham, J. and Locker, A. (in press): The terrestrial vertebrate remains from the excavations at the castle; Barnard Castle. In D. Austin and P. Bowland (eds), *Excavations at Barnard Castle, 1974–1981*. London.

Jope, E.M. 1963: The regional cultures of medieval Britain. In I.L. Foster and L. Alcock (eds), *Culture and Environment*. London, 327–54.

Jope, E.M. and Threlfall, R.I. 1958: Excavation of a medieval settlement at Beere, North Tawton, Devon. *Medieval Archaeology* 2, 112–40.

Keene, D.J. 1982: Rubbish in medieval towns. In A.R. Hall and H.K. Kenward (eds), *Environmental Archaeology in the Urban Context*. London, 26–30.

Kennedy, P.A. (ed.) 1963: *Nottinghamshire Household Inventories*. Thoroton Society Record Series, 22.

Kerridge, E. 1967: *The Agricultural Revolution*. London.

Kershaw, I. 1973a: *Bolton Priory. The Economy of a Northern Monastery*. Oxford.

Kershaw, I. 1973b: The great famine and agrarian crisis in England, 1315–1322. *Past and Present* 59, 3–50.

Keynes, R. 1983: Malthus and biological equilibria. In J. Dupaquier and A. Fauve-Chamoux (eds), *Malthus Past and Present*. London, 359–64.

King, A.C. 1984: Animal bones and the dietary identity of military and civilian groups in Roman Britain, Germany and Gaul. In T.F.C. Blagg and A.C. King (eds), *Military and Civilian in Roman Britain*. Oxford, 187–217.

Kirk, R.E.G. (ed.) 1892: *Accounts of the Obedientars of Abingdon Abbey*. Camden Society, London.

Knowles, D. 1963: *The Monastic Order in England*. Cambridge.

Kosminsky, E.A. 1956: *Studies in the Agrarian History of England in the Thirteenth Century*. Oxford.

Kussmaul, A. 1981: *Servants in Husbandry in Early Modern England*. Cambridge.

Labarge, M.W. 1980: *A Baronial Household of the Thirteenth Century*. Brighton.

Lamb, H.H. 1977: *Climate: Present, Past and Future*. London.

Lamb, H.H. 1985: Climate and landscape in the British Isles. In S.R.J. Woodell (ed.), *The English Landscape, Past, Present and Future*. Oxford, 148–67.

Lambrick, G. forthcoming: *Excavations at Mount Farm, Berinsfield*.

Lambrick, G. and Robinson, M. 1979: *Iron Age and Roman Riverside Settlements at Farmoor, Oxfordshire*. London.

Langdon, J. 1982: The economics of horses and oxen. *Agricultural History Review* 30, 31–40.

Langdon, J. 1984: Horse hauling: a revolution in vehicle transport in twelfth- and thirteenth-century England? *Past and Present* 103, 37–66.

Langdon, J. 1986a: *Horses, Oxen and Technological Innovation: the Use of Draught Animals in English Farming from 1066 to 1500*. Cambridge.

Langdon, J. 1986b: Ox-shoeing on English desmesnes, 1200–1500. *Tools and Tillage* 5, 173–9.

Le Patourel, H.E.J. 1974: The use of horses. In M. Ryder, Animal remains from Wharram Percy. *Yorkshire Archaeological Journal* 46, 51–2.

Le Roy Ladurie, E. 1972: *Times of Feast, Times of Famine*. London.

Le Roy Ladurie, E. 1981: *The Mind and Method of the Historian* (tr. S. Reynolds and B. Reynolds). Brighton.

Lee, L., Seddon, G. and Stephens, F. 1976: *Stained Glass*. New York.

Lee, R.D. 1973: Population in pre-industrial England: an econometric analysis. *Quarterly Journal of Economics* 87, 581–607.

Lee, R.D. 1986: Population homeostasis and English demographic history. In R.I. Rotberg and T.K. Rabb (eds), *Population and Economy: Population History from the Traditional to the Modern World*. Cambridge, 75–100.

Lennard, R. 1959: *Rural England, 1086–1135*. Oxford.

Levitan, B. 1982: The faunal remains. In P. Leach, *Ilchester. Volume I: Excavations 1974–5*. Bristol, 269–84.

Levitan, B. 1984a: Faunal remains from Priory Barn and Benham's Garage. In P. Leach, *The Archaeology of Taunton*. Bristol, 167–93.

Levitan, B. 1984b: The vertebrate remains. In S. Rahtz and T. Rowley, *Middleton Stoney*. Oxford.

Linnard, W. 1982: *Welsh Woods and Forests: History and Utilization*. Cardiff.

Lloyd, T. 1977: *The English Wool Trade in the Middle Ages*. Cambridge.

Lloyd, T. 1978: Husbandry practices and disease in medieval sheep flocks. *Veterinary History* 10, 3–13.

Locker, A. 1977: Animal bones and shellfish. In D.S. Neal, Excavations at the Palace of Kings Langley, Hertfordshire 1974–76. *Medieval Archaeology* 21, 160–2.

Lowndes, R.A.C. 1967: A medieval site at Millhouse in the Lune Valley. *Transactions of the Cumberland and Westmorland Antiquarian and Archaeological Society* 67, 35–50.

MacGregor, A. 1985: *Bone, Antler, Ivory and Horn*. London.

Madge, S. and Fry, E.A. (eds) 1903–10: *Inquisitions* Post Mortem *for Gloucestershire*. British Record Society, 30 and 40.

Maguire, D., Ralph, N. and Fleming, A. 1983: Early land use on Dartmoor – palaeobotanical and pedological investigations on Holne Moor. In M. Jones (ed.), *Integrating the Subsistence Economy*. Oxford, 57–106.

Maltby, M. 1979: *The Animal Bones from Exeter, 1971–75*. Sheffield.

Maltby, M. 1982: Animal and bird bones. In R.A. Higham, J.P. Allan and S.R. Blaylock, Excavations at Okehampton Castle, Devon. Part 2 – the Bailey. *Devon Archaeological Society Proceedings* 40, 114–35.

Malthus, T.R. 1798: *An Essay on the Principle of Population*. London.

Markham, G. 1649: *Farewell to Husbandry*. London.

Mate, M. 1980: Profit and productivity on the estates of Isabella de Forz (1260–92). *Economic History Review* 33, 22–31.

Mate, M. 1985: Medieval agrarian practices: the determining factor? *Agricultural History Review* 33, 22–31.

Mayes, P. and Butler, L. 1983: *Sandal Castle Excavations*. Wakefield.

McCloskey, D.N. 1976: English open fields as behaviour towards risk. *Research on Economic History* 1, 124–70.

McKintosh, M.J. 1986: *Autonomy and Community: the Royal Manor of Havering, 1200–1500*. Cambridge.

McLean, T. 1981: *Medieval English Gardens*. London.

Mead, W.R. 1954: Ridge and furrow in Buckinghamshire. *Geographical Journal* 120, 34–42.

Meirion-Jones, G. 1973: The long-house: a definition. *Medieval Archaeology* 17, 135–7.

Metcalf, D.M. 1977: A survey of numismatic research into the pennies of the first three Edwards (1279–1344) and their continental imitations. In N. Mayhew (ed.), *Edwardian Monetary Affairs 1279–1344*. Oxford, 1–31.

Michelmore, D.H.J. (ed.) 1981: *The Fountains Abbey Lease Book*. Yorkshire Records Society 140.

Millar, E.G. (ed.) 1932: *The Luttrell Psalter*. London.

Miller, E. 1966: La société rurale en Angleterre Xe–XIIe siècles. *Agricultura e Mondo in Occidente nell' Alto Medievo*. Spoleto, 111–34.

Miller, E. 1971: The twelfth and thirteenth centuries: an economic contrast? *Economic History Review* 25, 1–14.

Miller, E. 1975: Farming in northern England during the twelfth and thirteenth centuries. *Northern History* 11, 1–16.

Miller, E. and Hatcher, J. 1978: *Medieval England: Rural Society and Economic Change 1086–1338*. London.

Moffet, L.C. (in preparation a): The medieval cereals and weeds from School Road, Alcester.

Moffet, L.C. (in preparation b): The botanical evidence from late Saxon and early medieval Stafford. In M.O.H. Carver (ed.) *Early Medieval Stafford*.

Moffet, L.C. (in preparation c): Cultivated plants and domesticated activities: the evidence from the plant remains at Dean Court Farm.

Moffet, L.C. (in preparation d): The evidence for free threshing tetraploid wheat in Britain.

Moorhouse, S. 1983: Documentary evidence and its potential for understanding the inland movement of medieval pottery. *Medieval Ceramics* 7, 45–88.

Morgan, K.O. (ed.) 1984: *The Oxford Illustrated History of Britain.* Oxford.

Morris, C. 1977: Plague in Britain. In *The Plague Reconsidered: a New Look at its Origins and Effects in 16th and 17th Century England.* Local Population Studies Supplement. Matlock, 37–48.

Morris, C.A. 1980: A group of early medieval spades. *Medieval Archaeology* 24, 205–10.

Morris, C.A. 1981: Early medieval separate-bladed shovels from Ireland. *Journal of the Royal Society of Antiquaries of Ireland* 111, 50–69.

Morris, C.A. 1983: A late Anglo-Saxon hoard of iron and copper-alloy artefacts from Nazeing, Essex. *Medieval Archaeology* 27, 27–39.

Morris, C.A. 1984: Anglo-Saxon and Medieval Woodworking Crafts – the Manufacture and Use of Domestic and Utilitarian Wooden Artefacts in the British Isles, 400–1600 AD. Unpublished PhD thesis, University of Cambridge.

Morris, J.E. 1901: *The Welsh Wars of Edward I.* Oxford.

Munby, J. 1985: Portchester and its region. In B. Cunliffe and J. Munby, *Excavations at Portchester Castle. Volume IV: Medieval, the Inner Bailey.* London, 270–95.

Murphy, P. 1985a: Environmental reports. In M. Atkin, A. Carter and D.H. Evans, Excavations in Norwich 1971–1978, part 2. *East Anglian Archaeology* 26, 66–9.

Murphy, P. 1985b: The plant remains. In M. Atkin, Excavations on Alms Lane (site 302N). *East Anglian Archaeology* 26, 228–34.

Murphy, P. (unpublished): Hill Hall, Essex, plant macrofossils.

Musty, J., Algar, D.J. and Ewence, P.F. 1969: The medieval pottery kilns at Laverstock, near Salisbury, Wiltshire. *Archaeologia* 102, 83–150.

Musty, J. and Algar, D.J. 1986: Excavations at the deserted medieval village of Gomeldon, near Salisbury. *Wiltshire Archaeological and Natural History Magazine* 80, 127–69.

Myhre, B. 1982: Agrarian development, settlement history and social organization in south-west Norway in the Iron Age. In K. Kristiansen and C. Paludan-Muller (eds), *New Directions in Scandinavian Archaeology.* Copenhagen, 224–71.

NCE 1967–79: *The New Catholic Encyclopaedia* 17 volumes. New York.

Newton, K.C. 1969: A source for medieval population statistics. *Journal of the Society of Archivists* 3, 543–6.

Nightingale, M. 1953: Ploughing and field shape. *Antiquity* 27, 20–6.

Noddle, B. 1975: The animal bones. In C. Platt and R. Coleman-Smith, *Excavations in Medieval Southampton 1953–1969.* Leicester, 332–9.

Noddle, B. 1976: Report on the animal bones from Walton, Aylesbury. In M. Farley, Saxon and medieval Walton, Aylesbury: excavations 1973–4. *Records of Buckinghamshire* 20, 269–87.

Noodle, B. 1977: Mammal bone. In H. Clarke and A. Carter, *Excavations at King's Lynn, 1963–1970.* London, 378–99.

Noddle, B. 1980: Animal bones. In P. Wade-Martins, North Elmham Park. *East Anglian Archaeology* 9, 375–412.

O'Connor, T.P. 1982: Animal bone from Flaxengate, Lincoln *c.*870–1500. *The Archaeology of Lincoln* 18.1. London.

O'Connor, T.P. 1984: Selected Groups of Bones from Skeldergate and Walmgate. *The Archaeology of York* 15.1. London.

O'Donoghue, B. 1982: *The Courtly Love Tradition*. Manchester.

Ohlin, G. 1974: No safety in numbers: some pitfalls of historical statistics. In R. Floud (ed.), *Essays in Quantitative Economic History*. Oxford, 59–78.

Orwin, C.S. and Orwin, C.S. 1967: *The Open Fields* third edition. Oxford.

Oschinsky, D. 1971: *Walter of Henley and other Treatises on Estate Management and Accounting*. Oxford.

Owen, A.E.B. (ed.) 1981: *The Records of a Commission of Sewers for Wiggenhall*. Norfolk Record Society 48.

Page, F.M. 1936: *Wellingborough Manorial Accounts*. Northamptonshire Record Society 8.

Palliser, D.M. 1982: Civic mentality and the environment in Tudor York. *Northern History* 18, 78–115.

Palliser, D.M. and Pinnock, A.C. 1971: The markets of medieval Staffordshire. *North Staffordshire Journal of Field Studies* 11, 49–63.

Parain, C. 1966: The evolution of agricultural technique. In M.M. Postan (ed.), *The Cambridge Economic History of Europe* 1 second edition. Cambridge.

Parry, M.L. 1978: *Climatic Change, Agriculture and Settlement*. Folkestone.

Parry, M.L. 1985: Upland settlement and climatic change. In D. Spratt and C. Burgess (eds), *Upland Settlement in Britain*. Oxford, 35–50.

Partridge, M. 1969: *Early Agricultural Machinery*. London.

Partridge, M. 1973: *Farm Tools through the Ages*. Reading.

Passmore, J.B. 1930: *The English Plough*. Oxford.

Pearsall, D. and Salter, E. 1973: *Landscapes and Seasons of the Medieval World*. London.

Peate, I.C. 1934: Severn eel traps. *Man* 34, 153–4.

Pelham, R.A. 1936: Fourteenth-century England. In H.C. Darby (ed.), *An Historical Geography of England before AD 1800*. Cambridge, 230–65.

Penn, S.A.C. 1987: Female wage earners in late fourteenth-century England. *Agricultural History Review* 35, 1–14.

Percival, J. 1921: *The Wheat Plant*. London.

Perkins, J.A. 1977–8: The sickle, the scythe, and the physical characteristics of migratory harvest workers. *Ethnologia Europaea* 10, 88–97.

Pernetta, J. 1973: The animal bones. In M. Robinson, Excavations at Copt Hay, Tetsworth, Oxfordshire. *Oxoniensia* 28, 112–15.

Pesez, J.M. 1975: Une maison villageoise au XIVe siècle: les structures. *Rotterdam Papers* 2, 139–50.

Petit, P.A.J. 1968: *The Royal Forests of Northamptonshire*. Northamptonshire Record Society 23.

Phillips, G. 1980: The fauna. In P. Armstrong, Excavations in Scale Lane, Lowgate 1974. *East Riding Archaeologist* 6, 77–85.

Phythian-Adams, C. 1977: *The Fabric of the Traditional Community*, II.5. Milton Keynes.

Plat, H. 1601: *The New and Admirable Art of Setting Corne*. London.

Platt, C. 1969: *The Monastic Grange in Medieval England*. London.

Platt, C. and Coleman-Smith, R. 1975: *Excavations in Medieval Southampton 1953–*

1969, I. Leicester.

Platts, G. 1985: *Land and People in Medieval Lincolnshire*. Lincoln.

Poos, L.R. 1981: Plague mortality and demographic depression in later medieval England. *The Yale Journal of Biology and Medicine* 54, 227–34.

Poos, L.R. 1983: Population and Resources in Two Fourteenth-century Essex Communities: Great Waltham and High Easter 1327–1389. Unpublished PhD thesis, University of Cambridge.

Poos, L.R. 1985: The rural population of Essex in the later middle ages. *Economic History Review* 38, 515–30.

Poos, L.R. and Smith, R.M. 1984: 'Legal windows on to historical populations'?: recent research into demography and the manorial court in medieval England. *Law and History Review* 2, 129–52.

Porter, J. 1975: A forest in transition: Bowland 1500–1650. *Transactions of the Historical Society of Lancashire and Cheshire* 125, 40–60.

Porter, S. 1983: Farm transport in Huntingdonshire, 1610–1749. *Journal of Transport History* 3, 35–45.

Postan, M.M. 1966: Medieval agrarian society in its prime: 7. England. In M.M. Postan (ed.), *The Cambridge Economic History of Europe* 1 second edition. Cambridge, 548–632.

Postan, M.M. 1973: *Essays on Medieval Agriculture and General Problems of the Medieval Economy*. Cambridge.

Postan, M.M. 1975: *The Medieval Economy and Society*. Harmondsworth.

Postan, M.M. 1978: A note on the farming out of manors. *Economic History Review* 31, 521–5.

Postan, M.M. and Titow, J.Z. 1973: Heriots and prices on Winchester manors with statistical notes on Winchester heriots by J. Longden. In M.M. Postan (ed.), *Essays on Medieval Agriculture and General Problems of the Medieval Economy*. Cambridge, 107–49.

Postgate, M.R. 1973: Field systems of East Anglia. In A.R.H. Baker and R.A. Butlin (eds), *Studies of Field Systems in the British Isles*. Cambridge, 281–324.

Power, E. 1941: *The Wool Trade in English Medieval History*. Oxford.

Pryor, F., French, C., Crowther, D., Gurney, D., Simpson, G. and Taylor, M. 1985: The Fenland project No. 1. Archaeology and environment in the Lower Welland Valley. *East Anglian Archaeology* 27.

Rackham, J. 1978: The faunal remains. In P.V. Addyman and J. Priestly, *Five Castle Excavations*. London.

Rackham, J. (in press): The animal bones. In D. Austin, *The Deserted Medieval Village of Thrislington, County Durham: Excavations 1973–4*. London.

Rackham, O. 1976: *Trees and Woodland in the British Landscape*. London.

Rackham, O. 1978: Archaeology and land-use history. *Essex Naturalist* new series 2, 16–57.

Rackham, O. 1980: *Ancient Woodland*. London.

Rackham, O. 1986: *The History of the Countryside*. London.

Rahtz, P.A. 1959: Holworth medieval village excavation 1958. *Proceedings of the Dorset Natural History and Archaeological Society* 81, 127–47.

Rahtz, P.A. 1969: Upton, Gloucestershire, 1964–1968. Second report. *Transactions of the Bristol and Gloucestershire Archaeological Society* 88, 74–126.

Rahtz, P.A. 1976: Buildings and rural settlement. In D.M. Wilson (ed.), *The Archaeology of Anglo-Saxon England*. London, 49–98.

Rahtz, P.A. and Hirst, S.M. 1976: *Bordesley Abbey*. Oxford.

Ramskou, T. 1957: Lindholm Hoje third preliminary report for years 1956–57. *Acta Archaeologia* 28, 193–201.

Rau, R. 1968: *Briefe des Bonifatius Willibalds Leben des Bonifatius*. Darmstadt.

Ravensdale, J.R. 1984: Population changes and the transfer of customary land on a Cambridgeshire manor in the fourteenth century. In R.M. Smith (ed.), *Land, Kinship and Life-cycle*. Cambridge, 197–226.

Razi, Z. 1980: *Life, Marriage and Death in a Medieval Parish: Economy, Society and Demography in Halesowen, 1270–1400*. Cambridge.

RCHM 1960: Royal Commission on Historic Monuments, Excavations in the west bailey at Corfe Castle. *Medieval Archaeology* 4, 29–55.

RCHM 1968: Royal Commission on Historic Monuments, *West Cambridgeshire*. London.

RCHM 1970a: Royal Commission on Historic Monuments, *Shielings and Bastles*. London.

RCHM 1970b: Royal Commission on Historic Monuments, *Central Dorset*. London.

RCHM 1970c: Royal Commission on Historic Monuments, *South-east Dorset*. London.

RCHM 1975: Royal Commission on Historic Monuments, *North-east Northamptonshire*. London.

RCHM 1981: Royal Commission on Historic Monuments, *North-west Northamptonshire*. London.

RCHM 1982: Royal Commission on Historic Monuments, *South-west Northamptonshire*. London.

Rees, S. 1979: *Agricultural Implements in Prehistoric and Roman Britain*. Oxford.

Rees, S. 1981a: *Ancient Agricultural Implements*. Aylesbury.

Rees, S. 1981b: Agricultural tools: function and use. In R. Mercer (ed.), *Farming Practice in British Prehistory*. Edinburgh, 66–84.

Rees, U. (ed.) 1985: *The Haughmond Cartulary*. Cardiff.

Regenos, G.W. (ed.) 1959: *The Book of Daun Burnel the Ass*. Austin, Texas.

Reynolds, P. 1981: New approaches to familiar problems. In M. Jones and G. Dimbleby (eds), *The Environment of Man: the Iron Age to the Anglo-Saxon Period*. London, 19–49.

Richards, J. 1978: *The Archaeology of the Berkshire Downs*. Reading.

Richardson, G. 1979: King's Stables, an early shieling on Black Lyne Common, Bewcastle. *Transactions of the Cumberland and Westmorland Antiquarian and Archaeological Society* 79, 19–27.

Richardson, H.G. and Sayles, W.O. (eds) 1953: *Fleta* 2. Selden Society 72.

Ridgard, J. 1985: *Medieval Framlingham: Select Documents 1270–1524*. Suffolk Records Society 27.

Roberts, B.K. 1973: Field systems of the west midlands. In A.R.H. Baker and R.A. Butlin (eds), *Studies of Field Systems in the British Isles*. Cambridge, 188–231.

Roberts, B.K. 1977: *Rural Settlement in Britain*. London.

Roberts, B.K. 1985: Village patterns and forms: some models for discussion. In D. Hooke (ed.), *Medieval Villages*. Oxford, 7–26.

Robinson, M. 1973: Excavations at Copt Hay, Tetsworth. *Oxoniensia* 38, 41–115.

Robinson, M. 1984: 33 St Aldates. Agricultural debris against the Norman bridge. In B. Durham, The Thames crossing at Oxford: archaeological studies 1978–9. *Oxoniensia* 49, 78–9.

Robinson, M. (in preparation): Molluscan evidence for pasture and meadowland on the floodplain of the upper Thames basin.

Roden, D. 1968: Woodland and its management in the medieval Chilterns. *Forestry* 41, 59–71.

Roden, D. 1973: Field systems of the Chiltern Hills and their environs. In A.R.H. Baker and R.A. Butlin (eds), *Studies of Field Systems in the British Isles*. Cambridge, 325–76.

Rowley, R.T. 1982: Medieval field systems. In L.M. Cantor (ed.), *The English Medieval Landscape*. London, 25–55.

Rowley, R.T. 1986: *The Landscape of the Welsh Marches*. London.

Russell, J.C. 1948: *British Medieval Population*. Albuquerque.

Russell, J.C. 1958: Late ancient and medieval population. *Transactions of the American Philosophical Society* 48, 1–152.

Russell, J.C. 1969: Population in Europe 500–1500. In *Fontana Economic History of Europe* 1, 25–70.

Russell, J.C. 1985: *Late Ancient and Medieval Population Control*. Philadelphia.

Ryder, M.L. 1974: Animal remains from Wharram Percy. *Yorkshire Archaeological Journal* 46, 42–52.

Ryder, M.L. 1983: *Sheep and Man*. London.

Sabine, E.L. 1934: Latrines and cesspools of medieval London. *Speculum* 9, 303–21.

Sadler, P. (in press): Faunal remains. In J. Fairbrother, *The Manor of Faccombe, Netherton*. Oxford.

Sahlins, M. 1976: *Culture and Practical Reason*. London.

Salzman, L.F. 1923: *English Industries of the Middle Ages*. Oxford.

Salzman, L.F. (ed.) 1955: *Ministers' Accounts of the Manor of Petworth, 1347–1353*. Sussex Records Society 55.

Salzman, L.F. 1957: A note on shepherds' staves. *Agricultural History Review* 5, 91–4.

Sandler, L.F. 1974: *The Peterborough Psalter in Brussels and other Fenland Manuscripts*. London.

Sawyer, P.H. 1965: The wealth of England in the eleventh century. *Transactions of the Royal Historical Society* 15, 145–64.

Sawyer, P.H. 1976: Introduction: early medieval settlement. In P.H. Sawyer (ed.), *Medieval Settlement: Continuity and Change*. London, 1–10.

Sawyer, P.H. 1978: *From Roman Britain to Norman England*. London.

Sawyer, P.H. 1979: Medieval English settlement: new interpretations. In P.H. Sawyer (ed.), *English Medieval Settlement*. London, 1–8.

Sayce, R.U. 1936: The investigation of British agricultural implements. *Man* 34, 63–6.

Scaife, R.G. 1982: Pollen report. In P. Mills, Excavations at Broad Sanctuary, Westminster. *Transactions of the London and Middlesex Archaeological Society* 33, 360–5.

Schofield, R.S. 1986: Through a glass darkly: the 'Population History of England' as an experiment in history. In R.I. Rotberg and T.K. Rabb (eds), *Population and Economy:*

Population and History from the Traditional to the Modern World. Cambridge, 11–34.

Schofield, R.S. and Wrigley, E.A. 1979: Infant and child mortality in the late Tudor and early Stuart period. In C. Webster (ed.), *Health, Medicine and Mortality in Tudor and Stuart England.* Cambridge, 61–95.

Schofield, R.S. and Wrigley, E.A. 1986: Introduction. In R.I. Rotberg and T.K. Rabb (eds), *Population and Economy: Population and History from the Traditional to the Modern World.* Cambridge, 61–95.

Schumer, B. 1984: *The Evolution of Wychwood to 1400: Pioneers, Frontiers and Forests.* Leicester.

Sébillot, P. 1984: *La Faune.* Paris.

Seebohm, F. 1905: *The English Village Community* fourth edition. London.

Sheail, J. 1971: *Rabbits and their History.* Newton Abbot.

Sheail, J. 1972: The distribution of taxable population and wealth in England during the early sixteenth century. *Transactions of the Institute of British Geographers* 55, 111–26.

Sheppard, J.A. 1975: Medieval village planning in northern England: some evidence from Yorkshire. *Journal of Historical Geography* 2, 3–20.

Simpson, W.G. 1981: Excavations in field 05124, Maxey, Cambridgeshire. *Northamptonshire Archaeology* 16, 34–64.

Singer, C., Holmyard, E.J., Hall, A.R. and Williams, T.I. (eds) 1956: *A History of Technology* 1. Oxford.

Singer, C., Holmyard, E.J., Hall, A.R. and Williams, T.I. (eds) 1957: *A History of Technology* 2. Oxford.

Skeat, W.W. (ed.) 1882: *The Book of Husbandry by Master Fitzherbert 1534 edition.* London.

Slater, T. 1979: More on the wolds. *Journal of Historical Geography* 5, 213–18.

Smith, A. 1863: *An Inquiry into the Nature and Causes of the Wealth of Nations* new edition. Edinburgh.

Smith, B.S. 1964: *A History of Malvern.* Leicester.

Smith, C.T. 1965: The Cambridge region: settlement and population. In J.A. Steers (ed.), *The Cambridge Region 1965.* Cambridge, 133–61.

Smith, R.M. 1978: The population and its geography in England 1500–1730. In R.A. Dodgshon and R.A. Butlin (eds), *An Historical Geography of England and Wales.* London, 199–238.

Smith, R.M. 1979: Some reflections on the evidence for the origins of the 'European marriage pattern' in England. In C. Harris (ed.), *The Sociology of the Family: New Directions for Britain.* Keele, 74–112.

Smith, R.M. 1981: The people of Tuscany and their families in the fifteenth century: medieval or Mediterranean? *Journal of Family History* 6, 107–28.

Smith, R.M. 1982: Rooms, relatives and residential arrangements: some evidence in manor court rolls 1250–1500. *Medieval Village Research Group Annual Report* 30, 34–5.

Smith, R.M. 1983a: Hypothèses sur la nuptialité en Angleterre aux XIIIe-XVIe siècles. *Annales Economies, Sociétés, Civilisations* 38, 107–36.

Smith, R.M. 1983b: Some thoughts on hereditary and proprietary rights in law under customary land in thirteenth- and early fourteenth-century England. *Law and History Review* 1, 95–128.

Smith, R.M. 1984a: Some issues concerning families and their property in rural England. In R.M. Smith (ed.), *Land, Kinship and Life-cycle*. Cambridge, 1–86.

Smith, R.M. 1984b: Families and their land in an area of partible inheritance, Redgrave, Suffolk 1260–1320. In R.M. Smith (ed.), *Land, Kinship and Life-cycle*. Cambridge, 135–96.

Smith, R.M. 1986a: Marriage processes in the English past: some continuities. In L. Bonfield, K. Wrightson and R. Smith (eds), *The World We Have Gained: Histories of Population and Social Structure*. Oxford, 43–99.

Smith, R.M. 1986b: Women's property rights under customary law: some developments in the thirteenth and fourteenth centuries. *Transactions of the Royal Historical Society* 26, 165–94.

Smith, R.M. (forthcoming): Demographic disequilibrium in later medieval England: some thoughts on female nuptuality.

Smyth, J. 1883: *Lives of the Berkeleys* 3 volumes. Gloucester.

Sparke, I.G. 1976: *Old Horseshoes*. Aylesbury.

Stamper, P.A. 1980: Barton Blount: climatic or economic change: an addendum. *Annual Report of the Moated Sites Research Group* 7, 43–7.

Stamper, P.A. 1983: The medieval forest of Pamber, Hampshire. *Landscape History* 5, 41–52.

Standish, J. (ed.) 1914: *Inquisitions* Post Mortem *relating to Nottinghamshire*. Thoroton Society, Record Series 4.

Statutes of the Realm 1819–28 11 volumes. London.

Steane, J.M. 1974: *The Northamptonshire Landscape*. London.

Steane, J.M. 1975: The medieval parks of Northamptonshire. *Northamptonshire Past and Present* 5, 211–33.

Steane, J.M. 1984: *The Archaeology of Medieval England and Wales*. London.

Steane, J.M. 1985: Bernwood forest – past, present and future. *Arboricultural Journal* 9, 39–55.

Stebbings, G.L. 1982: *Darwin to DNA, Molecules to Humanity*. San Francisco.

Steel, T. 1975: *The Life and Death of St Kilda*. Glasgow.

Steensberg, A. 1936: North-west European plough-types of prehistoric times and the middle ages. *Acta Archaeologica* 7, 244–80.

Steensberg, A. 1983: *Borup, AD 700–1400: a Deserted Settlement and its Fields in South Zealand, Denmark*. Copenhagen.

Stenton, F. (ed.) 1957: *The Bayeux Tapestry*. London.

Stephenson, M. 1983: Wool Yields in Medieval England. Paper presented to the Anglo-American Conference on Medieval Economy and Society. Exeter.

Still, L. and Pallister, A. 1967: West Hartburn 1965. *Archaeologia Aeliana* 45, 139–48.

Stokes, E. and Drucker, L. 1939: *Warwickshire Feet of Fines*. Dugdale Society, 15. London.

Straker, V. 1979: Late Saxon and late medieval plant remains from Marefair, Northampton. Ancient Monument Laboratory Reports 2867.

Suttie, J.M. and Hamilton, W.J. 1983: The effect of winter nutrition on the growth of young Scottish red deer. *Journal of Zoology* 210, 153–9.

Taylor, C.C. 1966: Strip lynchets. *Antiquity* 40, 277–82.

Taylor, C.C. 1975: *Fields in the English Landscape*. London.

Taylor, C.C. 1978: Aspects of village mobility in medieval and later times. In S. Limbrey and J.G. Evans (eds), *The Effect of Man on the Landscape: the Lowland Zone*. London, 126–34.

Taylor, C.C. 1983: *Village and Farmstead: a History of Rural Settlement in England*. London.

Taylor, C.C and Fowler, P.J. 1978: Roman fields into medieval furlongs? In H.C. Bowen and P.J. Fowler (eds), *Early Land Allotment*. Oxford, 159–62.

Thawley, C. 1981: The mammal, bird and fish bones. In J.E. Mellor and T. Pearce, *The Austin Friars, Leicester*. London, microfiche.

Thirsk, J. 1957: *English Peasant Farming*. London.

Thirsk, J. 1964: The common fields. *Past and Present* 29, 3–29.

Thirsk, J. 1967a: The farming regions of England. In J. Thirsk (ed.), *The Agrarian History of England and Wales* 4. Cambridge, 1–112.

Thirsk, J. 1967b: Farming technique. In J. Thirsk (ed.), *The Agrarian History of England and Wales* 4. Cambridge, 161–99.

Thirsk, J. 1978: *Economic Policy and Projects*. Oxford.

Thirsk, J. 1984: *The Rural Economy of England*. London.

Thomas, K. 1983: *Man and the Natural World*. London.

Thompson, H. 1960: The deserted medieval village of Riseholme, near Lincoln. *Medieval Archaeology* 4, 95–108.

Thrupp, S. 1965: The problem of replacement rates in late medieval England. *Economic History Review* 14, 113–28.

Titow, J.Z. 1961: Some evidence of thirteenth-century population growth. *Economic History Review* 14, 101–19.

Titow, J.Z. 1962: Some differences between manors and their effects on the conditions of the peasantry in the thirteenth century. *Agricultural History Review* 10, 113–28.

Titow, J.Z. 1972: *Winchester Yields*. Cambridge.

Tits-Dieuaide, M.-J. 1981: L'évolution des techniques agricoles en Flandre et en Brabant du XIVe au XVIe siècle. *Annales Economies, Sociétés, Civilisations* 36, 362–81.

Tits-Dieuaide, M-J. 1984: Les campagnes Flamandes du XIIIe au XVIIIe siècle, ou le succès d'une agriculture traditionelle. *Annales Economies Sociétés, Civilisations* 39, 590–610.

Tomlinson, P.R. 1985: Use of vegetative remains in the identification of dyeplants from waterlogged 9th–10th century AD deposits at York. *Journal of Archaeological Science* 12, 269–83.

Tomlinson, P.R. (in preparation): Vegetative plant remains from waterlogged deposits identified at York.

Trevelyan, G.M. 1942: *Illustrated English Social History* 1. New York.

Trow-Smith, R. 1957: *A History of British Livestock Husbandry to 1700*. London.

Twigg, G. 1984: *The Black Death: a Biological Reappraisal*. London.

Tylecote, R.F. 1986: *The Prehistory of Metallurgy in the British Isles*. London.

Unwin, T. 1981: Rural marketing in medieval Nottinghamshire. *Journal of Historical Geography* 7, 231–51.

Veale, E. 1957: The rabbit in England. *Agricultural History Review* 5, 85–90.

VCH 1907a: *Victoria History of the County of Berkshire* 2.

VCH 1907b: *Victoria History of the County of Essex* 2.

VCH 1954: *Victoria History of the County of Leicestershire* 2.

VCH 1976: *Victoria History of the County of Yorkshire, East Riding* 3.

VCH 1979: *Victoria History of the County of Staffordshire* 6.

VCH 1985a: *Victoria History of the County of Shropshire* 11.

VCH 1985b: *Victoria History of the County of Somerset* 5.

VCH 1988: *Victoria History of the County of Sussex* 6.

VCH (forthcoming): *Victoria History of the County of Shropshire* 4.

Vinogradoff, P. 1892: *Villainage in England.* Oxford.

von Strassburg, G. 1960: *Tristan.* Hardmondsworth.

Wacher, J. 1966: Excavations at Riplingham, East Yorkshire 1956–7. *Yorkshire Archaeological Journal* 41, 608–69.

Wade-Martins, P. 1980: Village sites in Launditch hundred, Norfolk. *East Anglian Archaeology* 10.

Walmsley, J.F.R. 1968: The *censarii* of Burton Abbey and the Domesday population. *North Staffordshire Journal of Field Studies* 8, 73–80.

Watts, L. and Rahtz, P.A. 1984: Upton Deserted Medieval Village, Blockley, Gloucestershire, 1973. *Transactions of the Bristol and Gloucestershire Archaeological Society* 102, 141–54.

Webb, J. 1854: *A Roll of the Household Expenses of Richard de Swinfield, Bishop of Hereford.* Camden Society, London.

Webster, L. and Cherry, J. 1972: Medieval Britain in 1971. *Medieval Archaeology* 16, 147–212.

West, B. 1982: Spur development: recognizing caponised fowl in archaeological material. In B. Wilson, C. Grigson and S. Payne (eds), *Ageing and Sexing Animal Bones from Archaeological Sites.* Oxford, 255–62.

West, J. 1964: The Administration and Economy of the Forest of Feckenham during the Early Middle Ages. Unpublished MA thesis, University of Birmingham.

West, S. 1985: West Stow. The Anglo-Saxon Village. *East Anglian Archaeology* 24.

Westley, B. 1977: Animal bones. In K. Barton and E. Holden, Excavations at Bramber Castle, Sussex, 1966–7. *Archaeological Journal* 134, 67–8.

Wheeler, A. 1969: *The Fishes of the British Isles and North-west Europe.* London.

Wheeler, A. 1977: Fish bone. In H. Clarke and A. Carter, *Excavations at King's Lynn 1963–1970.* London, 403–8.

Wheeler, A. 1984: Fish bones. In P. Leach, *The Archaeology of Taunton.* Bristol, 193–4.

Wheeler, A. and Jones, A.K.G. 1976: Fish remains. In A. Rogerson, Excavations on Fullers Hill, Great Yarmouth. *East Anglian Archaeology* 2, 208–25.

Wheeler, R.E.M. (ed.) 1954: *London Museum Medieval Catalogue.* London.

Whitaker, I. 1958: The harrow in Scotland. *Scottish Studies* 2, 149–70.

White, K.D. 1967: *Agricultural Implements of the Roman World.* Cambridge.

White, L. 1962: *Medieval Technology and Social Change.* Oxford.

White, T.H. 1951 *The Goshawk.* London.

Whitman, F.H. 1982: *Old English Riddles.* Ottawa.

Wilkinson, M. 1979: The fish remains. In M. Maltby, *Faunal Remains on Urban Sites: the Animal Bones from Exeter.* Sheffield, 74–81.

Wilkinson, M. 1982a: Fish. In T. O'Connor, Animal bones from Flaxengate, Lincoln *c.*870–1500. *The Archaeology of Lincoln*, 18.1, 4–6.

Wilkinson M. 1982b: Fishbones. In R.A. Higham, J.P. Allan and S.R. Blaylock, Excavations at Okehampton Castle, Devon. Part 2- the Bailey. *Devon Archaeological Society Proceedings* 40, 135–8.

Willerding, U. (in preparation): Palaeo-ethnobotanical researches on houses from medieval and early modern times.

Williams, A. 1978: *Backyard Farming*. London.

Williams, J.P. 1984: Marriage among the Customary Tenants of the Bishops of Winchester, 1297–1366. Unpublished fellowship dissertation, Trinity College, Cambridge.

Wilson, B. 1980: Animal bone and shell. In N. Palmer, A beaker burial and medieval tenements in the Hamel, Oxford. *Oxoniensia* 45, 198, Fiche E04-F11.

Wilson, B. 1983: Animal bones and shell. In C. Halpin, Late Saxon evidence and excavation of Hinxey Hall, Queen Street, Oxford. *Oxoniensia* 48, 68–9, Fiche D11–E13.

Wilson, C.A. 1984: *Food and Drink in Britain*. Harmondsworth.

Wilson, D.G. 1979: Horse dung from Roman Lancaster; a botanical report. *Archaeo-Physika* 8, 331–50.

Wilson, D.M. 1976: Craft and industry. In D.M. Wilson (ed.), *The Archaeology of Anglo-Saxon England*. Cambridge, 253–81.

Wilson, D.M. 1981: *The Anglo-Saxons* third edition. Harmondsworth.

Wilson, D.M. and Hurst, J.G. 1964: Medieval Britain in 1962 and 1963. *Medieval Archaeology* 8, 231–99.

Wilson, D.M. and Hurst, J.G. 1965: Medieval Britain in 1964. *Medieval Archaeology* 9, 170–220.

Wilson, D.M. and Hurst, J.G. 1969: Medieval Britain in 1968. *Medieval Archaeology* 13, 230–87.

Woods, P. 1962: The investigation in 1957 of strip lynchets north of the Vale of Pewsey. *Wiltshire Archaeological Magazine* 57, 163–71.

Wormald, F. (ed.) 1960: *The St Albans Psalter*. London.

Wrathmell, S. and Wrathmell, S. 1974–5: Excavations at the moat site, Walsall 1972–4. *South Staffordshire Archaeological and Historical Society* 16, 19–53.

Wright, D. 1970: Broadcast sowing in England. *The Countryman* 74, 84–8.

Wright, S. 1976: Barton Blount: climatic or economic change? *Medieval Archaeology* 20, 148–52.

Wrigley, E.A. 1978: Fertility strategy for the individual and the group. In C. Tilly (ed.), *Historical Studies of Changing Fertility*. Princeton, 135–54.

Wrigley, E.A. 1983: Malthus's model of a pre-industrial economy. In J. Dupaquier, A. Fauve-Chamoux and E. Grebenik (eds), *Malthus, Past and Present*. London, 111–24.

Wrigley, E.A. 1986: Elegance and experience: Malthus at the bar of history. In D. Coleman and R.S. Schofield (eds), *The State of Population Theory: Forward from Malthus*. Oxford, 46–64.

Wrigley, E.A. 1987: No death without birth: the implications of English mortality in the early modern period. In R. Porter and A. Wear (eds), *Problems and Methods in the History of Medicine*. London, 133–50.

Wrigley, E.A. and Schofield, R.S. 1981: *The Population History of England 1541–1871: a Reconstruction*. London.

Yaxley, D. 1980: The manors and the agrarian economy. In P. Wade-Martins, North Elmham Park. *East Anglian Archaeology* 9, 561–634.

Yealland, S. and Higgs, E. 1966: The economy. In R.H. Hilton and P.A. Rahtz, Upton, Gloucesterhire, 1959–1964. *Transactions of the Bristol and Gloucestershire Archaeological Society* 85, 139–43.

Youngs, S., Clark, J. and Barry, T. 1984: Medieval Britain and Ireland in 1983. *Medieval Archaeology* 28, 203–65.

Index

Note: **Emboldened** page numbers refer to illustrations, diagrams, or maps.